VOLCANOES

POWER AND MAGIC

VOLCANOES

POWER AND MAGIC

KÖNEMANN

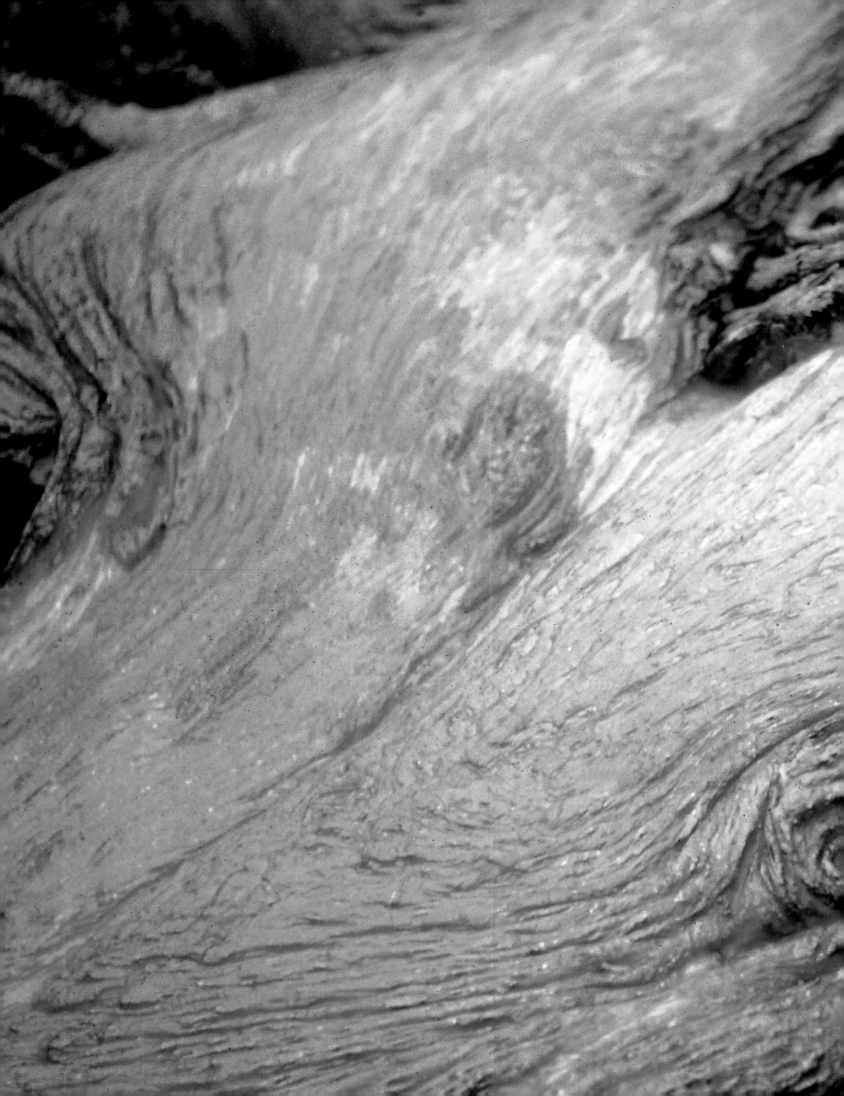

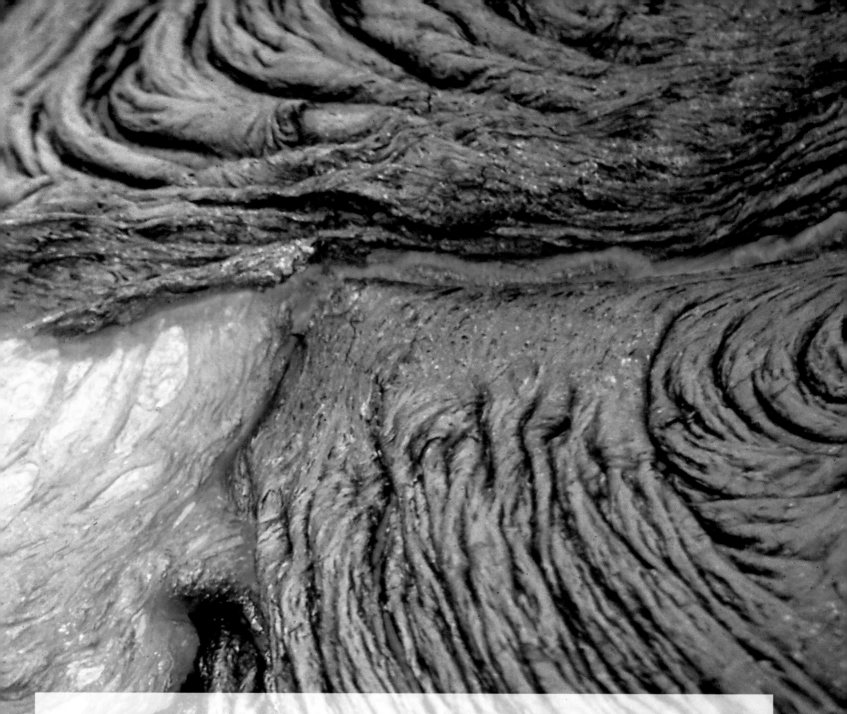

© 1996 Losange
General editor: Daniel Obert
Scientific consultant: Frédéric Lécuyer
Original title: Fabuleux Volcans

© 2001 for the English edition:
Könemann Verlagsgesellschaft mbH
Bonner Strasse 126, D-50968 Cologne

Translation from French: Dick Nowell for SMALL PRINT
Editing: Naomi Laredo and Karin Fancett
Project management and typesetting: SMALL PRINT,
Cambridge, England

Project coordination: Nadja Bremse-Koob
Production: Ursula Schümer

Printing and binding: Mateu Cromo Artes Gráficas, Madrid

Printed in Spain

ISBN 3-8290-5620-6

10 9 8 7 6 5 4 3 2 1

CONTENTS

FIRE IN THE EARTH

Map of the volcanoes mentioned in this book   10–11
Kilauea, *by Marie-Christine Hamond and Karim Kelfoun*   12–15
Mount Saint Helens, *by Jacques Durieux*   16–21
Nevado del Ruiz, *by Frédéric Maciejak*   22–23
Mount Pelée, *by Alain Gourgaud*   24–25
Heimaey, *by Olgeir Sigmarsson*   26–27
Etna, *by Frédéric Lécuyer*   28–29
Piton de la Fournaise, *by Jacques Durieux and Frédéric Lécuyer*   30–35
Pinatubo, *by Jacques Durieux*   36–45
Mount Colo, *by Frédéric Lécuyer*   46–47
Merapi, *by Alain Gourgaud*   48–51
Sakurajima, *by Frédéric Lécuyer*   52–53
Rabaul, *by Marie-Christine Hamond and Karim Kelfoun*   54–55

HOW VOLCANOES WORK

by Frédéric Lécuyer

Introduction   59
Volcanoes in legend   60–61
The history of volcano science   62–68

Plate tectonics   69–86
The structure of the earth   70–71
From continental drift to plate tectonics   72–73
Volcanic activity and tectonic plates: world map   74–75
Volcanic activity and plate tectonics   76–77
Volcanoes in subduction zones   78–79
Volcanoes on the mid-ocean ridges   80–83
Volcanoes at hot spots   84–86

The origin of magma   87–96
From magma to lava   88–89
Oceanic basalts   90–91
Subduction-zone basalts   92–93
Mid-plate basalts   92–93
Magma transport and storage   94–95
The carbonatites of Ol Doinyo Lengai   96

The mechanics of volcanic eruptions   97–113
Eruption mechanisms   98–99
The range of eruption types   100–101
The products of eruptions   102–103
The life story of an andesitic stratovolcano   104–105
The life story of a shield volcano   106–107
Secondary volcanic phenomena   108–109
Large-scale volcanic structures   110–113

Volcanoes in the solar system, *by Frédéric Maciejak*   114–115

LIVING WITH VOLCANOES

by Jean-Louis Cheminée

The hazards of volcanoes   118–133
Major volcanic disasters and their causes   120–121
The seven principal volcanic hazards   123–133
Volcanoes and air safety   126–127

Volcano surveillance and the forecasting of eruptions   134–153
Volcanological observatories: their work and development   135–140
The volcanological observatories of the IPGP   137–139
The techniques of volcano surveillance and eruption forecasting   140–153

Conclusion, *by Jean-Louis Cheminée*   154–155

Glossary   156
Index   157–159
Picture credits   160
Metric units   160

**FIRE
IN THE
EARTH**

MAP OF THE VOLCANOES

Drawing up a list of the volcanoes to include in a book like this one may not seem a particularly difficult task – but then, 1511 new volcanoes have become active in just the last ten thousand years! The Smithsonian Institution, publisher of *Volcanoes of the World*, a catalog of the most active volcanoes, has listed no fewer than 414 eruptions involving loss of life, and 101 leading to evacuations, between 1974 and 1993! Scientists have dated over 7880 eruptions to the period since 8000 B.C.

So, in fact, the problem is how to choose: each of these volcanoes has some claim on our attention, or at least that of the many volcanologists working in every corner of the globe. We cannot even list them all, but we have covered as broad a selection as possible, though we would have liked to include many more!

Augustine

Mt. Saint Helens

Crater Lake

Yellowstone

Shasta

Lassen Peak

Paricutín

Soufrière de la Guade

Mt. Pele

Nevado del Ruiz

Teahitia

Kilauea

Mauna Loa

El Misti

Huaynaputina

MacDonald

El Chichón

Arenal

Poas

△ Volcanoes described in detail on pages 12–55

▲ Other volcanoes mentioned

MENTIONED IN THIS BOOK

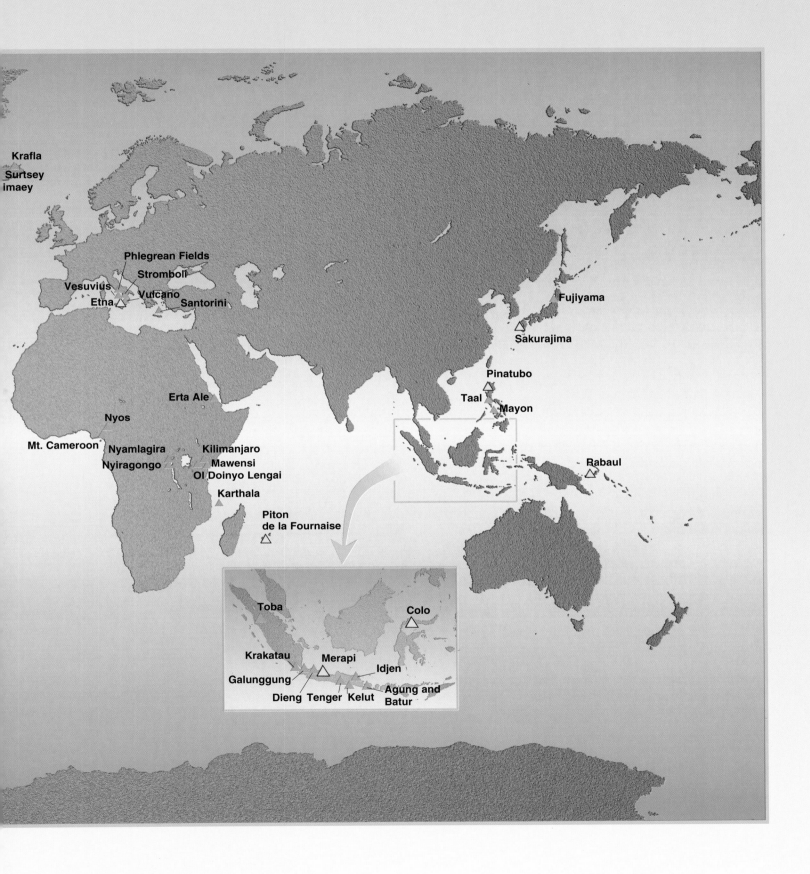

KILAUEA

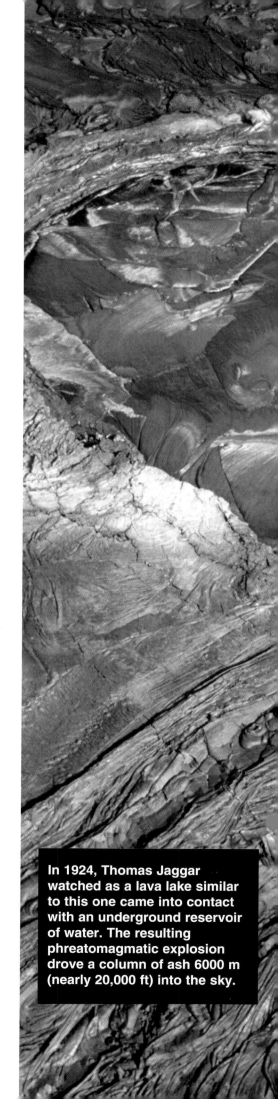

Standing shoulder to shoulder with Mauna Loa, Kilauea rises 1220 meters (4000 feet) above sea level. It has very gently sloping sides, nowhere steeper than 6°, making it a perfect example of a shield volcano, a type formed by the layering of very free-flowing basaltic lava. Most of the lava (over 65%) first flows through lava tunnels, before spreading out to create "ropy lava" formations (also called pahoehoe lava).

At the volcano's summit is a distinctive caldera 3.5 kilometers (2 miles) across and 150 meters (500 feet) deep. In the southwestern sector of the caldera is a pit-crater (an area of ground collapse) known as Halemaumau, or "the domain of ferns."

Kilauea is also remarkable for the rift zone that runs right across it, with two branches starting at the summit and running to the east and to the southwest respectively. On the surface, the path of the rift is marked by old cones of scoria, lakes of solidified lava – and active eruptions.

It has been deduced from geophysical data that an irregularly-shaped reservoir of magma about 4 kilometers (2.5 miles) beneath the summit of Kilauea supplies both the main chimney and the network of fissures in the rift zone.

An eventful history

Records of Kilauea's eruptions begin as late as the 19th century, and are mainly due to the work of missionaries stationed in Hawaii. William Ellis described the eruption of 1823, and Titus Coan devoted himself to studying the volcano's activity from 1840 to 1874. Their observations were followed by those of the mineralogist and explorer James Dana.

Between them, the three men reported virtually constant activity at Kilauea's summit between 1823 and 1924, revealing a cyclical pattern of subsidence and refilling of the caldera, as well as occasional lateral outpourings.

In 1912, the scientist Thomas Jaggar built a volcanological observatory on the caldera's rim, which is still there today. From here, he witnessed an eruption of the explosive type in 1924, a rare event for a volcano that had been thought "quiet." This phreatomagmatic (steam/magma) eruption produced a column of ash rising to over 6000 meters (nearly 20,000 feet), and emptied the lava lake which until then had filled the Halemaumau Crater.

For some time after this, activity was more episodic, and was confined to either the caldera or the rift zone on the volcano's eastern flank. The year 1968 marked the start of a new period of intense activity, most of it taking place along the same branch of the rift zone. The eruption that began in earnest in May 1969 and continued, with a few quieter spells, until June 1974 gave rise to the crater of Mauna Ulu, "the mountain that grows." An estimated 185 million cubic meters (240 million cubic yards) of lava was expelled during this period of eruption, some of which flowed into the sea.

In 1924, Thomas Jaggar watched as a lava lake similar to this one came into contact with an underground reservoir of water. The resulting phreatomagmatic explosion drove a column of ash 6000 m (nearly 20,000 ft) into the sky.

- **Location:** Island of Hawaii (USA, Pacific Ocean)
- **Altitude:** 1220 m (4000 ft) above sea level, but rising 6750 m (22,140 ft) above the surrounding ocean floor
- **Diameter at base:** 180 x 75 km (112 x 47 miles)
- **Volcano type:** basalt shield volcano, hot spot
- **Most frequent activity types:** Hawaiian (the source of this term), fissure eruptions, lava fountains, formation of lava lakes
- **Eruptions:**
  Earliest eruptions 200,000 years ago.

  Most recent eruption: 1983 to date.
- **Points of interest:**
  The history of Kilauea began 200,000 years ago and falls into five phases:

  200,000 to 2000 years ago: volcano formed and grew in height.

  2000 years ago:
  Powers Caldera formed, 8 x 6 km (5 x 3.75 miles), filling gradually until 1790.

  1790:
  Modern Caldera, 5 x 3.5 km (3 x 2 miles), formed by ground collapse.

  1790 to 1960:
  activity mainly confined to the summit craters.

  1960 to present:
  activity located mainly on the volcano's flanks.

The eruption of 1983

However, the longest-lasting and most productive eruption in Kilauea's recorded history is the one that began in 1983. At least fifty major eruptive episodes have been observed and recorded since that year.

Initially, a fissure eruption appeared midway along the eastern rift zone in January 1983. For nearly three and a half years, activity took the form of lava fountains, which at their climax reached a height of over 500 meters (1650 feet). In this process, magma is flung into the air by the force of released gases. It may then form flows of still-molten lava, or may fall back to earth as solidified fragments, which build up a heap of scoria. This is how the cone called Pu'u 'O'o was formed around the vent where these fountains erupted, some 19 kilometers (12 miles) below Kilauea's summit.

In July 1986, activity shifted to an area 3 kilometers (2 miles) further east, again in the volcano's eastern rift zone. Now centered on Kupaianaha, the event entered an "effusive phase" that lasted for five and a half years. During the episode of November 1991, the lava flow was estimated at 12 million cubic meters (15.5 million cubic yards) a day, and its temperature reached almost 1100°C (2000°F). In February 1992, activity at Kupaianaha ceased, giving way to occasional eruptions on the western side of Pu'u 'O'o, where the crater filled to become a lava lake. In all, the lava produced by this event between 1983 and 1996 covered a surface of 82 square kilometers (32 square miles), in places to a depth of 25 meters (82 feet)! The island of Hawaii had grown by around 150 hectares

Venting of gas from the magma below through fissures produces lava fountains, which can reach heights of 500 m (1650 ft).

Lava lakes, like this one in the Pu'u 'O'o Crater, are not common. They are linked to effusive mechanisms and fill or empty according to the volcano's mood, containing or releasing lava flows that sometimes reach all the way to the sea.

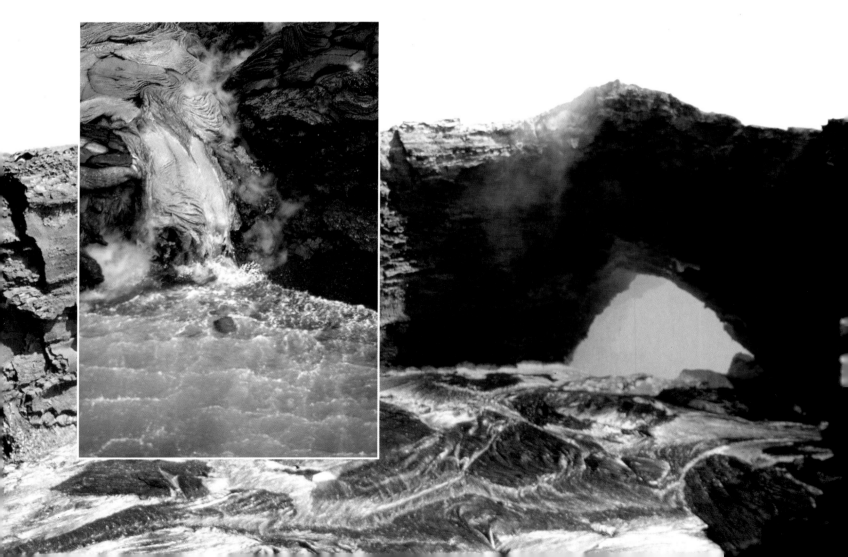

THE MYTH OF THE GODDESS PELE

For Hawaiians, Kilauea ("the rising cloud of smoke") has always been the favorite haunt of Pele, an awesome divinity who symbolizes youth and beauty. Sometimes she appears to the inhabitants of the Big Island of Hawaii as a lovely young woman; but at other times, to put them to the test, she takes the form of an ugly old hag. Tales are told of how her anger destroys those who are so bold as to cross her, for it is she who causes the mountain to erupt. How else could such unbridled outbursts be explained, except as the whim of some goddess? Tradition even maintains that it is Pele's hair that sparkles forth from the lava fountains, and her body whose lines the lava flows trace out.

But the existence of Kilauea can be accounted for by geological processes well known to scientists, and has no need of legend to explain it. Like all the other volcanoes of the Hawaiian archipelago, Kilauea lies on the volcanic range that runs across the ocean from southeast to northwest, rising out of the central region of the Pacific plate. Each new volcano has risen in turn above the same mantle plume and then moved away with the drift of the Pacific plate (see the diagrams on p.85), so that the further southeast, the younger the volcano. Kilauea, at just under 200,000 years old, is one of the most recent productions of this "hot spot" mechanism.

(370 acres), but the gaining of this new land has been offset by the devastation of a considerable area of forest and grassland.

What is more, where lava flows have approached the inhabited coastal area, they have caused a great deal of damage to property. The lava advances only slowly in this zone – moving at 4 to 5 kilometers (2.5 to 3 miles) per hour – so the local people and emergency services have had time to organize evacuations: they have even relocated domestic oil tanks for fear of explosions and, still more remarkably, moved a whole church to preserve their place of worship from the flames. By 1996, a total of 180 homes had been overwhelmed, and to the southwest of the island's capital, Hilo, the picturesque little town of Kalapana, which had so often been threatened in the past, was eventually obliterated by the all-engulfing lava.

Kilauea remains active to this day, enabling volcanologists from all over the world to profit from the exceptionally good conditions it offers for studying and recording eruptions. As a result of such unusually close scrutiny by scientists, 99% of the volcano's eruptions can now be predicted. ∎

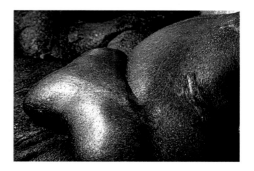

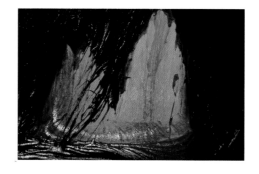

The very free-flowing lava produced by Kilauea gives rise to some weird formations, such as hummocks of "pudding lava" (left) and long-drawn-out "lava strands" (right), which look rather like melted cheese.

MOUNT SAINT HELENS

U ntil 1980, Mount Saint Helens was one of the natural jewels of the American West, towering at a height of 2950 meters (9680 feet) over lake and river, forest and prairie. Its shape and its snowy summit earned it the nickname of the American Fujiyama, and it made a splendid sight rising out of the clouds that rolled in from the Pacific.

The native people who had lived near Mount Saint Helens for thousands of years gave it a wide berth: they called it *Tah-one-lat-clah*, "the smoking mountain."

An active past

Mount Saint Helens is a large stratovolcano belonging to the Pacific Ring of Fire. It was highly active during the 19th century, and from 1832 to 1857 was more or less constantly in eruption. The region was not densely inhabited, so few people saw these eruptions, and the memory of them faded quickly. Then, for more than a century, the mountain's behavior gave every reason to believe it was harmless.

Nevertheless, the volcano attracted the interest of a few geologists, and in 1978 Dwight Crandell and Donal Mullineaux published the results of a very detailed study, concluding that "There could be an eruption before the end of this century" (see page 151). The volcano was soon to show how right they were.

Warning signs

After 123 years of slumber, the initial signs that Mount Saint Helens was awakening came in March 1980: an earthquake with a magnitude of 4.2 was the first of a long series of shocks, and by March 25 many hundreds were being recorded every day. The volcano made the front pages on March 27, for at 12:36 p.m. a violent explosion was heard throughout the region, and Mount Saint Helens began to hurl out jets of steam and ash.

A group of journalists who visited the summit by helicopter saw a ring of black cinders surrounding a hole at the top of the snow-capped mountain, and great chasms which bore witness to the volcano's return to life.

Throughout April, explosion after explosion enlarged the crater, and the ash gradually turned the snow a dirty brown. Scientists following these developments in detail quickly realized that these were phreatic explosions (involving groundwater which turns to steam), and that they were gradually breaking up the ancient dome. A continuous tremor (regular shocks, caused by magma rising in its channels) began to be felt, suggesting that fresh magma was filling the whole structure of the volcano.

The mountain's shape was also changing markedly: the magma forcing its way up through the volcano formed a protrusion at the summit. By May 12, this spike was growing at a rate of 1.5 meters

- **Location:** Washington (USA)
- **Altitude:** 2550 m (8360 ft); 2950 m (9680 ft) before May 18, 1980
- **Diameter at base:** 8.5 km (5.25 miles)
- **Volcano type:** andesitic stratovolcano, subduction zone, cordillera type
- **Most frequent activity types:** explosions, debris avalanches
- **Eruptions:**
  Earliest eruptions 40–50,000 years ago.
  Ten recorded eruptions since the 17th century.
  Most recent eruption: 1991.
- **Points of interest:**
  May 18, 1980, was one of the most significant dates in modern volcanology. For the first time, volcano scientists had the opportunity to observe a major destabilization of a volcanic edifice. On the mountain's north slope, 2.7 km³ (0.65 cu. miles) of material from a cone that had lasted over 2200 years broke up in a few minutes, freeing pressurized gases within the mass of lava (cryptodome) that had been trapped inside it.

  In less than half a minute, a supersonic blast flattened forests over an area of more than 600 km² (230 sq. miles), and the great sheets of debris from the volcano's sides formed an avalanche that left behind an "avalanche caldera."

  This climax was followed by pyroclastic flows, alternating with the formation of new domes.

Following the cataclysm of May 18, 1980, a succession of cloud columns rose into the sky over Mount Saint Helens, as further Plinian eruptions destroyed each new dome that formed within the caldera.

(5 feet) a day, and it had already reached a length of 200 meters (650 feet).

As soon as the tremors had started, the US Forest Service had closed off access to the mountain, for fear that falling debris might cause avalanches. From March 27 onwards, scientists from the US Geological Survey began to produce more precise forecasts, and they recommended an exclusion zone 30 kilometers (20 miles) in radius around the volcano. Finally, the state of Washington decided to evacuate two zones: the first became totally off-limits, and access to the other was restricted.

On Saturday, May 17, the volcanologist David Johnston came on duty at the Coldwater II station, relieving his colleague Harry Glicken (who later lost his life in the explosion of another volcano, Mount Unzen in Japan, in June 1991). It was a fine, sunny spring weekend, and nature seemed smiling and at peace – but there was a rude awakening to come.

IN THE HEART OF THE CASCADE RANGE

The unusually fearsome and sudden Mount Saint Helens eruption served as a reminder that the whole Cascade Range to which the mountain belongs is volcanic, and capable of violent eruption. From Lassen Peak, northeast of San Francisco, to Mount Garibaldi (British Columbia) in the north, this range is part of the Pacific Ring of Fire. Although many of these majestic mountains had in the past given indications that could have been seen as warnings of trouble to come, they had certainly not been paid enough attention.

Mount Rainer, for instance, 80 kilometers (50 miles) north of Mount Saint Helens, gives off smoke and vapor, melting its covering of ice into strange shapes. Mount Hood, 100 kilometers (60 miles) in the other direction, breathes sulfurous vapors from its fumaroles ... and Mount Mazama too, best known for its impressive 600-meter (1970-foot) deep caldera, Crater Lake, should have drawn attention to the potential violence of this volcanic range. Indeed, 6000 years ago, Mount Mazama had covered the whole northeast of what is now the United States with ash. In May, 1915, Lassen Peak produced a dark gray cloud that rose to a height of 11 kilometers (7 miles), and showered ash as far as 300 kilometers (200 miles) away; however, in 1915 international attention was preoccupied with other events ...

In 1969, after the first eruptions of Arenal, a volcano in Costa Rica similar in many ways to mountains in the Cascade Range, the geologist Dwight Crandell warned the authorities about the crouching monsters that lay not far from population centers (Portland, for instance), and the need to take account of this potential hazard.

In 1969, and again in 1972 and 1977, steps were taken to set up surveillance stations and monitor seismic activity. The system came into operation in March 1980, by which time there were 58 stations in the network; just one was on Mount Saint Helens.

■ **Gray area: volcanic deposits less than 2 million years old**

May 18, 1980: the climax

At seven in the morning, from his observation post 8 kilometers (5 miles) from the volcano, David Johnston radioed his latest observations to the Vancouver control center. Seismic activity, ground deformation, sulfur dioxide (SO_2) emissions: the whole picture was much as it had been for several weeks now. One day, he had been heard comparing the mountain to a bomb with a lighted fuse and remarking that, unfortunately, nobody knew how long it was.

Suddenly, at 8:32 a.m., he came on the radio again: "Vancouver, Vancouver, this is it!" Then silence. Nothing was ever found of David Johnston, his equipment, his car, or his camp.

The eruption of Mount Saint Helens had begun in earnest.

Everything happened within the first minute of this cataclysmic eruption, and it reached maximum power extremely quickly. A major seismic shock (magnitude 5.1) broke open the swelling that had appeared near the summit, and the whole north face crumbled, forming a huge avalanche of debris that raced down the mountainside. The pressure that had built up inside the cryptodome (the dome hidden inside the volcano) at last escaped: the gases decompressed almost instantly. There were two simultaneous explosions: one plume rose directly upward into the sky, and another emerged sideways, on the volcano's flank. Water was turning to steam with incredible violence, and the plume from the lateral explosion caught up and overtook the initial debris avalanche. This cloud swept irresistibly over slopes and peaks, driven by an unimaginably powerful force, and moving at nearly 1100 kilometers (680 miles) per hour.

The temperature inside the cloud, as it spread more than 25 kilometers (15 miles) from the volcano, was as high as 260°C (500°F). The blast uprooted every tree in an area of 600 square kilometers (230 square miles). It is estimated that this sideways blast lasted for just thirty seconds, but the avalanche of debris that followed carried with it ash, rocks, lumps of ice, and uprooted trees.

These forests surrounding Mount Saint Helens were the home of giant sequoias, some over 60 m (200 ft) tall and up to 5 m (16 ft) thick. Coming from as far as 25 km (15 miles) away, the blast mowed them down.

TRUE STORIES FROM MOUNT SAINT HELENS

Harry Truman and his cats

Mount Saint Helens came up against the extreme stubbornness of an 84-year-old man. Harry Truman lived in a shack on the shore of Spirit Lake, right in the red zone, the priority evacuation area. After a magnitude 5 earthquake shook the region, he admitted to a visiting friend that he was afraid, but declared that nothing was going to budge him from his home. "I'm a part of this mountain," he said, "and the mountain's a part of me."

Along with his sixteen cats, Harry Truman perished in the eruption of Mount Saint Helens, which he had regarded as his lifelong friend.

The saga of the Moore family

Mike and Lu Moore and their two children were camping 20 kilometers (12 miles) from the north face of the volcano on the very day of the eruption. Mike Moore had taken care to stay well within the officially-designated safety zone, sheltered by high ridges, and it was this wise precaution that saved the lives of all four.

A little after 8:30 a.m. on May 18, 1980, the family was aroused by a dull rumbling, instantly followed by an immense, swirling ash cloud. They barely had time to take shelter in a neighboring cabin, and lay there swaddled in blankets, their faces covered in damp cloths, as the ash cloud passed overhead.

They could hear stones bombarding the cabin roof ... and when calm returned, they came out into an ashen world, coated with gray powder. They tried to reach their car, but could not get through the tangle of uprooted trees, and were forced to spend the night in the midst of this devastation before eventually being found, next morning, by a rescue helicopter.

In all, more than two billion cubic meters of debris piled up in Spirit Lake and in the river, which was blocked for nearly 30 kilometers (20 miles). The rubble was deposited more than 180 meters (nearly 600 feet) thick in places. Mud flows followed, from the melting of ice and snow: these carried cinders and rocks as far as 45 kilometers (28 miles) from the volcano. Within 15 minutes, the vertical plume of ash was 25 kilometers (15 miles) high, and ash continued being thrown up for nine hours without a pause. Twenty minutes after the explosion, the sound waves from Mount Saint Helens were heard in Seattle.

Once the paroxysm had subsided, the volcano could be seen once more. On the summit of Mount Saint Helens, a new crater 1.5 by 3 kilometers (1 mile by 2 miles) wide and 700 meters (2300 feet) deep had formed. The explosion had blown the top off the mountain, leaving it 400 meters (1300 feet) lower. Sixty people had died, 300 kilometers (200 miles) of road had been destroyed, and several thousand trees had been pulverized. Over 6500 deer and elk, 200 black bears, and countless birds and small mammals had been killed. Nothing moved for miles around.

New domes would later form in the crater, and new explosions would tear them apart, continuing until 1986. But none of these explosions matched the power of the one on May 18, 1980, which delivered an estimated 27,000 times the energy of the Hiroshima bomb. ■

For the first time in the history of volcanology, scientists were able to watch as the whole side of a volcano slipped away. In just a few moments, Mount Saint Helens lost 400 m (1300 ft) of its height, and a horseshoe-shaped gash 3 km (2 miles) across and 700 m (2300 ft) deep split open its northern slope.

The force of the explosion was augmented by the melting of ice and snow, which mingled with the ash, and followed by powerful mud slides. Pouring down the mountainsides, they swept away houses, wrapped trucks around trees, and overwhelmed everything in their path.

NEVADO DEL RUIZ

Picture an Andean cordillera landscape in western Colombia, with sparse vegetation, bare rocks, and snow-capped peaks. The huge andesitic stratovolcanoes, separated by deep valleys, bear witness to the subduction zone that lies beneath. Here, Nevado del Ruiz has been piling up its immense structure for the last few thousand years: about 55 kilometers (34 miles) in diameter and 5321 meters (17,453 feet) high, the mountain is crowned by an icecap that covers 25 square kilometers (10 square miles). It rises some 5000 meters (16,400 feet) above the cultivated and densely-populated plain of the River Magdalena, about 70 kilometers (43 miles) to the east, and more than 3000 meters (9850 feet) above the flat valley of the Cauca to the west. Until the disaster of November 13, 1985, Nevado del Ruiz was not much talked of around the world, but on that day it became famous. Only two previous eruptions had been recorded in the annals of the region's inhabitants: one in 1595, when six hundred people had been killed by debris flows (lahars) which came down the Guali and Lagunillas valleys as far as the Magdalena, and one in 1845, when a lahar obliterated Ambalema and a thousand of its inhabitants, just 30 kilometers (20 miles) uphill from the site where Armero then lay, peaceful and prosperous, on the deposits of earlier lahars. The volcano had then entered an inactive phase that lasted until 1984.

25,000 dead in just a few hours

Toward the end of 1984, the volcano reawoke. Earthquakes shook its peak, the fumaroles grew hotter, and there were some minor phreatic eruptions. This modest activity continued until the end of August 1985, when the earthquakes increased in frequency. On September 11, the volcano belched out hot cinders for seven hours, covering the summit and melting enough ice to produce a lahar, which then swept down the valley of the River Azufrado, covering a distance of around 27 kilometers (17 miles) in barely one hour: a terrible warning. On November 10 the seismic tremors became continuous, a clear indication that the magma was nearing the summit. On the 13th, the region was lashed by a torrential down-pour of rain, and just before 3 p.m. a phreatic eruption threw up ash which fell some hours later on the towns of Mariquita and Armero, over 45 kilometers (28 miles) to the northeast and east of the mountain respectively. Toward 9 p.m., the magma eruption began: a column of ash 8 kilometers (5 miles) tall formed, accompanied by some small pyroclastic flows (hot ash flows). Though this erup-tion was a modest one for this type of volcano, it melted more than 5% of the icecap, and this huge melt, swollen by the rain and by water from the small lakes that filled the mountain's summit craters, mingled with the accumulated ashy material to produce torrential lahars. They poured down the valleys radiating from the summit,

A volcano makes the headlines: in 1985, a gigantic mud flow from Nevado del Ruiz submerged the town of Armero. There was a lesson to be learned from this disaster: the need for scientists and governments to work more closely together.

- **Location:** Colombia
- **Altitude:** 5321 m (17,453 ft)
- **Volcano type:** andesitic cordillera stratovolcano (subduction zone)
- **Most frequent activity type:** explosive, with pyroclastic flows

rapidly accelerating to speeds of 30 to 35 kilometers (19 to 22 miles) per hour.

It took barely two hours for the deadly flows of debris to reach the inhabited areas more than 60 kilometers (38 miles) from the point of eruption. Huge torrents of mud, rocks, and enormous tree trunks swamped the streets of Chinchina (to the west) and Armero (to the east), sweeping away everything in their path. The consequences were tragic: 25,000 dead, many thousands injured, 15,000 cattle killed. The roads were blocked; electricity and telephone lines were cut; and homes, hospitals, schools, and factories were almost completely destroyed. The entire rural economy had been ruined: in the space of just a few hours, Nevado del Ruiz had risen to fourth place in the grim list of the most lethal volcanoes of the past century.

An avoidable catastrophe

The first intimations of eruptive activity had occurred twelve months before, and seismographs had been set up around the volcano. By October, a risk chart had been drawn up. And yet a baleful procession of adverse factors brought these preparations to nothing. The scientists' communiqués were not clear – were contradictory, even – and so had little credibility with the authorities and the public. The authorities, not knowing when the eruption would take place, waited until the last minute before raising the alarm, fearing the high economic and political cost of an evacuation ordered too soon, or ordered unnecessarily. Worse still, the government was too busy consolidating its own political power, and fighting the drug traffickers, to pay full attention to an eruption that had, in any case, already been going on for over a year. To cap it all, the bad weather, the lateness of the hour, and the repeat screening of a particularly important football match all helped to slow the spreading of the alarm. With hindsight, it is quite clear that many lives could have been saved. ∎

MOUNT PELÉE

In the early hours of May 8, 1902, everything was quiet in Saint-Pierre on the Caribbean island of Martinique. But at 8 a.m. the town was rocked by a violent explosion, heard up to 600 kilometers (370 miles) away, and a few minutes later Saint-Pierre, one of the finest towns in the Caribbean, was obliterated by a "nuée ardente," or glowing cloud, rolling down from Mount Pelée, the volcano dominating the bay. Over 28,000 people were killed, in what was to remain the worst volcanic disaster of the 20th century.

On August 10 of the same year, another nuée ardente claimed over a thousand further victims in the nearby township of Morne-Rouge.

- **Location:** Island of Martinique (Caribbean)
- **Altitude:** 1397 m (4582 ft)
- **Volcano type:** andesitic stratovolcano, subduction zone, island arc
- **Most frequent activity type:** explosive, with destruction of domes (gave its name to the Pelean type of eruption)
- **Eruptions:**
  Earliest eruptions 25,000 years ago.
  Most recent eruptions: 1902–05, 1929–32.
  25 known eruptions in the last 6000 years.

A well-advertised disaster

Warning signs of the cataclysm were seen as early as 1889: small fumaroles appeared around the top of the volcano, which at that time contained a hollow, the caldera known as l'Étang Sec, "the dry pool." At the start of 1902, this fumarole activity intensified: in particular, a strong smell of hydrogen sulfide began to emanate from the western flank of the volcano. This was where earlier, quite minor hydrovolcanic eruptions had taken place in 1792 and 1851, known as "phreatic" eruptions because they involved the superheating of underground water. The first phreatic explosion of 1902 came on April 24. Earth tremors were felt, and a plume of steam and ash formed. The social and political life of Saint-Pierre was hardly touched by these events, unsettling though they were – and very close by: the volcano's peak is only 7 kilometers (4 miles) from the town. The first round of elections for the legislature, on April 27, had been inconclusive, and attention was focused on the second round, due to take place on May 11.

On May 2, cinders rained down on the small neighboring town of Le Prêcheur, and some of its inhabitants came to Saint-Pierre to take

refuge. The local authorities played down the danger – because of the election campaign!

On May 3, it was Saint-Pierre's turn to wake up under a light dusting of gray ash. Two days later, the crater of l'Étang Sec burst, releasing a wave of destruction. At the mouth of the River Blanche, the Guérin factory with its twenty-five workers was buried under 6 meters (20 feet) of mud. As this flood reached the sea, it launched a mini-tsunami at the harbor of Saint-Pierre, sowing panic among the townspeople. On May 6, in spite of the Mayor's reassurances, some people left the town. The next day, the volcano was quiet, and a committee of scientists pronounced that "Mount Pelée presents no more danger to the town of Saint-Pierre than Vesuvius does to Naples." At 8 a.m. on May 8, Saint-Pierre was wiped from the map: just two people survived. One of these, named Ciparis, was in jail at the time. Protected by the thick walls of his cell, he lived to show off his burns in a circus for many years to come.

What devastated the town of Saint-Pierre, together with an area of 58 square kilometers (23 square miles) around it, was a "nuée ardente" expelled from the top of the volcano. The expression was coined by the French volcanologist Alfred Lacroix, who was sent on an official investigation of the disaster scene in June 1902. Nuées ardentes (a term still used to refer to a pyroclastic flow accompanied by a hot ash cloud) are associated with the growth and subsequent destruction of a dome of viscous lava (in this case, andesitic lava). The nuée ardente thrown up by Mount Pelée, a mixture of dome fragments and expanding gases, roared down the slope at high speed, reaching the town in just a few minutes. A dome was outgrowing the crater and began to collapse, causing small, incandescent avalanches. Its progress was followed in detail by Lacroix until September 1903.

By the end of 1902, a lava spike on the top of the dome had grown to a length of 260 meters (850 feet); it then crumbled. The dome continued to collapse, producing further nuées ardentes similar to or smaller than those of May 8. The largest occurred on May 20 (completing the destruction of the town), June 6, July 9, and August 30, 1902. The last of these laid waste a further 56 square kilometers (22 square miles) to the east of the volcano, including part of the small township of Morne-Rouge. ∎

Like the claw of a dragon struggling to climb out of the earth, this spike rose 260 m (850 ft) out of the volcano's summit.

HEIMAEY

- **Location:** Island of Heimaey (Iceland)
- **Altitude:** Helgafell (The Sacred Hill), 225 m (740 ft); Eldfell (Fire Hill), 215 m (705 ft) after the 1973 eruption
- **Volcano type:** fissure eruption volcano, mid-ocean (mid-Atlantic) ridge zone, with additional hot spot
- **Most frequent activity type:** Hawaiian (lava fountains and aa-type flows) and Strombolian (regular explosions)
- **Eruptions:**

  Formation of Helgafell: 5500 years ago.

  Most recent eruption: January–June 1973.

On January 23, 1973, a little before 2 a.m., one of Iceland's most destructive eruptions began, right next to the country's main fishing port. It was on Heimaey, the only inhabited island in the Vestmannaeyjar archipelago. Soon after midnight, while most of the island's five thousand inhabitants were asleep, storm force 12 winds from the southeast whipped up the sea into such a fury that almost the entire fishing fleet of sixty or seventy vessels remained in the harbor. A little later that night, the wind dropped and veered, now blowing the clouds due north.

Incandescent waves

Everything seemed calm when, just before two, the town's central police station received a telephone alert: an eruption was beginning near the harbor. The police rushed to the eastern end of town. There, less than 400 meters (440 yards) from the nearest homes, an erupting fissure 1600 meters (one mile) long was belching out fountains of lava which formed a curtain of fire, in places as much as 150 meters (500 feet) tall.

The lava was flowing to the east and northeast, and one flow had already reached the sea. The cinder deposits (tephra) were already quite heavy, but luckily the wind was blowing the fallout north, sparing the town and its houses for that night. The fire-alarm sirens were sounded, while wailing police and fire service cars toured the streets to wake up the townspeople, who were, remarkably, still asleep! Just after the stroke of two, the evacuation began, and the inhabitants streamed toward the harbor. There lay the boats immobilized by the evening's storm, and people quickly climbed into them to escape from the eruption zone. For the first few hours, the fissure produced almost 200 cubic meters (260 cubic yards) of magma per second; most of it emerged as lava flows, but thin streams were spewed northward into the sky, over the boats carrying the people of Heimaey. The crack extended for a length of 100 meters (110 yards) beneath the sea, and the contact between

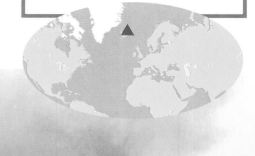

The eruption began with a curtain of fire pouring out of a fissure less than 400 m (440 yds) from people's homes – an incredible sight.

magma and water produced Surtseyan (hydrovolcanic) explosions. The wind showered the village with ash so dense that the few people who were still there to observe could not see their own hand at arm's length! Volcanic bombs fell on roofs and in through windows, starting fires.

A blanket of cinders

As the days went by, bombs weighing 200 to 300 kilos (440 to 660 pounds) were hurled 700 meters (760 yards) from the fissure, falling on the town. The layer of black cinders was over 3 meters (10 feet) thick in some parts of town, and roofs gave way under the weight. In early February, activity died down considerably. Directly over the spot where the fissure had been, there now stood a Strombolian cone 215 meters (705 feet) tall, which was later given the name Eldfell. On February 4, further north along the line of the crack, a small underwater eruption cut the island's brand-new drinking-water pipeline and the power-supply cable linking Heimaey with the rest of Iceland. That same day, a worrying development occurred: the lava flow changed direction and began to advance on the town. The new direction of the burning flood threatened the harbor entrance, which was already in danger of being blocked at low tide, since the lava had advanced 70 meters (76 yards) into the harbor. When the tide came in, the water came into contact with the lava flow and turned to steam; pressure from this steam caused explosions and fragmented the lava itself into small secondary cones, though these had no deep lava sources beneath them. At times, the explosions were so violent that people thought a new phase of eruptions had begun, right there in the harbor.

Battling against the volcano

On February 6, the authorities decided that Heimaey harbor must be saved at all costs. The battle began: under scientific direction, sea-water began to be pumped onto the glowing lava to make it set more quickly. The first attempt seemed promising, so every water pump that could be found in Iceland was put into service, as well as many from overseas. It was a four-month struggle, a dance to the rhythm of constantly shifting pumps and hoses, before the advance of the lava front began to slow down and eventually stopped. The harbor of Heimaey had been saved, and hope rekindled among the towns-people, many of whom returned to set about digging out their homes from under the blanket of ash.

The eruption ended on June 26, after five months of volcanic activity. It had produced nearly 230 million cubic meters (300 million cubic yards) of volcanic products in the form of flows, not to mention another 20 million (26 million cubic yards) of tephra ejected by the volcano, and had destroyed 417 houses. The cinders were later used to improve the airport runways, and to build new roads in the extension of the town to the west.

The lava flow had added 13.5 square kilometers (5.25 square miles) to the surface area of Heimaey island, and had erected a natural barrier against the southeasterly wind. The inhabitants still spray the lava flow with water and recover the steam produced in this way, which they use to heat their homes – and a brand new open-air swimming pool! ■

Blackout: dark lapilli covered everything. Houses and vehicles were swallowed up by the island on which they stood!

ETNA

A great warship edges along the coast in full sight of Taormina, when a dull rumbling is heard; the drummer quickens his pace, and the trireme from the great city of Athens hastens along. The thick dark folds of cloud hanging over Etna's snowcaps can mean only one thing: Hephaestus has rekindled his fire, the forge of the gods is at work, and woe betide any human who lingers in the neighborhood!

Myth and reality

A couple of thousand years later, ruins are all that remain of the ancient Hellenic empire – but Etna is still there. Still standing on the east coast of Sicily, and still active, as it has been for nearly 300,000 years. Etna, 3315 meters (10,900 feet) high and about 50 kilometers (30 miles) in diameter at its base, was one of the first volcanoes to be studied and recorded. It is a basalt shield volcano, but not very typical of its kind, located right above the spot where some major faults in the continental crust converge, at the edge of the great African plate.

Its history falls into a number of broad divisions: the first major episode took place under water and the latest left a gaping scar, the Valle del Bove ("Valley of the Ox"). This is a horseshoe-shaped caldera opening to the east, and seems to have evolved over a long period – many tens of thousands of years, in fact – before finally reaching its present size, 15 kilometers (9 miles) from north to south. At present, Etna has four central craters, and it is here that most of the eruption activity takes place. Additionally, however, large amounts of lava frequently well up from huge radial cracks that appear on the mountain's flanks; on many occasions these have destroyed, or threatened to destroy, fields, villages, and towns planted on the Sicilian monster's slopes.

The eruption of 1991–92: "Thanks – for nothing!"

When a new eruption from one of these fissures began in December 1991, a little to the south of the volcano's summit craters, nobody was worried. It was very high up, well away from the inhabited areas: the aa-type flows were contained within the Valley of the Ox. A few days later, however, in January 1992, the source of the lava moved along a crack to the southeast, and this time the fiery mass was emerging only 2200 meters (7200 feet) up. Even this would not have seemed disastrous, except that two centuries earlier, in 1792, an almost identical development had led to the total obliteration of the small town of Zafferana Etnea. The danger of an eruption outside the Valley of the Ox was very real: just three years before, in 1989, a parallel crack had opened up and spread well beyond the caldera. One of the first tasks for Professor Franco Barberi's team of volcanologists was to install sniffers for CO_2 and radon: these would give advance warning of magma rising anywhere along the fault.

The points where the 1991–92 lava flows emerged were in fact all within the great horseshoe-shaped depression, but the volume of

Like a ribbon of fire, the glowing flood of molten rock snakes its way down the side of Etna ... Hephaestus' forge is back at work!

- **Location:** Island of Sicily (Italy)
- **Altitude:** 3315 m (10,900 ft)
- **Diameter at base:** approx. 50 km (30 miles)
- **Volcano type:** basalt shield volcano (ill-defined geology)
- **Most frequent activity type:** Strombolian (regular explosions) and Hawaiian (episodic lava fountains, frequent and copious lava flows from fissures)
- **Eruptions:**
  Earliest eruptions 300,000 years ago.
  Most recent eruption: the 1991–92 flow, with explosive activity in the summit craters until 1996.
- **Point of interest:**
  Etna, the largest active volcano in Europe, has been in virtually continuous activity for the last two thousand years.

lava was so great that it soon spilled over the caldera's boundary walls and overran Val Calanna, the last barrier before Zafferana. The mountaindwellers of Etna did not wait for scientific advice: they piled up an earth dike with bulldozers and earthmovers, and this held back the flow until April 7, 1992; but then it was breached. The operation was repeated five times over the next 2 kilometers (1.25 miles), but each dike was overcome by the flow sooner or later. In fact, what was happening was that, although the source of the lava was at 2200 meters (7200 feet), it had formed a natural tunnel starting 200 meters (650 feet) further down. The lava flowed through this tunnel, reappearing about 970 meters (3200 feet) lower still as re-emergent sources, known as *bocche effimere* or "temporary mouths," whose location changed from day to day. As long as it was flowing within the tunnel, the lava could remain at an extremely high temperature, between 950 and 1050°C (1740 and 1920°F), which meant that it stayed quite fluid and the scorching lava front was able to advance to the very gates of Zafferana.

The Italian team of volcanologists quickly decided that the problem had to be tackled further up, at the point where the lava entered the tunnel. The theory was simple: divert the flow so that it could no longer flow in. The lava would still have the same distance to cover, but now it would be in the open air, where it would cool and thicken. The techniques used were many and varied: one was to open up the side of the flow with dynamite. The most original idea, though, was one that had never been tried before and required immense resources. US army helicopters began to shuttle back and forth over the glowing lava of Etna, carrying one- and three-ton blocks of concrete, with which the scientists hoped to block the tunnel entrance.

These various efforts had some success in slowing the lava flow, so that in the end only a few acres of vines and a hut that served as a seasonal shelter for grape-pickers were destroyed. But it was this hut that provoked the melodramatic episode for which this particular eruption of Etna will be remembered ...

The Sicilians, no doubt disappointed by the ineffectiveness of their own earth dikes, were of the opinion that the Italian government had not spent enough money or made enough effort to save Zafferana. On the wall of the ruined hut, they inscribed a trenchant message to the government: *"Grazie governo,"* "Thanks – for nothing!" The media picked it up, of course, thereby simply adding fuel to the flames. ∎

Diggers and earthmovers (above) are pressed into service, as the town of Zafferana comes under threat. Where the lava flows into self-made tunnels (inset below), helicopters are used (below) in an attempt to block the tunnel entrances with concrete.

PITON DE LA FOURNAISE

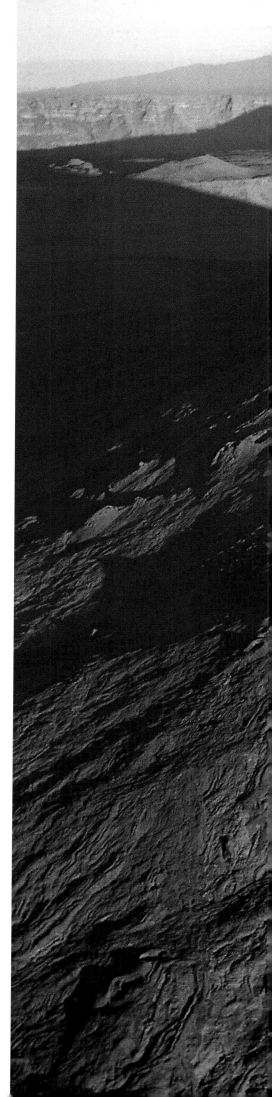

The island, alone and uninhabited in the middle of the Indian Ocean, had no name as yet, when naval officers landed in the early 17th century to take possession in the name of the King of France. In 1663, Louis Payen and a handful of men set about making the place habitable, and five years later the first colonists arrived on the "Isle Bourbon," which was only much later to be renamed Réunion. Piton de la Fournaise, the active volcano on the island, has been under observation ever since then, and has attracted visits from many famous scientists because of its almost uninterrupted activity.

A place full of history ...

Jean-Baptiste Bory de Saint-Vincent was the first to describe the volcanic activity of the region, in 1801. He also named the various craters after leading thinkers of the time, giving his own name to the main crater (then filled with a lava lake), which thus became the Bory Crater. He had as his guide Joseph Henry Hubert, whose job was to assist the French colonial administrator Pierre Poivre in his efforts to develop food and spice production. Hubert handed over his detailed observational records to Bory, who used them to illustrate his own work, *Travels in the Four Great Islands of the African Sea*, published in 1804.

... with a modern observatory!

It was early in the 20th century that Alfred Lacroix first suggested setting up a volcanic observatory to keep watch on Piton de la Fournaise. Finally built in 1979, two years after the village of Piton-Sainte-Rose was partially destroyed, the observatory was commissioned in 1980. It is less than 15 kilometers (9 miles) from the summit, and one of the most modern in the world, equipped not only to provide a better understanding of past volcanic activity on Réunion, but also, with its networks of seismometers, magnetometers, tiltmeters, and geochemical monitoring devices, to predict future eruptions: it has forecast all of the two dozen or so that have occurred since it came into service.

Piton de la Fournaise is a basalt shield volcano (see pages 106–7). Half a million years old, it is often compared with Kilauea (pages 12–15), but though both are near-perfect examples of the shield type in its fullest development, Piton de la Fournaise has a few distinctive eruption characteristics and structural

The volcano's activity is concentrated at its summit, where there is a huge depression 9 km (5.5 miles) in diameter. Within this are the two main pit-craters, the Bory Crater and (shown here) the Dolomieu Crater.

- **Location:** Island of Réunion (Indian Ocean)
- **Altitude:** 2631 m (8630 ft) above sea level and a further 4000 m (13,000 ft) above the ocean floor
- **Diameter at base:** 200–240 km (125–150 miles)
- **Volcano type:** hot spot
- **Most frequent activity type:** Hawaiian, fissure and effusive eruptions
- **Eruptions:**

  Earliest eruptions 530,000 years ago.

  Most recent eruption: 1992.
- **Points of interest:**

  Piton de la Fournaise ("Furnace Peak") is the active strato-volcano on Réunion. Though this volcano only became active 530,000 years ago, the first eruptions from the whole volcanic complex go back 2.1 million years. That phase created the northeastern part of the island, Piton des Neiges, and ended 220,000 years ago. Activity is now almost entirely concentrated on this peak, in the Fouqué enclosure, a huge depression 9 km (5.5 miles) in diameter and 100–300 m (330–990 feet) deep, open to the southeast. At its center are the two main craters: Bory, 200–350 m (220–380 yards) wide, already there by the 16th century, and Dolomieu, 700–1000 m (760–1100 yards) wide, created in 1766. Some eruptions also occur along the great radial and circular faults, causing damage but presenting little danger to life.

features that make it unique. Almost all of its eruptions come from fissures, concentrated mainly in two linear zones of weakness that slice down into the heart of the mountain. These structures, to the northeast and southeast of the central Dolomieu Crater, are known as "rift zones," and channel most of the magma that finds its way to the surface. The current hypothesis is that they are in fact symptoms of an immense landslide: the whole eastern side of the volcano is subsiding under its own weight.

This is not the first time such an event has occurred. Three thousand years ago, probably at the time when the caldera known as the Fouqué enclosure was formed, this same section of the mountain gave way and 20 to 30 cubic kilometers (5 to 7 cubic miles) of material slipped down, leaving behind a huge U-shaped depression open to the east, the Fouqué enclosure and the Grand-Brûlé. The landslide extended all the way under the sea. Today's fractured zones of weakness extend well beyond the Fouqué enclosure on both sides, and give rise to eruptions such as those of 1977 (to the northeast: Piton de Sainte-Rose) and 1986 (to the southeast). These eruptions outside the enclosure pose a threat to native villages in the area.

The 1986 eruption

Like some 97% of the eruptions on Piton de la Fournaise, this one began within the enclosure, in December 1985. Lava fountains and fluid lava flows alternated in the Dolomieu Crater until the start of February 1986, when a relatively quiet period ensued. At that point, the lava covered the whole floor of the crater, and it was estimated that the volcano had produced 7 million cubic meters (9 million cubic yards) of basalt. The partial vacuum left by the exit of this volume of material from the magma chamber caused a deflation of the summit, recorded by the observatory down on the Plaine des Cafres. Calm seemed to have been restored, and nothing further happened until mid-March. On March 17 and 18, the observatory gave the alarm: the volcano was swelling! The eastern side of the Dolomieu Crater had shifted 10 centimeters (4 inches): something was up.

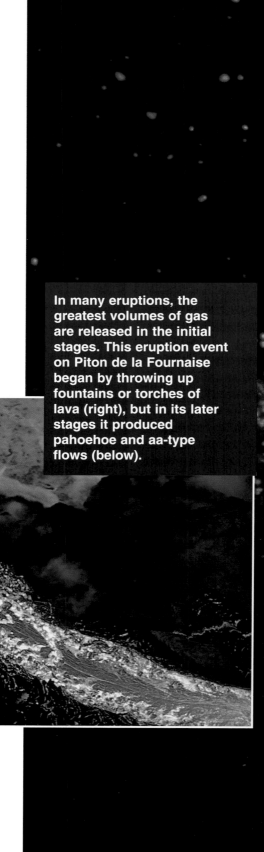

In many eruptions, the greatest volumes of gas are released in the initial stages. This eruption event on Piton de la Fournaise began by throwing up fountains or torches of lava (right), but in its later stages it produced pahoehoe and aa-type flows (below).

The next day, not only did the lava begin flowing again at Dolomieu, but a crack 700 meters (760 yards) long also opened outside the enclosure, to the southeast and more than 1200 meters (3900 feet) lower down, on a peak known as Piton de Takamaka (altitude 1070 m/3500 ft). Lava was flowing toward the sea, at speeds of between 100 and 300 meters (110 and 330 yards) per hour. The two hundred or so unfortunate people living in traditional houses downslope from the fissure had to be evacuated. This crack continued

erupting until March 23. Eight homes were destroyed, and the main road that encircles the island was crossed in two places by the lava, which eventually flowed into the sea.

While this was happening, a new fault opened up close to the shore, just 120 meters (390 feet) above sea level. The cracks spread rapidly over the ground, extending 800 meters (half a mile) up the side of the volcano after just a few hours. The road was cut and cut again by gaping cracks that grew with every new shudder of the earth. The steaming gaps hindered access by the rescue services, and the metal plates put down to bridge them constantly needed replacing. On March 24, the lava burst forth. It poured straight into the nearby waters of the Indian Ocean at a temperature of 1160°C (2120°F), and what an encounter that was! Water and fire did battle amid a salvo of violent explosions, giving off plumes of red steam and eventually producing a new tongue of land. When peace returned, the island was larger by a bare and bristling 30 hectares (74 acres) of black rock.

All this time, the eruption up in the Dolomieu Crater had been continuing. On March 28, the seismic activity became so intense that it sent the monitoring network completely haywire. The summit deflated slightly and then, on March 29, produced a sudden, violent phreatomagmatic explosion that formed a pit-crater within the central crater.

In April 1986, all activity came to an end – so far as this eruption was concerned, at least. But Piton de la Fournaise never stays inactive for long: 160 eruptions have been recorded since the island was first inhabited, and almost one per year since the observatory's surveillance began. The frequency of these eruptions makes this one of the world's most active volcanoes, and an ideal open-air laboratory for the volcanologists of the IPGP (the Paris Institute for Global Geophysics). ∎

The great free-flowing streams of lava produced by Piton de la Fournaise often cut the main road around the island, and on occasion they obliterate homes that lie in their path.

Earth is born where fire and water meet! In 1986, lava flows created 30 hectares (74 acres) of new land in the ocean, but the waves have since eroded over half of it. From this ceaseless struggle between the elements, Réunion has arisen.

- **Location:** Island of Luzon (Philippines)
- **Altitude:** 1760 m (5770 ft) until 1991; now 1490 m (4890 ft)
- **Diameter at base:** 30–50 km (20–30 miles)
- **Volcano type:** subduction zone, island arc
- **Most frequent activity type:** only eruption event known in historical times began in 1991: explosive, Plinian, with formation of caldera
- **Eruptions:**

  Earliest eruptions 1.1 million years ago.

  Most recent eruptions: 1991–95.

  No activity for 500 years before 1991.
- **Points of interest:**

  Pinatubo was practically unknown before 1991, not having erupted for nearly 500 years; it did not even figure in the list of known active volcanoes. Its geology is not at all well understood, and it was a complete surprise when the mountain became active.

  The first signs of activity came in August 1990, after a violent earthquake had rocked Luzon the month before. However, it was on April 2, 1991, that a plume of steam and some outflows of ash announced the beginning of the eruption proper. When it was over, the volcano had a new caldera, where the summit of the mountain had caved in to a depth of some 650 m (2100 ft) over a tract 2.5 km (1.5 miles) wide.

PINATUBO

Pinatubo, one of the twenty-one active volcanoes in the Philippines, is 1.1 million years old. Located midway along the volcanic arc that follows the island of Luzon's western shore, it was, at a height of 1760 meters (5770 feet), the tallest volcano in the range.

Before 1991, the mountain was heavily furrowed by erosion and its slopes were covered with extremely dense forest, gashed here and there by canyons from which great rivers issued. Apart from a zone of thermal activity at the mountain's foot, there was nothing in this landscape to proclaim its volcanic nature – nor did human memory recall any eruptions in the last five hundred years.

Some 15,000 people had their homes in small villages around the foot of the mountain, and 500,000 others lived in towns nearby. There were also two important US military bases in the area: Clark Air Base and Subic Bay, housing a total of nearly 30,000 people. On the slopes of the volcano itself, 500 families of Aetas, the original occupants of the island, combined a nomadic life with a little farming, growing coffee, bananas, and orchids. They depended directly on the rivers and forest of Pinatubo for their survival. The whole scene was to be utterly devastated by a series of events that began when explosions were heard coming from the mountaintop on the afternoon of April 2, 1991.

Advance warning

These phreatic explosions went on for several hours. Vast areas of forest were destroyed, and dust and lumps of ancient lava were thrown out. Craters formed on the north face of the summit dome, and the next day a row of large fumaroles appeared along the same axis. The authorities were immediately alerted, and a race between the volcano and the scientists began. Experts from PHIVOLCS (the Philippines Institute of Volcanology and Seismology) knew very well how dangerous their volcanoes were: they all had a propensity to explode, so it was immediately decided to evacuate the 5000 people living within 10 kilometers (6 miles) of Pinatubo's summit.

The scientists quickly set up an initial seismographic network around the volcano: between 40 and 140 seismic shocks were recorded daily. Foreign experts arrived to help their Filipino colleagues, and together they hastily constructed the brand-new Pinatubo Volcano Observatory (PVO). At the same time, they carried out a complete geological survey of the mountain, so that by studying former eruptions they could draw up a picture of what the coming one would be like. It was not long before this portrait began to take on horrific features: over the last few thousand years, Pinatubo had experienced some extremely violent explosive episodes, with abundant pyroclastic flows leaving deposits more than 20 kilometers (12 miles) from the crater.

These deposits had given rise to lahars – flows of mud and debris – broad enough to smother all the nearby lowlands. This data was plotted on a map that illustrated the manifold dangers threatening

The eruption left Pinatubo scarred by a caldera 2.5 km (1.5 miles) across. Above this gaping hole, many dark, swirling Plinian cloud columns rose more than 15 km (9 miles) into the air.

The coming eruption began to present a more and more terrifying picture. Seeing the size of the giant Plinian cloud columns, which might easily herald a pyroclastic flow, the authorities followed scientific advice and established an evacuation zone extending 40 km (25 miles) around the volcano.

the area, to give the civil and military authorities the information they needed in order to decide what precautions they should take. And, of course, there was the task of convincing them that these dangers were genuine.

Not long before, the volcanologists Maurice and Katia Krafft had lost their lives in an explosion on another volcano, Mount Unzen, in Japan: the eyes of the world, therefore, were on the Japanese volcano and the huge pyroclastic avalanches that continued to burst from its dome. Before their deaths, the two scientists had made a video describing the various hazards presented by volcanoes, and this played a crucial role in bringing home to the Philippines authorities, and indeed the whole local population, what they were up against. Copies of the video cassette were made, and soon more than 80 cassettes were in circulation, explaining and illustrating what could happen at Pinatubo, and what the consequences of an eruption might be.

From June 3 onward, events began to move faster: explosions, ash

Ash covers everything: plants die of suffocation, and the sky is blackened for several days by the plume from the eruption. People do their best to protect themselves and to salvage whatever they can: here, a peasant cuts and dusts off a few canes of sugar, all that is left for the surviving livestock to eat.

In the ash-filled darkness, the inhabitants flee from the area, leaving almost everything behind. These peasants, abandoning farm and crops, take with them whatever they can: a bundle of belongings and a few head of cattle.

In the wake of the eruption, a typhoon ... The downpour turns water and ash into torrents of mud that sweep away villages, roads, bridges, and rail tracks. In some of the valleys, the mud flows extend as far as 40 km (25 miles) from the volcano.

fallout, and earth tremors all intensified. On June 5, the scientists decided to move to alert level 3: "Eruption possible within the fortnight."

The next day, a massive deformation of the summit was recorded: it was swelling further and further. On June 7, a violent explosion sent a plume of ash and steam as high as 7 kilometers (4 miles) into the air. Alert level 4 was activated: "Eruption possible in the next twenty-four hours," and further evacuations began at the foot of the volcano.

Convincing people of the danger was no longer the greatest obstacle to these evacuations: media attention was now squarely on Pinatubo. The problem was how to reach the Aetas, who lived in remote parts of the forest. The Franciscan sisters set off to explain the situation to them, and gradually they trickled in to join the others in the refugee camps.

Military authorities at the two US bases were a little harder to convince: the Gulf War had just been won, and they were not going to be overawed by a mere volcano! In the end, though, Maurice and Katia Krafft's images won them over as well.

From June 8 through 12, the dome at the summit was observed to be growing further, as constant explosions belched out ashes.

On June 9, the alert level was raised to 5: "Eruption in progress." The radius of the evacuation zone was enlarged to 20 kilometers (12 miles), and another 25,000 people left the area. The next day, Clark Air Base was evacuated, with the departure of 14,000 US military personnel and their dependants. Only the volcanologists remained in position to maintain their constant watch on the mountain.

Massive explosions

The first major explosive eruption occurred on June 12: a plume of ash was thrown 19 kilometers (nearly 12 miles) into the air. It was accompanied by minor pyroclastic flows on the northern side, a mixture of gases, drops of lava, and solid particles. The evacuation radius was then moved out to 30 kilometers (19 miles), displacing 58,000 people in total.

Between June 12 and 15, more and more such explosions occurred, although most were not visible to the observers, since the volcano was hidden by cloud or darkness – or the air was so full of ash that the mountain could not be made out. All that the scientists knew of these explosions was what they learned from their seismographs and from the traces of the plumes on those radar sets that were still operational.

On June 14, the weather cleared and the volcano's summit reappeared, wreathed in plumes from the explosions that were issuing from several vents. The next morning, laterally-spreading explosions were reported, apparently coming from the base of the dome: it was feared the dome itself would soon break up.

Night for day. One of the last remaining inhabitants clears his roof of accumulated ash. Nearly all of the six hundred dead were crushed in collapsing houses and cars which could not take the weight of their ash covering, once it had become soaked with rainwater.

The Aetas, original inhabitants of the island living in remote mountain areas, fled under a rain of "head-sized rocks from the sky." They were accommodated in refugee camps 10 km (6 miles) from the crater, but then had to move again on June 12 to new camps 30 km (19 miles) away.

The level of alert was raised once again, and this time the evacuation area was extended to 40 kilometers (25 miles) around: the last people to be evacuated were moved in a hurry. Driven by the prevailing easterly wind, ash from the explosions now covered the western part of Luzon island, though most of it fell into the sea and some even reached China.

A typhoon was on its way, however, and the wind was changing. As the ash fallout began to affect the center of the island, people started leaving the region in great numbers without prompting.

The town of Olongapo, 45 km (28 miles) from the crater, was buried under a layer of ash that built up with each new explosion until it was around 15 cm (6 ins) deep.

June 15, 2:30 p.m. – darkness at noon

Just one seismograph was still working on the mountain: the others, located around the cone, had all been destroyed. Lumps of rock 4 centimeters (1.5 inches) across were hailing down 20 kilometers (12 miles) from the crater. The weather had closed in again, and the volcano could no longer be seen. Sudden changes in atmospheric pressure indicated that a gigantic explosion was taking place; satellites and radar images told the same story. It was early afternoon, yet night was steadily creeping across the land ...

A fallout of ash over the whole region was blocking out the sunlight. A gigantic plume rose 30 kilometers (19 miles) into the sky – according to some, it was 40 kilometers (25 miles) high. At over 10 kilometers (6 miles) up, in the stratosphere, this plume billowed out in a mushroom cloud over 500 kilometers (300 miles) wide. At this altitude, the ash was picked up by the jet stream, to be carried almost right round the globe.

While these explosions were taking place, pyroclastic flows were hurtling down the mountainside. The glowing rivers carved through the landscape, their deposits filling valleys, leveling out the ridges, and piling up debris. They completely engulfed the forest and the abandoned villages, as well as those remaining Aetas whom it had been impossible to contact, or who had refused to leave.

Just as the volcano was reaching the height of its activity, Typhoon Yunya hit the island of Luzon. Violent winds transported quantities of ash over great distances, and Manila airport had to be closed for many days, though it was 100 kilometers (60 miles) away.

The huge quantities of water that rained down loosened the ash and pyroclastic flow deposits, unleashing destructive torrents of mud (lahars) that laid waste the area, in places extending more than 40 kilometers (25 miles) from the crater.

The typhoon-borne rain saturated the coating of ash that covered everything, making it much heavier: trees broke, electric pylons collapsed, and the roofs of houses gave way. Many people who had survived until then by taking refuge indoors or in cars were now crushed to death.

And afterward ... a deserted landscape

At the end of June 1991, the volcano was still active, but its plume of ash rose no more than 15–20 kilometers (9–12 miles) high. It became possible, with caution, to approach the area again and make a preliminary assessment of the damage. The entire summit of the volcano had disappeared, and where it had been there was now a caldera caused by the collapse of the ancient chimney, a huge crater 2.5 kilometers (1.5 miles) wide and 650 meters (2100 feet) deep. A mantle of ash lay 10 centimeters to 1 meter (4 to 40 inches) thick over an area of 4000 square kilometers (1560 square miles), even though most of the ash had fallen into the South China Sea.

Extensive pyroclastic flows had completely overrun the volcano's flanks. For 16 kilometers (10 miles) all around the crater, they had left deposits 50–200 meters (160–650 feet) deep, and their total volume was estimated at 6 or 7 cubic kilometers (1.5–1.7 cubic miles). All the vegetation had been destroyed, the valleys had been filled in, and the rivers were carving themselves new beds. The landscape that was home and life to the Aetas had disappeared from the surface of the earth ...

And yet, one year on, life was already beginning to reclaim ascendancy in this desolate landscape. Nature will always spring up again, and people will rebuild.

Study of the deposits revealed that they had probably originated from the emission of some 4 or 5 cubic kilometers (1–1.2 cubic miles) of magma, almost ten times as much as at Mount Saint Helens. This was the second largest eruption of the 20th century, surpassed only by Katmai (Novarupta) in 1912, which created the Valley of Ten Thousand Smokes in Alaska. Pinatubo's eruption prompted the largest-scale evacuation ever organized: over 300,000 people left the area. The death toll was 600, but without the evacuation the figure could easily have been over 20,000. Many human lives were saved by a combination of the volcano scientists' ability to keep on top of events, close collaboration between them and the national authorities, and, above all, the fact that the local inhabitants had a clear understanding of the decisions taken. Without such highly effective communication, a major disaster could not have been averted and the handling of Pinatubo would not have become, as it has done, an example for the rest of the world to follow. ■

One year on from the eruption, and life has resumed its course (above). The tropical forest that clothed the volcano's slopes has disappeared, and in its place is snow-white ash. For a decade or so, every season, the rains will go to work on the eruption deposits, causing new mud slides (lahars) and reshaping the landscape. Jeepneys like this one (left) – the local public transport – make their way over the flooded tracks that snake across these deposits. The forest debris of charred trunks and branches is swept along by the lahars. Making the best they can of a terrible situation, the Filipinos are extracting this charcoal, one of the few "benefits" of the eruption (inset).

MOUNT COLO

To the far north of the island of Sulawesi, on the calm waters of the Gulf of Tomini, there is a dusting of islands. Lying a little apart from the others, the jewel of this Togian archipelago, Una-Una, is the only one of volcanic origin. It is the richest of them all, because it is the most fertile. Sheltered from the Pacific and its angry moods, as well as from the bloodthirsty pirates who haunt the Celebes sea close by, the people of Una-Una have established copra plantations, and the lower slopes of the volcano Colo are densely covered with coconut palms.

Precursors of disaster

At the start of the 1980s, some 7000 people were living prosperously on the mountainside. Their lives were peaceful, and the 507-meter (1663-foot) volcano seemed no threat. Nevertheless, as early as 1951, Neumann van Padang, a geologist with the volcanological service of the colonial Dutch East Indies government, had drawn attention to the fact that an eruption in 1898 had thrown out more than 2.2 million cubic meters (2.8 million cubic yards) of ash, its fallout affecting an area of 303,000 square kilometers (118,000 square miles).

In 1900, the central crater had seen considerable activity. Powerful explosions, Vulcanian in type at first and then Strombolian, created turmoil in the atmosphere, and dense plumes formed over the island. Volcanic activity remained moderate, though, and calm returned to Una-Una – until April 1961, when a single seismic shock was felt. A crater lake formed, fed by rainwater, with fumaroles along its southern edge that quickly covered the whole area with a yellow carpet of sulfur.

This, for the more adventurous islanders, was a new source of interest and profit: the sulfur was used for whitening sugar, for making matches, and locally for the preparation of a traditional medicine, an excellent remedy for skin conditions. A couple of cabins were erected inside the crater, and people engaged in a lively business carrying down blocks of sulfur. Like many of the country's volcanoes, Mount Colo was looked on by the Indonesians as one of nature's gifts.

Although the local population failed to heed the volcano's warning signals, the Volcanological Survey of Indonesia (VSI) was on the alert and concerned enough to install a seismograph at this remote site. Thanks to this precautionary measure, at the start of 1982 the scientists detected considerable seismic activity directly beneath the island, which intensified as the year wore on. Then, on July 8, 1983, the first phreatomagmatic explosions vaporized the water in the crater lake and blew the unfortunate sulfur-gatherers' cabins to matchwood. The seismographs continued to record fresh shocks, at a rate of between nine and eleven a day, until July 15. In the following few days the number of shocks increased dramatically, rising to thirty or forty seismic events per day.

The volcanologists were ready for action, and the eight villages on the island's shores were evacuated. The villagers were sent to

- **Location:** Island of Una-Una, Sulawesi (Indonesia)
- **Altitude:** 507 m (1663 ft)
- **Volcano type:** andesitic stratovolcano (ill-defined geology, probably island arc)
- **Most frequent activity type:** explosive: phreatic and/or phreatomagmatic

neighboring islands, and from there dispersed all over northern Sulawesi.

By July 23, when the climax came, the volcanologists were the only people left on the island. Within just three minutes, pyroclastic flows had destroyed everything within 3 kilometers (nearly 2 miles) of the crater. Another three minutes, and the "tongue" of a pyroclastic flow, channeled along a riverbed, cut the village of Una-Una itself in two, to the terror of the Indonesian volcanologists who had remained on duty in the village in order to observe the eruption. They escaped only by fleeing as fast as they could and, in the end, swimming to rejoin their boats, which were keeping a prudent distance.

An island under surveillance

The whole western side of the volcano was devastated. To the east, only two villages escaped total destruction; the others were razed to the ground. The island was declared a danger zone, and all access was officially forbidden until 1986. Only then was it possible for the inhabitants to begin again, gathering copra from the coconut palms that had survived; even then, restrictions were put in place to prevent too rapid a recolonization. Only 200 people were allowed to live on the island, and for periods of not more than two months. Rotas were organized, and some of the houses that were still standing were refurbished.

Twelve years on, these restrictions remained in force on Una-Una: the area was still considered a volcanic high-risk zone, and with good reason. New plantations of palms have sprung up, but the environment is even now a living reminder of the catastrophe. The luxuriant vegetation invading the great Mosque and the empty shells of grand houses serves as a warning that human beings count for little enough when the earth unleashes its full powers. The message of Mount Colo is that the lives of thousands can be saved only by unremitting vigilance. ∎

Over half of the rich and verdant island of Una-Una was destroyed on July 23, 1983, by pyroclastic flows from the erupting Mount Colo. On the beach, the radial blast mowed down trees and leveled houses.

Splendor and decadence: the ruins of magnificent houses abandoned as nature reasserts itself, all still in the shadow of danger from Mount Colo.

MERAPI

Indonesia, with its more than one hundred and eighty volcanoes, is truly a volcanologist's paradise! Fascinating they may be, but they also present a real hazard to the people who live there. Merapi (an Indonesian word meaning "fiery red"), in central Java, is a great andesitic volcano 28 kilometers (17 miles) in diameter at its base, which is 500 meters (1640 feet) above sea level, and rises to 2911 meters (9550 feet). It dominates the great Javanese city Yogyakarta, with its one million inhabitants. The city is in fact built in part upon ancient deposits from Merapi, and lies only 20 kilometers (12 miles) from the crater at its summit. This makes Merapi potentially the most dangerous volcano in all of Java, since nearly 1.5 million people are at risk in case of an eruption. The volcano is surprisingly densely populated for one so greatly feared, with over 1500 inhabitants per square kilometer (3900 per square mile), twice the average density for Java as a whole. One third of this number, nearly 500,000 people, are directly threatened by current activity in the volcano. However, although the people who are at risk or have been evacuated are encouraged to settle in less heavily populated parts of Indonesia (through the inducements of the "transmigration" policy), Javanese peasants remain very attached to their own farms, in spite of the risks. And indeed, in Indonesia as elsewhere, volcanoes have been of great service to agriculture. Merapi is no exception: its ash enriches the soil, and this "fertilizer from the sky" makes it possible to gather as many as three harvests in one year! This is the unavoidable paradox of the Indonesian volcanoes: they are both benefactors of agriculture and fearsome killers.

A high-risk volcano

Merapi is a volcano in constant activity, and its quiescent periods never last more than a few years. It has a remarkable pattern of eruptions, in the region of twenty to thirty each century. Its history has only recently been documented: a young volcano, less than 100,000 years old, it has always been predominantly explosive and has produced major eruptions right up to recent times. An example is the great Saint Helens-type eruption (of a type named after that of Mount Saint Helens in 1980: see pages 16–21) that destabilized the whole southwestern side of the mountain: a landslide involving many cubic kilometers of material formed a gigantic debris avalanche that affected areas as far as 29 kilometers (18 miles) from the summit. This uncovered the near-surface magma pocket under the southwestern slope, and it exploded savagely in a devastating blast whose destructive force was felt for hundreds of miles around the volcano. Such events are exceptional, but they can occur more than once in the life of a stratovolcano, as happened at La Soufrière (Guadeloupe) between 11,000 and 3000 years ago. The date of this event at Merapi is still uncertain, but it was between 8000 and 2000 years ago. Huge Plinian eruptions causing heavy fallout of ash and pumice over a wide area have also occurred at Merapi, as recently as the 15th century. The resulting ash and mud flows reached the site of

Bathed in the light of the setting sun, Merapi rises out of the palm plantations. The mountain's imposing presence has inspired the Javanese to weave a halo of legends around it ...

- **Location:** Island of Java (Indonesia)
- **Altitude:** 2911 m (9550 ft)
- **Diameter at base:** 28 km (17 miles)
- **Volcano type:** andesitic stratovolcano, subduction zone, island arc (Sunda island arc)
- **Most frequent activity type:** broadly Pelean: explosive activity, with dome formation and ejection of incandescent boulders, and destruction of domes accompanied by pyroclastic flows and nuées ardentes
- **Eruptions:**

  Earliest eruptions approx. 60,000 years ago.

  Most recent eruptions: 1994 (nuées ardentes) to 1996 (incandescent boulders ejected from dome).
- **Point of interest:**

  Merapi is currently the most dangerous of the 128 active volcanoes in the Indonesian archipelago.

present-day Yogyakarta. The temple of Sambisari, which dates from the 9th century, lies 24 kilometers (15 miles) from the crater and was excavated in the 1980s from beneath more than 8 meters (26 feet) of ash that had all come from Merapi.

The pattern of activity at Merapi has been constant for many centuries now: viscous andesitic lava accumulates to form domes, either inside a crater or on the mountainside – that is, on a steep slope. The domes become unstable owing to their own weight, and this gives rise to the types of activity characteristic of Merapi. Observers, mainly from the Volcanological Survey of Indonesia (VSI), describe three phenomena associated with the growth and collapse of these domes. First, avalanches occur, often incandescent ones known in Indonesia as *guguran*. These are entirely gravity-driven: boulders, varying in volume from one cubic meter (1.3 cubic yards) to several hundreds, break away from the dome and hurtle down the slopes, shattering as they bounce. During the night of February 10/11, 1992, there were as many as five to twenty-five such avalanches an hour, and the boulders traveled 300 to 800 meters (330 to 880 yards).

The second phenomenon, a type of pyroclastic flow, also results from the collapse of a dome without any initial explosion. These Merapi-type pyroclastic avalanches (known locally as *awan panas*) move silently, apart from a slight whistling from escaping gases.

Thirdly, pyroclastic flows of a different type are caused by an initial explosion. They produce a vertical plume as they roll noiselessly down the slope, channeled by the valleys.

Merapi's major recorded eruptions have in many cases been preceded by long periods of apparent dormancy, but these are deceptive, for the longer things are quiet, the more dangerous the awakening will be. The principal eruptions in historical times occurred in 1822, 1872, and 1930–31. The 1822 event carved out a huge crater 600 meters (2000 feet) deep. In 1872, after three years of calm, Merapi threw up an eruption column that reached a height of 9000 meters (30,000 feet) and then fell back, producing pyroclastic flows unlike those originating directly from dome activity. This is the only instance of such an eruption type in Merapi's recent history. In 1930–31, seven years of peace were terminated by pyroclastic flows that extended for 15 kilometers (over 9 miles) and killed 1369 people.

Merapi's activity is cyclical, with a period of about fifty or sixty years between major eruptions. Since the latest of these had occurred in 1930–31, another disastrous eruption could be expected at any time. Lesser eruptions are frequent, though, and the authorities have set up a four-level alert system for warning the public of the hazards.

– The first level means "Beware": it is issued at the first signs of activity.
– Level 2, "Redouble vigilance," recommends voluntary evacuation.
– Level 3 is "Prepare for evacuation of the hazard zone."
– Level 4 means "Imminent danger of pyroclastic flows or lahars." This is the highest level of alert, involving rapid, organized evacuation.

Lahars (mud flows: see page 128) can cause as much damage as any other volcanic phenomenon, and are among the most dangerous.

November 22, 1994 (above): Pyroclastic flows lay waste the southern slopes of Merapi, halting only after 6 km (nearly 4 miles).
The morning after (below): Volcanologists from the VSI (Volcanological Survey of Indonesia) visit the scene to estimate the volume of the deposits. There is a danger that they might produce mud slides.

The 1994 event at Merapi

There had been pyroclastic flow eruptions at Merapi in 1984 and 1992, and since then the mountain had remained highly active: the dome at the top had grown to a record size, a sure harbinger of a major eruption with devastating consequences.

During the night of August 22/23, Merapi's impressive bulk, lit by a full moon, was clearly visible from the Plawangan observatory facing the volcano's southern flank. The dome had outgrown the summit crater, and pieces broke away from it every now and then in noisy, but not incandescent avalanches. At times their point of origin, at the base of the dome on the south side, would glow red. As the dawn broke, a glance at the valley that ran southwest from the base of the dome showed all too clearly what might happen. The dome was breaking up on that side over a length of nearly a kilometer (1100 yards): if boulders accumulated at the foot of the slope, they would not stop any pyroclastic flows that followed, but might well divert them into the next valley, that of the Boyong, which ran due south. The southern slopes of the volcano and the town of Kaliurang, which had escaped harm for decades, would be in the direct line of fire – as would the observatory itself! It was a worrying situation, for the dome had grown huge: much of it had spilled out of the crater and was poised at the top of a very steep slope. It could easily become unstable, but when? The slightest nudge from the rising magma might release either an avalanche of boulders or a major pyroclastic flow, without further warning.

On November 22, 1994, at 10:30 a.m., pyroclastic flows began to race down the southern flank of Merapi. They traveled 6 kilometers (nearly 4 miles) down the valley of the Boyong: one village, 5 kilometers (3 miles) from the summit and 100 meters (325 feet) above the valley floor, was partially destroyed. Some sixty people were killed and nearly three hundred others injured, most of them burned by hot gases. Hundreds of houses were destroyed, and thousands of head of livestock perished. About six thousand people had to be evacuated, most of them living along the Boyong river, because of the risk of lahars. The shock wave broke a number of windows at the Plawangan observatory, which was 4 kilometers (2.5 miles) from the summit and 200 meters (650 feet) above the Boyong valley, and one of the VSI's technical team suffered minor burns. The observatory was moved and reinstalled at Kaliurang. ∎

BENEATH THE MENACING GIANT

The novel feature of the 1994 eruption was the "rolling cloud" that accompanied the pyroclastic flows, causing extensive damage to the ridge areas, which normally escape destruction: the flows themselves (as in 1984) remained in the valleys. This eruption was reminiscent of the one experienced at Mount Pelée on May 8, 1902: it was less violent, to be sure, but villages that had been thought safe behind their protecting ridges must from now on be considered at risk from a type of cloud that flows over obstacles in the terrain.

A year on from the eruption, the situation remained unchanged: the dome, though partly destroyed in 1994, was continuing to grow, and the threat was still very real. A major eruption could happen at any time.

Merapi is Indonesia's best-watched volcano. Many of its eruptions are forecast, not least because of a seismographic network that detects rising magma. However, the challenge for the scientists is to predict not only the timing of coming eruptions, but above all their severity. Yet how can one forecast the strength of an avalanche or a tempest? Because this question cannot be answered reliably, Merapi remains a particularly dangerous volcano.

SAKURAJIMA

According to an ancient legend, Japan rests on the back of a sleeping giant catfish. When he is disturbed, the islands move, and his writhing violently shakes the archipelago of the Rising Sun. This was how, in the days of shogun and samurai, the elders would explain the frequent earthquakes that afflict the whole region.

The 130 million Japanese, who live with volcanoes every day, are familiar with natural disasters, but the inhabitants of Kyushu, in southern Japan, have taken an unusually thorough approach to this strange form of cohabitation.

An island at the mercy of its volcano

The volcano Sakurajima rises 1117 meters (3665 feet) above the city of Kagoshima, some 6 kilometers (nearly 4 miles) away, and has been closely intertwined with human history since the 8th century. It is an andesitic stratovolcano in the Aira caldera, and is one of the world's most active volcanoes. Since the beginning of the 20th century, there have been eleven periods of eruption, including two well-remembered episodes, in 1914 and in 1946, during which heavy lava flows poured down the mountainside toward the villages of Sakurajima and Shirahama.

Activity in the central craters has been uninterrupted since 1955: there, one violent explosion follows another at a quite frightening

- **Location:** Island of Kyushu (Japan)
- **Altitude:** 1117 m (3665 ft)
- **Diameter at base:** 10 km (6 miles)
- **Volcano type:** andesitic stratovolcano, island arc (subduction zone)
- **Most frequent activity type:** explosive; frequent Vulcanian eruptions
- **Eruptions:**
  Earliest eruptions 7750 years ago.
  Most recent eruption: 1955 to date.

Sakurajima (below) was an island, but the 1914 eruption turned it into a peninsula. It has the classic shape of an andesitic stratovolcano. Dense black clouds rise from it, subjecting the city of Kagoshima (right), about 6 km (4 miles) away, to a continuous rain of mineral dust.

rate. In 1986, for instance, they reached a frequency of five hundred a year. The shock waves shatter house and car windows on the Sakurajima peninsula, and sometimes as far away as Kagoshima. Most of the lava bombs and boulders fall within 2 kilometers (1.25 miles) of the summit, but some of them reach inhabited areas, and the two thousand permanent residents of the peninsula can find their houses roofless and gutted.

As for the 100,000 townspeople of Kagoshima, they endure a lavish dusting from the plume's fallout. Yet strangely enough, nobody wants to leave the place. It was decided in 1960 to build a volcanological observatory just 3 kilometers (under 2 miles) from the action, but the hail of projectiles that fell too often for comfort forced the volcano scientists from Kyoto University into a prudent withdrawal. Since 1978, there has been a new observatory at a more respectful distance of 5 kilometers (3 miles). On the other hand, an underground shelter with 250 meters (820 feet) of tunnels has been converted into an advance post, with completely automated monitoring and observation systems. A battery of video cameras and photographic equipment is linked to a seismograph which sets them recording as soon as it detects a particular pattern of seismic waves.

Since 1982, the volcano has also been covered by networks of instruments that detect ground deformation, earth shocks, and the widening of selected fissures (see page 152). This network transmits directly to the observatory's computers, which automatically evaluate the degree of risk. There are three alert levels: "vigilance required," "critical," and "danger." Sakurajima's constant activity throughout the 1980s gave ample opportunity to demonstrate that this equipment, which is among the most sophisticated in the world, can also be relied upon. Nevertheless, when the Red Alert signal rings at the volcanology station, it is reassuring to know that a human being still acts as the final link in the chain and sets the evacuation in motion.

A disciplined response

In order to reduce the likelihood of having to resort to evacuation, the local authorities on Sakurajima have constructed strange concrete bunkers which look oddly like bus shelters. The purpose of these reinforced structures, though, is not to protect people against rain, but against the basalt bombs hurled from the craters.

Every year, on January 12, most of the residents join in a dress rehearsal for the evacuation that has been planned in case of a major eruption. The emergency drill is full-scale and carried out in real time. To speed up evacuation, twenty boarding quays and a helicopter landing pad are kept in permanent readiness, just as the schoolchildren of Sakurajima must carry their hard hats with them all year round.

The authorities have thought of everything – but they are well aware that, although a daytime evacuation should go off without a hitch, an eruption at night, especially during one of the region's many storms, could create serious difficulties and might even turn into a tragedy. One can only hope that the *kami kase*, or Divine Winds, which have long protected Japan by loosing typhoons on its enemies, will keep the people of Sakurajima safe from harm. ■

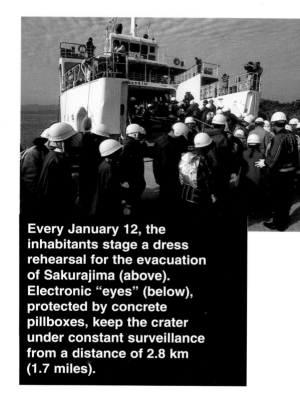

Every January 12, the inhabitants stage a dress rehearsal for the evacuation of Sakurajima (above). Electronic "eyes" (below), protected by concrete pillboxes, keep the crater under constant surveillance from a distance of 2.8 km (1.7 miles).

RABAUL

On September 10, 1767, while exploring the waters of Melanesia to the north of what would later be named Papua New Guinea, the British seafarer Philip Carteret observed an enormous plume of smoke, and concluded immediately that it must be a volcanic phenomenon of some kind. This was the first historical record of the volcano complex known as Rabaul, at the northeastern point of the island of New Britain.

Like the other volcanoes in the Bismarck Sea, Rabaul marks a sensitive geological zone where a number of tectonic plates meet, some in subduction. This situation produces intense seismic activity, and gives rise to an extremely explosive type of volcanic activity associated with acidic magma.

Rabaul, from volcano city ...

The Western colonists who settled in the region at the end of the 19th century were completely ignorant of the risks. The town of Rabaul was built in 1905 and became quite prosperous after the First World War: the site chosen, at the head of Blanche Bay, was ideally suited to the establishment of a port. The topography of the area, though, should have alerted the colonists to the fact that the bay was located right in the center of an active caldera – and that caldera had been formed by ground collapse due to gigantic ignimbrite eruptions that had occurred every 2000 to 3600 years. Between these major events there had been lesser eruptions which, though brief, were often violent and spectacular.

... to ghost town

A seismic crisis affected the area from 1971 on, causing marked changes in ground profiles and continuing until it reached a climax between 1983 and 1985. This episode did not end in an eruption, but on September 19, 1994, a new phase of intense activity began, heralded by a number of earthquakes. The inhabitants were put on alert and given the order to evacuate: 30,000 people left the town in an orderly manner by the routes that had been designated in the emergency plans.

At first light the next morning, scientists at the volcanological observatory were sweeping the bay with binoculars when they noticed a major swelling in the caldera's floor. It had risen some 5 meters (16 feet) owing to the upthrust of ascending magma, bringing coral reefs into view above the surface of the water. The volcano Tavurvur began to erupt at 6:15 a.m., and soon produced a tall column of ash. Another volcano in the complex, Vulcan, erupted in its turn at 7:45 a.m.

It was fortunate that the town was empty of people. Fallout rained down on Rabaul, covering it with dirty-whitish mineral dust. Two high plumes of ash and gases rose above the town to a height of nearly 16 kilometers (10 miles), and major discharges of static electricity sent lightning flashes zigzagging across these pillars of cloud. The fine ash made it impossible to see, and it became very

- **Location:** Island of New Britain (Papua New Guinea)
- **Altitude:** 688 m (2257 ft)
- **Diameter of collapsed caldera:** 12 ˘ 15 km (7.5 ˘ 9.3 miles)
- **Volcano type:** caldera, subduction zone, island arc
- **Most frequent activity types of the active volcanoes in the caldera:** Tavurvur and Vulcan often erupt together; explosive eruptions (Vulcanian and Plinian), sometimes phreatomagmatic
- **Eruptions:**
  7000 years ago: formation of first caldera.

  1400 years ago: formation of second caldera.

  Most recent eruption: 1994 to date (Tavurvur and Vulcan).

AN EVENTFUL PAST

In 1878, underwater volcanic activity in the western area of the bay made the seawater boil, and a Plinian cloud column then formed. The pumice fallout was lighter than water and covered the sea with a floating layer 2 meters (6.5 feet) thick, rendering the bay inaccessible to shipping. Within a few days, the island of Vulcan rose from this flotsam.

On May 29, 1937, the 1878 eruption scenario was repeated, but this time it directly threatened the town of Rabaul. Plinian fallout from the island of Vulcan caused considerable damage and left the town surrounded by a desolate landscape, where palms with broken fronds remained standing like huge folded umbrellas. Streets and homes were buried under ash, and the death toll was around five hundred. The volcanic upheavals caused a tsunami which devastated the port. The next day, Tavurvur, on the other side of the caldera, produced its own plume. After three days of intense activity, a new structure, also named Vulcan, rose above the surface and bridged the gap between the coast and the original Vulcan island.

Tavurvur (top) and Vulcan combine forces to smother the town of Rabaul in mineral dust. Aircraft bogged down in the powdery mess (below) seem to be contemplating the erupting volcano beyond the end of the runway, while in the harbor (below), choked with floating pumice, navigation is impossible and ships lie on their sides.

difficult to move around the area. The airport was closed before all the planes could be removed to safety. All the hangars were blown down, and the runway disappeared under a thick mantle of ash. In line with the end of runway, less than 2 kilometers (1.25 miles) away, the cone of Tavurvur sputtered and roared. The harbor, which was even closer to the two volcanoes, soon became unnavigable: there was a blanket of pumice floating on the surface of its waters.

For four days, ash fell on the deserted town, burying it to a depth of 30 centimeters (one foot) in some districts and as much as 1.5 meters (5 feet) in others.

Then the eruption gradually subsided. The two volcanoes were still active, but producing smaller volumes of material, and the town was covered with no more than a perpetual cloud of fine dust.

The eruption of Tavurvur continues, though its activity is declining, and ground deformations are still being recorded throughout the Rabaul area. But far more worrying than these eruptive events on Tavurvur and Vulcan is the very real possibility that the whole caldera might once again cave in. ∎

HOW
VOLCANOES
WORK

HOW VOLCANOES WORK: INTRODUCTION

When else does nature appear so unbridled, or inspire so much fear and wonder, as during a volcanic eruption? Often the names of volcanoes are associated in our collective memory with death and destruction, yet the fascinating spectacle of an eruption can inspire us to look beyond its tragic effects. For as long as they have been observing such phenomena, human beings seem to have experienced this mixture of wonder and repulsion. Powerless before the monstrous wrath of these fiery giants, they have nevertheless asked questions, and from their tortured imaginings many interpretations have arisen, some rational and others less so.

Ancient peoples used to personify volcanoes, and some still retain a lively faith in these ancestral beliefs. The human mind has always been driven by a longing to understand, sometimes to the point of obsession. The unfortunate Empedocles, for instance, philosopher and scientist of classical antiquity, settled down by the rim of Etna's craters in order to try to understand these curious phenomena. Alas! he could not penetrate the volcano's mysteries, and hurled himself into a crater: the story goes that the volcano spat out one solitary sandal, as an ultimate insult to humanity.

Many centuries later, out of the ferment of philosophical and scientific culture, volcanology would eventually emerge. Since then, the struggle has been slightly less unequal, and instead of facing the dragon, as Saint George did, with nothing but a lance, the modern volcanologist of the 21st century is armed with new weapons: geophysics, geochemistry, and geology.

One day, perhaps, the tantrums of the beast will be understood well enough to be mastered! ■

SANTORINI AND THE MYTH OF ATLANTIS

In 1620 B.C., the most violent volcanic eruption of the last four thousand years took place at Thera (modern Santorini). Its repercussions were felt throughout the Mediterranean, and destroyed the Minoan civilization, which was then at its height.

Not until 1967 were the ruins of the town of Akrotiri discovered under the Santorini pumice. Little by little, the archeologists and geologists formulated, refined, and finally established their astounding hypothesis: if the Atlantis of legend ever existed, it must have been at Santorini!

The Atlantis myth has come down to us from antiquity in the form of accounts by Greek philosophers, notably Plato. In several of his works he tells of the disappearance of a powerful civilization which ruled the sea while the Pharaohs ruled the mainland. Plato speaks of elegant cities, of cultured Atlanteans building sumptuous palaces and establishing a unique form of social justice – and of how "in the space of just one day and one harrowing night the whole citizen body was swallowed down by the earth, and Atlantis was drowned beneath the sea." A whole civilization wiped out in one stroke!

The Santorini eruption created a caldera by ground collapse (see pages 110–13) and produced a number of Plinian cloud columns whose fallout can still be found, many inches thick, in Turkey. But much worse than that, it also caused an enormous tsunami over 30 meters (100 feet) high, which destroyed coastal towns – including, perhaps, those of the fabled and mysterious Atlantis.

The active volcano Nea Kameni occupies the center of the Santorini caldera, its dark flow deposits contrasting strangely with the neighboring cliffs of white pumice.

VOLCANOES

For thousands of years the fertile human brain has teemed with strange, hybrid creatures and has filled mythologies, stories, and legends with them. Nature, regarded as hostile even now, has always been the primary source of our dread, and volcanoes, with their thunderous activity, have contributed to this myth-making. The terror they have inspired has given birth to gods and devils, demons and dragons, whose noxious breath has befouled the four corners of the world.

North America

The peoples of Oregon used to believe that Mount Mazama sheltered the god of fire and Mount Shasta the god of snow. Naturally, the eternal conflict between the forces of good and evil broke out, and the head of Mount Mazama was blown off, leaving an enormous yawning pit, Crater Lake, to bear witness to the defeat of the Evil One.

Long afterward, scientists discovered that the caldera of Crater Lake was formed some 6000 years ago, which means that the Oregon tribes were indeed there to witness the event!

There is a Wyoming legend that connects with volcanoes in a roundabout way. The Devil's Tower, a rocky spike which is in fact an ancient volcanic pipe laid bare by years of erosion, is said to have risen from the ground in order to save seven little girls pursued by a bear. No doubt it was the vertical columns and clefts, common features in structures of this sort, that were interpreted as the marks of the bear's claws on the mountainside and gave rise to the legend.

South America

In the Aztec imagination, the volcanoes of Mexico began erupting in order to rid the land of the conquistadors who were profaning their temples. In Nicaragua, it was to appease the volcanoes – here also raised to the status of gods – that young maidens were thrown into the lava lake of Masaya.

In 1600, the volcano Huayna-putina poured out floods of ash and cinders on the Peruvian town of Arequipa. The Christian colonists thought this must be nothing less than the wrath of God foretold in the Apocalypse, while the Peruvians interpreted the eruption as their volcano joining the struggle against Spanish tyranny. They prepared to die, but were puzzled by the failure of another nearby volcano, El Misti, to erupt as well. Why was this volcano not helping its neighbor to oust the oppressor? At last they worked out the answer: El Misti had been renamed Mount Saint Francis, and this baptism had turned it into a Christian!

■ Crater Lake

Africa

In the Republic of Congo, according to local belief, Nyiragongo is the home of departed souls, while at Kilimanjaro in Tanzania the strange, dented apearance of Mawensi is attributed to the action of its giant neighbor Kobe, which is apparently affronted by Mawensi's promiscuity and chastises it with a great club.

Europe

Volcanic activity is common around the Mediterranean, and

■ Kilimanjaro

IN LEGEND

there are many eruption episodes scattered through the pages of Greek and Roman history. Mythology reflects popular belief, and so we find stories of Hephaestus, the Greek god of fire, having his palace in the belly of Etna: when the Cyclopes set to work forging arms for the gods, they make Etna's craters glow red.

The Romans, on the other hand, place their Vulcan, the equivalent of Hephaestus, at Vulcano in the Aeolian Isles. Etna, according to the great Virgil, is where the giant Enceladus was buried by Athene for having rebelled against the gods. His brother Mimas suffered the same fate at the hands of Hephaestus: his tomb lies beneath Vesuvius. Their desperate efforts to escape account for the tremors and earthquakes that come from beneath these mountains.

Later on, the Christian church appropriated the volcanoes for its own ends, making Etna the gate of Hell, while saints were revered as guardians that protected towns against diabolic attack from volcanoes.

In 1660 Saint Januarius, the patron saint of Naples, manifested his concern by making small dark crosses rain down on the slopes of Vesuvius: these pairs of pyroxene crystals, forming the shape of a cross, were hailed as a miracle.

■ Vesuvius

Asia

In Japan, monks of the Shinto religion live on the summit of Fujiyama, the sacred mountain. The monastery was founded around the year 800, and is a much-loved place of pilgrimage where believers may renew contact with nature and its divinities. Indonesia is perhaps the greatest cradle of volcano legends, as it is of volcanoes. Few indeed of its 128 active ones house no gods, goddesses, demons, or spirits. At the center of Java lives the man-mountain who appears among the cast of *wayang kulit*, the shadow theater. He is the greatest personage at Kraton, the royal palace at Yogyakarta: he is the sultan – but he is also the mountain, Merapi! His fate is closely bound up with those of the volcano and of Yogyakarta itself, and he remains very much alive even in the 21st century.

Other volcanoes too are inhabited by divinities and form the backdrop to sometimes curious ceremonies. Mount Bromo, in eastern Java, gets its name from the creator god of the Hindu pantheon, Brahma. Once a year, a great ceremony is held on the side of the mountain, and over a period of several days thousands of his worshippers come to pray, with festivities and sacrifices: goats, chickens, flowers, and money are all thrown into the crater.

■ Mount Bromo

The name of Mount Agung on Bali means "the One who rises above the Others." Bali has its own version of Hinduism, which views this volcano as a home of gods and demons. There is an immense temple complex at the foot of the mountain, where frequent ceremonies are held. ■

THE HISTORY OF VOLCANO SCIENCE

The forerunners: ancient and classical times

The Mediterranean, the undisputed cradle of Western culture, has long been the scene of frequent earthquakes and volcanic eruptions. It is hardly surprising, then, that the first known attempts to explain volcanoes have come down to us from classical antiquity. Yet, although the first writings we have on the subject are Greek, it is likely that earlier civilizations – such as those of Babylon the Great, Phoenicia, and the Hebrews – also made attempts to interpret volcanic eruptions.

The earliest-known scientific theories that offer an explanation of the earth and its capricious behavior date from the 6th century B.C. The Greek Thales, famous above all as a mathematician, thought of the earth as a disk floating on a vast ocean, and its upheavals as the result of that ocean's storms. His pupil, Anaximander, postulated a higher force in nature, giving rise to both heat and cold: he held that volcanic fires arose from the intimate mingling of these two opposing principles. As early as the 5th century B.C., two terms were in circulation that were fundamental to all the explanations offered by the ancients: air and fire. These two notions were to dominate all thinking on the subject until the 18th century of our own era, beginning perhaps with the unhappy Empedocles, born in 490 B.C. at Acragas in Sicily. Plato (428–348 B.C.) was a great traveler and witnessed an eruption of Mount Etna. He was immensely impressed, and speculated that a network of underground channels connected different regions: in these channels flowed a river of fire,

Pyriphlegethon, which supplied the lava produced at volcanic vents. Aristotle (384–322 B.C.) viewed the earth as a living organism, whose moods or "humors" found expression on the surface as earth tremors or volcanic eruptions. In his *Physics*, he is the first to use the term "crater" and explains eruptions by "the presence of a wind blowing within the earth, which reduces the air to particularly tiny particles which catch fire with shock and friction as they pass through narrow spaces." Strabo (58 B.C.–A.D. 21) deduced the volcanic nature of Vesuvius, although it was quite dormant at that time and covered with vegetation right up to the

In this imaginative depiction of the eruption of Vesuvius in A.D. 79, Simone Franco gives the volcano its present shape, with the famous cone at the summit that makes its profile as seen from Naples so familiar. However, the mountain had no such cone before the eruption, and was probably closer in shape to a typical andesitic stratovolcano.

summit. He also described a number of eruptions seen in the course of his incessant travels, not only in Greece, but also in the Aeolian Isles and Italy.

Those highly educated Romans who continued the studies of Greek philosophers set even greater store by rational explanations. There is a long poem called *Aetna*, which some say is by Virgil (70–19 B.C.), full of descriptions of the greatest active volcano known to the Mediterranean civilization of the time. Lucretius' view of its eruptions was that they were caused by winds that found themselves trapped within the hollow mountain and formed whirling vortices, growing hot through contact with the rocky walls and so producing flames, which issue from the crater or from long, straight cracks in the mountain. Ovid (43 B.C.–A.D. 17) describes Etna, on which the position of the vents is in fact constantly shifting, as "changing the airways of its breath."

In A.D. 62, the region of Naples was rocked by a violent earthquake. Seneca (4 B.C.–A.D. 65) was most impressed by the event, and often referred to it. His greatest contribution to volcano science, though, was to point out the importance of steam and gases in eruptions: he was the first to recognize them as the propulsive forces in explosions. His second stroke of genius was the idea that each volcano is supplied locally from a kind of enormous pocket of underground fire, a forerunner of our modern concept of magma chambers.

Pliny the Elder, in his *Historia Naturalis*, a discursive encyclopedia in thirty-seven volumes, lists the dozen or so active

volcanoes known in his time. He also tries to identify the warning signs of coming eruptions, concluding that calm air and sea precede the lighting of Vulcan's forge: this seems natural to him, since the winds are all trapped inside the mountain.

Always concerned for the well-being of his fellow creatures, Pliny hurried to the rescue of Pompeii's inhabitants when Vesuvius began to erupt in A.D. 79. We owe to this generous action (which cost him his life) our first detailed volcanological description: his nephew Pliny the Younger (A.D. 62–114) was a correspondent of Tacitus, and wrote to inform him of his uncle's death at Stabies. In the letter he describes the eruption with a naturalist's precision, which later earned him an honored place as one of the founding fathers of volcanology.

An age of darkness: from the Middle Ages to the end of the 17th century

During the Middle Ages, the all-powerful Church confined learning within monastic walls, and the Inquisition watched for heresy. Intellectuals whose ideas were out of line with Holy Scripture were pilloried – or, worse still, were often forced to recant their theories or face being burned at the stake as heretics. The monks viewed volcanoes as the gates of Hell, Satan's refuge. There were alchemists who had notions as to how they worked, but for the most part they kept quiet, and the Middle Ages almost entirely lost interest in the great mountains that spat fire. Nevertheless, in spite of the dangers, some noteworthy discoveries have come down to us even from those obscurantist times. Alexander Neckam (1157–1217) was the first to use the term "volcano" in its modern sense,

while Albertus Magnus (1207–80) conducted the first, rudimentary volcanic experiment.

On September 28, 1538, a volcano began to form in the middle of the town of Tripergola in the Phlegrean Fields. It was given the name of Monte Nuovo, and as it grew, reaching a height of 140 meters (460 feet) in the course of a week, so did the controversies. Some bold naturalists used it as evidence for their theory that the mountain ranges had sprung up very quickly. Georg Bauer (1494–1555), better known under the Latin version of his name, Agricola, considered that the fire inside the earth was due to sunbeams that penetrated its depths, apparently unhindered by the planet's solid crust. Giordano Bruno (1548–1600) was imprudent enough to end at the stake: he was held to have thrown doubt on the biblical Flood, for he had observed that volcanoes are often near the sea, and suggested that they might originate from an interaction between water and fire.

In the 17th century the theories of antiquity were rediscovered, and while Descartes offered a model of the earth's internal structure, Athanasius Kircher (1602–80) took up Aristotle's ideas once more. He pictured a world containing within it many pockets of fire, which fueled the vents of volcanoes. Toward the century's end, there were attempts to apply the findings of the emerging science of chemistry to the barely older study of volcanology. Almost simultaneously, Robert Hooke (1635–1703) and Martin Lister (1638–1711) formed · the

theory that fire might arise spontaneously from the reaction of pyrites and sulfur as they came into contact with the water and salt of the sea.

The 18th century had hardly begun when, wreathed in steam and fire, the island of Nea Kameni emerged in the middle of the Santorini caldera. A monk, Lazzaro Moro (1687–1740), took this and the formation of Monte Nuovo as evidence for his theory that all the mountains of the globe had arisen by being thrust up from below, and were volcanic in origin. While firmly convinced of the volcanic origins of the earth, by dint of a delicate intellectual side-shuffle he managed to avoid offending against Church doctrine by attributing the internal fires to an act of Divine will! Benoît Maillet (1656–1738) maintained, on the contrary, that all rocks had a marine origin, and that volcanoes are only by-products of the combustion of fat from animal remains trapped in sedimentary deposits. Maillet was a courageous thinker, but not a rash man: his theories were only published ten years after his death, under the pseudonym Telliamed, an anagram of his name. They launched a debate he could not have foreseen, and led to a fierce polemic among 18th-century thinkers over the origin of volcanoes and mountains. Watery or fiery: each had its advocates, known respectively as Neptunists and Plutonists.

Neptunists and Plutonists: the 18th century

The 18th century was the age of the naturalist. Tireless travelers,

This remarkable image of Mount Asama (Honshu, Japan) erupting in 1783 shows all the phenomena associated with such a volcanic eruption in stylized form. The artist obviously had quite extraordinary powers of observation.

these Enlightenment intellectuals made observation after observation, often with contradictory results. The ensuing arguments were lively, and sometimes even violent. It was this polemical energy that nourished the science of the age, not least the infant science of volcanology, which was then just taking its first faltering steps.

Count Buffon (1707–88) is probably one of the best known of these natural scientists. He says little about volcanoes, but that little is enough to give us a good summary of the view many of his mid-18th-century contemporaries held of them: "A cannon of huge proportions [...] spitting fire, flames, bitumen, sulfur, and molten metal from its mouth. The pyrites within effervesce on contact with air or water, and this causes the eruptions." He ends: "That is the natural scientist's account of volcanoes." He was convinced that volcanic activity was closely connected with the presence of large amounts of water, and suggested cutting off volcanoes from the sea by building great dikes all round them: that would, he thought, bring about their extinction more quickly. It should be pointed out in his defense that Buffon never had the opportunity to study a volcano, and that his theories about them were based on the works of other authors, both contemporaries and ancients.

The dispute between Plutonists and Neptunists may be said to have started on May 10, 1752, when Jean-Étienne Guettard (1715–86) presented a paper to the assembled members of the Académie des Sciences demonstrating that the mountains of the Auvergne region of France were in fact extinct volcanoes. He was a doctor, botanist, and mineralogist who had come to this conclusion about the nature of the Auvergne volcanoes while pioneering a geological survey of France. He had never set foot on an active volcano, either, but he

had with him various samples from Vesuvius and Etna. At Moulins, on the river Allier, he was stopped in his tracks by the sight of a fountain made from stone that reminded him strongly of his Vesuvius sample: it was the famous Volvic stone. All he needed to do was to find the place where it had been quarried, and he was soon able to show that the hill above Volvic (the Puy de la Nugère) was an ancient volcanic cone. Not long after, he climbed to the top of the Puy de Dôme and showed that all the cone-shaped hills of this range were accumulations of volcanic material, and not the waste heaps of immense forges dating from Roman times, as local legend would have it. He even went so far as to assert that these volcanoes were only dormant, and advised the local people to look out for certain signs that might give warning of an imminent eruption.

By proving that there were, or had been, volcanoes in the Auvergne, Guettard indirectly showed that they can exist at a distance from the sea, that is, independently of water. Nevertheless, he rather surprisingly explains the formation of basalts, especially the prismatic basalts, in terms of crystallization in a watery medium, as had Conrad Gesner (1516–65) before him in his 1550 publication *Fossils, Rocks, and Crystals*. In so doing, Guettard unwittingly split volcanologists into two camps, creating a rift that would persist for the rest of the century between the Neptunists (Neptune being the god of the sea), who favored a watery origin for volcanoes, and the Plutonists (from Pluto, god of the underworld), who argued for a fiery one.

It was a German, Abraham Gottlob Werner (1749–1817), who made the first move. His passion was mineralogy: he published a work on the classification of minerals entitled *Concerning the External Aspect of Fossils*, and

propounded a theory of rock formation called "geognosy." His views accorded with biblical accounts, most importantly that of the book of Genesis. He believed that the earth was cool, and always had been: this explained how at one time it was entirely covered by a great ocean. Rocks, therefore, had all originated by sedimentation or chemical precipitation in this immense ocean; none had been formed by fusion or melting. As for volcanoes, they were surface phenomena of little significance, caused no doubt by coal burning deep in the earth. Werner taught and defended his theory so brilliantly that he won it many passionate supporters and gave it a most promising start in life.

However, the Neptunists soon found an opponent in the Scottish doctor and chemist James Hutton (1726–97). He acquired a landed estate and began to take an interest in its geology as a leisure pursuit. He became an enthusiast and decided to devote all his time to science, founding a learned society in Edinburgh, the Oyster Club, which counted many of the famous scientists of the time among its members. Hutton studied ancient volcanic ranges in Scotland and made a number of observations, but did not immediately produce a theory as to their formation. His approach was in fact the exact reverse of Werner's, in that Werner sought observations that would confirm his theory, while Hutton was

■ James Hutton (1726–97)

looking for a hypothesis that would explain what he had observed. In 1795 he developed a theory which opposed the idea of the Flood and a limitless ocean. He maintained that there was no beginning, and no end, to the creation of the world, and in his work *A Theory of the Earth, with Proofs and Illustrations*, he set out the basic principles of Plutonism. Unhappily, he lacked any literary talent, and his work might have gone almost unnoticed if one of his disciples, John Playfair, had not set out his ideas afresh, a few years later, in a much clearer style. His *Illustrations of the Huttonian Theory of the Earth* gave Plutonism another chance.

According to Hutton, the earth's core is molten, for reasons not yet known, and is connected to volcanoes. It is this internal heat that melts rock and injects enormous quantities of igneous material into the earth's crust, each eruption relieving the pressure inside the globe.

The first reply to Hutton came from Richard Kirwan (1733–1812), who pointed to marine fossils which he claimed to have found in basalt. However, this "basalt" soon turned out to be a type of clay, fired by contact with lava. Robert Jameson, another Scottish mineralogist, went further still. He was the founder of a Wernerian natural history society in Edinburgh, where he was a professor at the University. The society published only works by authors who favored Neptunism.

The decisive arguments in this debate were provided by James Hall (1761–1832). Another mineralogist, but also a passionate experimenter, Hall learned that at some glassworks glass had been found to crystallize when cooled very slowly. He got hold of some of this crystalline material, heated it to melting point and, on cooling it, produced ... glass again. After many repeated experiments, he succeeded in producing either glass or crystals

at will, depending on the time he allowed for cooling. The result was the same when he used basalt, and in this way he proved that volcanic rocks also can be the outcome of a melting process. Later, visiting Vesuvius on his travels, he observed veins of lava that were more crystalline toward their center than at the edge. He deduced that this was lava that had been squeezed into clefts in the rock while molten: the surfaces that came into contact with the cold rock had cooled quickly and vitrified, while in the middle of the vein the lava had retained its heat longer and, cooling more slowly, had formed crystals.

Finally, George Watt (son of James Watt of steam engine fame) succeeded in synthesizing columnar basalt using a furnace. The igneous origin of volcanic rocks was no longer in doubt.

Aside from this dispute, many other observations and discoveries were made as the 18th century progressed. These provided a solid foundation for volcanology, a thoroughly modern science that is still young today. Even before Hutton published his ideas, Plutonism had a number of keen advocates in continental Europe, and all were convinced that studying the products of volcanic eruptions was the way to get at the truth. Among these well-known Plutonists was Nicolas Desmaret (1725–1815), who studied the same mountains as Guettard and made the first geological map of them. He demonstrated that basalt and molten lava are chemically one and the same, which was a considerable shock to received ideas. However, though a convinced Plutonist, Desmaret never engaged in polemic, but would simply invite his critics to

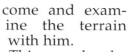

■ Déodat de Gratet de Dolomieu (1750–1801)

come and examine the terrain with him.

This was also the period of the great voyages of discovery, which opened up a vastly enlarged field of investigation for volcanologists. Captain Cook discovered Hawaii, Pallas traveled all over the Kamchatka peninsula: the entire globe was being crisscrossed repeatedly by natural scientists.

Colonel Jean-Baptiste Bory de Saint-Vincent (1778–1846) visited the Canary Isles before disembarking on the Isle Bourbon (present-day Réunion), where he did outstanding work on Piton de la Fournaise, describing and interpreting many features of the landscape formed by flowing lava. He gave names to this active volcano's principal craters, honoring famous scientists of his day, such as Dolomieu and Haüy – and without false modesty bestowed his own name on the central crater, which was active at that time and is known as the Bory Crater to this day.

Desmaret's ideas were taken up by Count Montlosier (1755–1838), who also studied the volcanoes of the Auvergne. He was the first to suspect that the melting of basalt was not the result of underground fires, although he did not offer an alternative explanation.

To Déodat de Gratet de Dolomieu (1750–1801), who witnessed several eruptions on Etna, Vesuvius, and Stromboli, it seemed clear that lava came from fluid magma which filled the inside of the earth. In the face of almost universal opposition, he maintained that the source of lava was the melting not of granite, but of different types of rock beneath the earth's crust. His scientific work was of outstanding quality, and makes him one of the founders of modern volcanology.

A friend of Dolomieu's, Sir William Hamilton (1730–1803), played a part which earned him similar eminence. He was British Ambassador to the court of Naples, and was so fascinated by Vesuvius that slanderers gossiped that he paid more attention to the volcano than to his charming wife, the famous Lady Hamilton – not a wise course in Naples! He climbed the mountain no fewer than sixty times, sometimes while it was active, and his book *Campi Phlegraei* was a great success with the scientific community of the day. He showed that volcanoes' cones are built up by the accumulation of fallout, and that basalt flows are not all the same, but can be of various types. He distinguished what we know as ropy lava from scoria and, like Dolomieu, thought that volcanoes were supplied from deep down, their "fire" being of a peculiar kind since it needed no air and "burned" even in underwater eruptions. Hamilton discovered that the great mushroom-shaped clouds are the result of magma coming into contact with water. He was also one of the first to be concerned with the effects of volcanic eruptions on people: he advised the evacuation of the Portici palace when it was threatened by a lava flow, and recommended clearing the roofs of Naples when the town was covered with ash. What is more, he was the first forecaster of eruptions, observing that the intensity of earth tremors increases as the eruption draws near: he can therefore be considered the first volcanologist to assess eruption risk.

By the end of the 18th century, the Neptunist theory was at its last gasp. It was finally buried by two of Werner's most prestigious pupils, von Humboldt and von Buch. Alexander von Humboldt (1769–1859) inherited a large fortune and set off for the New World as a Neptunist, but began to entertain doubts about the validity of Werner's theories. His work on volcanoes is all the more interesting since his observations were mainly undertaken in the Americas, a region that until then had not been studied at all. In the end he joined the Plutonists, declaring lava to be "mixtures of fluids, metals, alkalis, and earths." He also noticed that volcanoes are sited along great geological faults, forming volcanic mountain ranges, and he distinguished between major destructive earthquakes of tectonic origin and volcanic tremors, two concepts still in use today.

Leopold von Buch (1774–1853) was the most famous geologist of the early 19th century. He realized early on that there were many lava sources which could not be associated with the combustion of coal, since there was none in the region. After establishing this point in many places on his travels, notably in Albania and on Vesuvius, he too abandoned Vesuvius and Etna to study the volcanoes of the Auvergne. Tirelessly traveling around Europe for his research, he finally became convinced that Werner's ideas could not apply to volcano formation. However, he did not totally reject Neptunism until after Werner's death, out of respect for this master of a school of thought, admittedly a discredited one, who was also his own former teacher.

The emergence of modern volcanology

In the closing years of the 19th century, the final whistle was blown on the contest between Neptunism and Plutonism. However, no sooner was this heated dispute laid to rest than another controversy arose in the young science of volcanology: are craters formed by elevation or by accumulation?

The theory of the elevation of craters originated with von Buch, who in 1842 published a paper entitled *Observations on the Volcanoes of the Auvergne*, in which for the first time he stated his view of the origins of volcanoes. He maintained that volcanoes without craters, domes like Sarcoui, the Puy Chopine, and the Puy de Dôme, are formed by a kind of "swelling" or "bladder" of granite transformed into a rock which he called domite. An "internal volcanic force" was, he said, responsible for erecting these structures. He asserted that granite turns into domite, and that domite, when it melts, turns into basalt! Volcanoes which swell too much explode at the summit and collapse: that is the origin of craters. There are therefore two phases: an elevation phase (mountain-building) and an explosion of the summit area (formation of craters, known as *caldeiras* in the Azores and *calderas* in the Canaries). Applying his theories to Vesuvius, von Buch explained that the mountain rose out of the ground fully formed, and denied that accumulation played any part in the formation of relief topography.

These theories, passionately argued, won many followers among French natural scientists, but others were more sceptical, especially the British-born George Poulett Scrope (1797–1876).

An economist and politician by profession, Scrope was also a keen volcanologist and in 1825 wrote a work called *Considerations on Volcanoes* which set out the basic principles of modern volcano science. He made a painstaking study of the way cones form from the heaping up of scoria (cinders), and showed the importance of gases, above all water vapor, in the mechanism of eruptions. He noted that volcanoes are capable of producing more than one type of magma, and argued that this is because the chemistry of magma alters slowly while it is stored deep underground. He also considered that all eruptions must be through fissures. He thoroughly demolished von Buch's theory with its elevation craters, and also opposed that of Charles Daubeny (1795–1867), who suggested that the heat source for volcanic activity lay in an interaction between percolating groundwater and deep-lying sodium and calcium salts. Scrope believed that the heat was connected with the creation of the earth itself.

Somewhat later another Scot, Charles Lyell (1797–1875), the author of the first modern geological treatise *Principles of Geology*, came to support Scrope's ideas after reading his work and visiting a number of volcanoes. He spent a long time on Etna and did outstanding work there.

In 1831, a new volcanic island appeared in the Mediterranean, halfway between Sicily and Tunisia, and further undermined von Buch's elevation-crater hypothesis. Constant Prévost (1787–1856) announced, on returning from a scientific expedition to the island, that it was growing entirely by accumulation, and that no sign of "elevation" was to

■ **Ferdinand Fouqué (1828–1904)**

be seen. He used for the very first time an image which has survived to our day, comparing the explosions that accompanied this eruption to the uncorking of a bottle of champagne. Ferdinand Fouqué (1828–1904) finally laid the theory to rest in 1866, when he went to study the Santorini caldera and the eruption then taking place there on Nea Kameni. He discovered the traces of a town that dates from around 2000 B.C., buried beneath some 30 meters (100 feet) of accumulated pumice-type fallout. He was thus able to demonstrate without any doubt that the caldera had been formed by collapse after a massive explosion that had caused an immense amount of fallout. On his return

■ **Charles Sainte-Claire Deville (1818–81)**

home to resume teaching at the Collège de France, he declared that the notion of elevation craters should be abandoned once and for all.

At the end of the 19th century, attention was also turning to eruption gases. Charles Sainte-Claire Deville (1818–81) was the first to take gas samples, using sampling bottles, during an actual eruption – a very risky undertaking. To general amazement, he showed that the gases did not vary, as was thought, according to the volcano they came from, but that the proportions of their components depended on the stage of eruption at which the sample was taken. In 1912, it was again by sampling gases, with the use of long poles, at the Kilauea lava lake in Hawaii that Arthur Day (1869–1960) and Ernest Shepherd (1879–1949) were able to demonstrate the predominance of water vapor in gases of magmatic origin.

It was at this time that the microscopic study of rocks under polarized light and advances in chemistry began to make tentative contributions; before long, they would revolutionize the earth sciences. An event of great importance for volcanology was the eruption of Krakatau on August 27, 1883, causing a tsunami that killed between 30,000 and 40,000 people on the coasts of the Malay archipelago, in the Dutch East Indies. The Netherlands government sent Rogier Verbeek (1845–1926) to study the causes and the effects of this disaster, and the Royal Society of Great Britain dispatched its experts as well. For the first time ever, a volcanic eruption was properly studied in depth and on a large scale.

When Mount Pelée erupted in 1902, destroying the town of Saint-Pierre and killing 28,000 people, the press reported these events extensively, in detailed accounts drawn from a number of sources. This first encounter between volcanoes and the mass

media probably inspired many of the 20th century's most dedicated volcanologists.

Thomas Jaggar (1871–1953) was one of the first scientists on the spot after the eruption of Mount Pelée, and decided there and then to devote his life to the study of volcanoes so that, as he put it, "never again would a town be destroyed by a volcano." In 1912, on Kilauea in Hawaii, he built a volcanological observatory which in its day was one of the largest and most modern in the world.

Alfred Lacroix (1863–1948) was a professor of mineralogy at the National Museum of Natural History in Paris when

■ **Alfred Lacroix (1863–1948)**
Famous for his photographs and study of the eruption of Mount Pelée in 1902, Lacroix was made a member of the French Académie des Sciences in 1904, "propelled irresistibly by a volcano," as he himself liked to put it.

the French government sent him to the scene of the Mount Pelée eruption. His studies there, culminating in his work *Mount Pelée and its Eruptions*, elevated him to the very peak of his profession. In 1904 he was elected to the French Académie des Sciences – in his words, "propelled irresistibly by a volcano."

He drew up a classification system for volcanoes, later perfected and named the Lacroix classification by his followers. His photographs of what he named "nuées ardentes" (glowing clouds, pyroclastic flows accompanied by a hot ash cloud), as well as his studies of the phenomenon, became world famous and are even now referred to as models of precision. In 1932, he succeeded in getting an observatory set up on Mount Pelée.

In 1928, the Japanese established their first volcanological observatory on Aso San, followed by another on Asama. Around the same time, the Netherlands government sited a string of similar observatories around the

East Indies, and the Australians did the same at Rabaul in Papua New Guinea. Modern volcano science was installing "eyes and ears" all round the world to keep the fiery monsters under constant surveillance. Yet Etna, one of the first volcanoes to be studied, only got its observatory in 1953, thanks to the Swiss volcanologist Alfred Rittman (1893–1981).

Modern volcano science was now well established, and the scene was set for the greatest scientific challenge of all: from now on, each time the beast stirs, even though its sleep in the belly of the earth may have been long and deep, those who are dedicated to making sure that "never again would a town be destroyed by a volcano" will be there. Of course, theirs is necessarily a long-term mission, for their information is collected a little at a time, during the very events that are potentially so destructive. Sometimes it even demands the sacrifice of the boldest among them, whose passionate quest leads them to the limits of prudence, and beyond. ■

PLATE TECTONICS

This theory, conceived in the 1970s, has unified all the earth sciences, with volcanology taking its place alongside the rest as a fully-fledged scientific discipline. Although the theory is almost thirty years old as we move into the 21st century, it still provides the best model for understanding and interpreting the mechanisms that govern our planet.

THE STRUCTURE OF THE EARTH

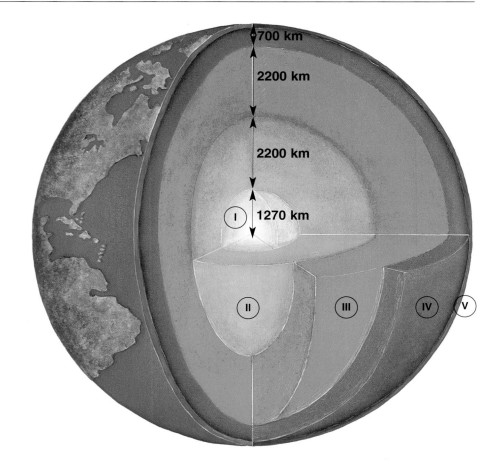

This model of the earth's structure appears in all the textbooks nowadays, and is taken for granted by most people. Yet direct observation of the planet's internal structure is totally impossible, and it has taken over a century of amassing seismic data, followed by the more recent development of techniques for physically modeling that data, to arrive at this apparently simple and obvious picture.

Our globe consists of three nested "spheres": the core (about 16% of the earth's volume), the mantle (82%), and the crust, both continental and oceanic (2% altogether).

It is most likely that this division of the earth into layers is the result of differences in the chemical composition of the various bodies that came together in space and fused to form the earth. Each of these layers is further subdivided according to physical differences within it.

The core

At the earth's center, the inner core is solid and at a very high temperature (approx. 5000°C or 9000°F). It is basically a lump of iron, containing roughly 4% nickel. The outer core surrounding it is liquid, and quite similar in its composition, though with a higher sulfur and oxygen content. Astrophysicists believe that the earth's magnetic field is due to the presence of this liquid zone deep inside the planet.

The mantle

This is the region where magmas originate. It contains most of the earth's mass, and is divided into two zones. The lower mantle consists of compact crystalline material, formed from iron and magnesium silicates in association with other iron and magnesium oxides. The upper mantle is also composed of iron

No.	Layer	State	Temperature	Composition
I	Inner core	Solid	5000°C (9000°F)	Iron and nickel
II	Outer core	Liquid	c.3500–2800°C (c.6300–5000°F)	Iron, silicon, and nickel (at the mantle boundary)
III	Lower mantle	Solid	c.2800–1700°C (c.5000–3100°F)	Silicates and oxides of iron and magnesium
IV	Upper mantle	Solid	c.1700–1300°C (c.3100–2400°F)	Silicates of iron and magnesium (olivine, pyroxene). A transition layer containing spinels and leucite separates the lower and upper mantles.
V	Crust	Solid	1300°C (2400°F) at deepest, cool at surface	Oceanic crust: basalt Continental crust: granite, granodiorite

THE TWO COMPETING MODELS
FOR CONVECTION IN THE MANTLE

A: Single-layer model, with a single convection system affecting the whole mantle.
B: Two-layer model, with two independent systems at different depths. One circulates in the lower mantle and the other in the upper mantle; they are separated by a discontinuity at a depth of 700 km (435 miles).

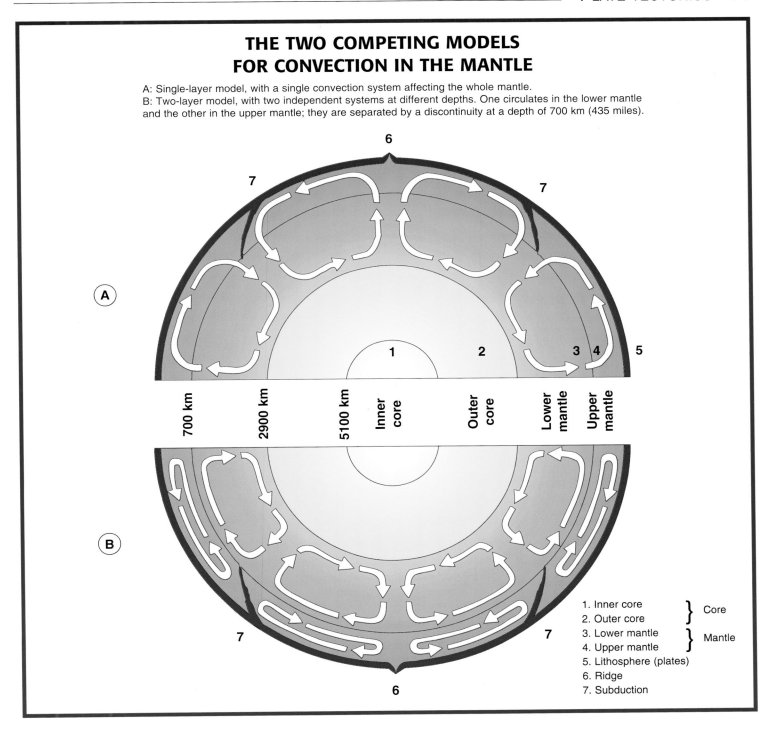

1. Inner core } Core
2. Outer core
3. Lower mantle } Mantle
4. Upper mantle
5. Lithosphere (plates)
6. Ridge
7. Subduction

and magnesium silicates, but associated with oxides of aluminum. Although solid, most of the mantle (known as the asthenosphere) is not rigid and can deform, moving rather like ice.

The lowest part of the mantle is hotter than the rest because of its contact with the very hot core. This temperature difference sets up huge convection currents, and it may be these that cause the lithospheric plates to move. At present, there are two competing models of the convection currents in the mantle, but both fit equally comfortably with the theory of plate tectonics (see pages 72–73). The uppermost part of the mantle, about 70 kilometers (43 miles) thick, is rigid because it is cooler. Together with the earth's crust, also rigid, it forms what is known as the lithosphere.

The crust
This cool top layer is much less dense. The basaltic oceanic crust, about 10 kilometers (6 miles) thick, is overlaid in continental areas by a continental crust, up to 50 kilometers (30 miles) thick, consisting mainly of granites. ∎

FROM CONTINENTAL DRIFT TO PLATE TECTONICS

It was at the beginning of the 20th century that Alfred Wegener (1880–1930) laid the foundations of the theory of continental drift. The idea was a stroke of genius, but it was ahead of its time, and had its ups and downs before finally becoming the key that opened the door to the plate tectonics hypothesis. That unifying theory, conceived in the late 1960s, succeeded in bringing all the earth sciences together, and volcanology plays a major role in this new synthesis, since one of the things that can now be explained is the distribution of volcanoes around the globe.

Continental drift

Wegener was a meteorologist and geophysicist: it was while watching icebergs break off from the parent ice sheet that he conceived the idea of continental drift. In his picture, the continents, consisting mostly of what was known as *sial*, a composite of *si*liceous and *al*uminous materials, floated like rafts on denser oceanic material made up of *sima*, compounds of *si*lica and *ma*gnesium.

When he published his theory in 1911, it was based primarily on arguments from shape and structure: what Wegener (and others before him, like A. Ortellius of Holland in 1596) had noticed was that the shape of the North American coastline more or less mirrors the outline of the European coast, and similarly with South America and Africa. Not only that, but mountain ranges and the great granitic shields have their counterparts on the other side of the divide.

Geologists put forward many additional arguments, based on paleontology and stratigraphy, to support Wegener's, and for more than twenty years it was geologists who most zealously defended his suggestion. It was, curiously enough, the geophysicists who could not accept the idea of major movements of the earth's crust and therefore strongly opposed the theory. At that time, in the first third of the 20th century, there was no known force that could drive movements on this scale, and for lack of such a motor Wegener had to abandon his idea. Not until the 1950s did

new propositions lead to its revival. Ironically, it was the geophysicists who now ensured its success, with the evidence from paleomagnetism: in that decade it was discovered that crystals which are sensitive to the earth's magnetic field, such as those of magnetite, preserve in their alignment a "fossil" record of the direction of the magnetic pole at the time when they crystallized out of cooling lava. By studying this record, the geophysicists found that the position of the continents relative to the magnetic poles had changed over time! It is true that the earth's magnetic poles oscillate in relation to the planet's axis of rotation, but greater changes than this could only be explained (ruling out major disturbances in the earth's rotation) by shifts in the position of the continents. Were such shifts still going on, the scientists wondered? And if so, what was driving them?

Sea-floor spreading

In 1962, the US geophysicist Harry Hammond Hess published the hypothesis that is still used today to account for continental drift. He brought in the idea of upward flows within the mantle providing new material, which emerges at the mid-ocean ridges and so adds to the surface of the ocean floor. The earth's crust on each side of the ridge moves with the shifting mantle beneath, taking with it ocean floor and continents alike.

On the surface of lava lakes such as this one on Erta Ale (Ethiopia), a solid skin forms and, under the influence of convection currents in the lake, provides a sort of scale model demonstrating how plate tectonics operates.

Since this spreading of the ocean floor implied an increase in the earth's surface area, it had to be compensated for: according to Hess, this occurs at the island-arc trenches. His idea enabled scientists to make sense of many of their observations, and set the framework for all research in the field during the decades that followed.

In recently-accumulated lava, which can be accurately dated, magnetite crystals point to the current position of the poles; but as one looks back in time, anomalies soon appear. The north magnetic pole, usually near the north pole of the globe, has reversed diametrically at certain points in the past, "flipping" to the south geographic pole for periods of varying length. These periods came to be known as "negative magnetic anomalies." Vine and Matthews had the idea of using the alternation between positive magnetic anomalies (when magnetic north coincides with geographic north) and negative ones as the basis of a time scale in which periods were demarcated by inversions of the magnetic poles: it would then be possible, they thought, to correlate the geological time scale with this. They matched their scale with the horizontal distribution of rocks on both sides of the mid-Atlantic ridge, and observed that the anomalies occurred symmetrically: the age of the ocean-floor basalts increases, the further they are from the ridge. Sea-floor spreading became an established fact, confirmed by the International Program of Ocean Drilling, IPOD. This determined the ages of the rocks with enough precision to give an idea of the rate of expansion (1 to 2.5 centimeters, or fi to 1 inch, per year in the case of the Atlantic). Local variations in speed revealed that this spreading is not taking place uniformly throughout the world's oceans: some parts of the ocean floor are moving faster

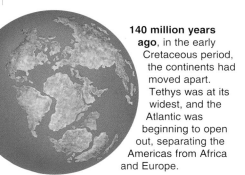

200 million years ago, at the beginning of the Jurassic period, today's continents had not yet separated, but formed a single block, alone in the ocean. Then a north–south divide appeared, forming another ocean, Tethys.

140 million years ago, in the early Cretaceous period, the continents had moved apart. Tethys was at its widest, and the Atlantic was beginning to open out, separating the Americas from Africa and Europe.

Today, the continents are still on the move. America is drifting away from Europe at an average rate of 3 cm (just over 1") per year.

Continental drift

than others. This led to a further enhancement of the theory: there had to be faults at right angles to the mid-ocean ridge, allowing the areas moving at different speeds to slide past each other. The existence of these "transform faults" was proved soon after by detailed seismic investigation.

The theory of plate tectonics

Within a few years, a number of facts had been established. There was no doubt that at the mid-ocean ridge – not only in the Atlantic, but in the Pacific too – our earth produces new sea-floor surface. Now this idea had to be integrated into the body of existing scientific knowledge. To start with, astronomers toyed with the idea of global expansion (an increase in the earth's volume), but the rate of increase

in sea-floor area was too high for that. There had to be regions compensating for it, where an area of the earth's crust equal to that newly created was being either swallowed up or pushed into folds. These crust-absorbing mechanisms in fact operate at the island arcs (the Philippines, Japan, Indonesia, etc.) and the great continental cordilleras (such as the Andes and the Rockies). This is where crust plunges deep into the mantle and is reabsorbed. But in the huge scars left by recent mountain-building, rocks are found that are typical of the ocean floor. These folded and layered rocks, in the Alps or the Himalayas, bear witness to the crumpling of what was once the bed of the ancient ocean (or oceans) known as Tethys.

At the end of the 1960s, MacKenzie, Le Pichon, and Isaaks put forward the suggestion, based on global seismic data, that the whole surface of the planet should be viewed as composed of plates. Each of these structural units, they argued, was separated from its neighbors by one of three types of boundary: crust formation zones (mid-ocean ridge or rift), crust absorption zones (subduction zones), and zones where one plate is moving past another (transform faults or transcurrent fault zones). Plate boundaries are deduced from the distribution of earthquake centers.

In 1968, Le Pichon envisaged no more than six main plates, but in the same year other researchers distinguished forty-eight, including many small ones. The basic idea of plate tectonics had gained general acceptance, but the detail, especially the number of plates, remains controversial even today, and the champions of microplates battle with the proponents of macroplates in a specialist dispute that has been going on ever since the beginning of the 1970s. ■

Plotting the positions of active volcanoes on a map of the world reveals how they are aligned along some of the plate margins. Above sea level, active volcanoes are found mainly in subduction zones. There are many such volcanoes in island arcs (such as Japan and Indonesia) and in cordilleras (such as the Cascade range in the USA and the Andes in South America). Very few show up at hot spots or mid-ocean ridges, but this is because almost all of their activity takes place beneath the ocean. The only known active rift in a continental region is the Great Rift in East Africa.

The mid-ocean ridges are completely submerged, except for Iceland, which rises above sea level because a hot spot here coincides with the mid-Atlantic ridge and reinforces its activity. Although hot spots are rare in continental regions, they are not restricted to plate margins. Most of the volcanoes associated with them do not even break the surface of the sea, but well-known ones that do are the Hawaiian islands and the island of Réunion.

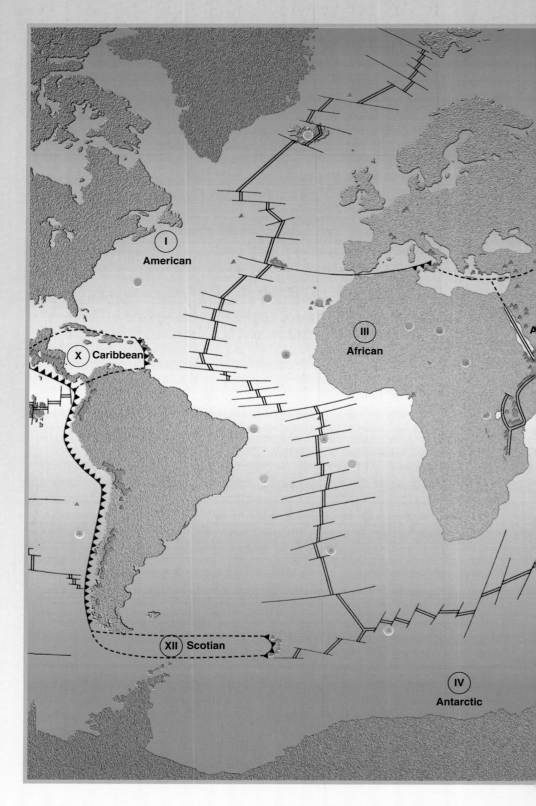

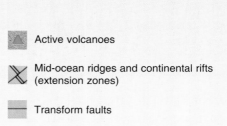

Active volcanoes

Mid-ocean ridges and continental rifts (extension zones)

Transform faults

Subduction zones (zones of compression)

Hot spots

 I – XIII Main plates

  Other plate boundaries (mountain ranges) and ill-defined, poorly-understood boundaries

TECTONIC PLATES: WORLD MAP

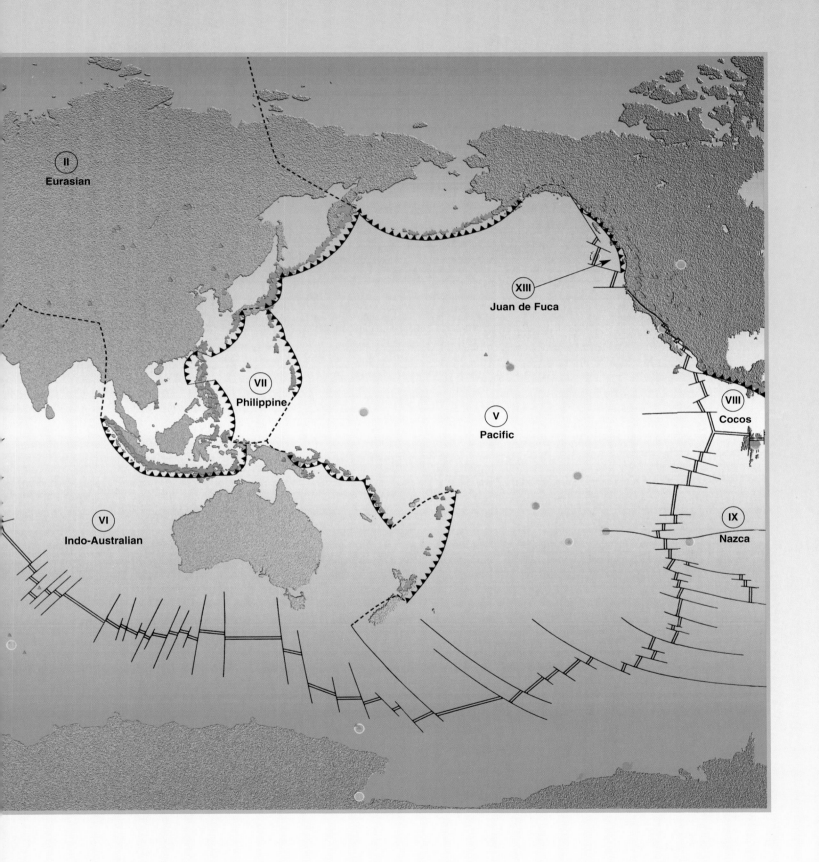

II
Eurasian

XIII
Juan de Fuca

VII
Philippine

VIII
Cocos

V
Pacific

VI
Indo-Australian

IX
Nazca

VOLCANIC ACTIVITY AND PLATE TECTONICS

For a long time, geologists regarded volcanic phenomena as rather insignificant, a kind of "skin disorder" of the planet, but the arrival of the plate tectonics theory in the 1970s changed all that. For the first time, volcanic activity fitted almost perfectly into an overall model of the earth, and the formation of mountain ranges and the distribution of volcanic structures around the globe could at last be explained. It is tectonic plates, especially their boundaries, that determine where volcanoes occur, and even the mechanisms by which magma is formed seem to fall into line with the theory.

Volcanic activity at the margins of diverging plates

The mid-ocean ridges – 60,000 kilometers or 37,000 miles long – form the longest range of volcanoes in the world. They are located at the boundaries between diverging plates, which are probably driven apart by convection currents in the mantle

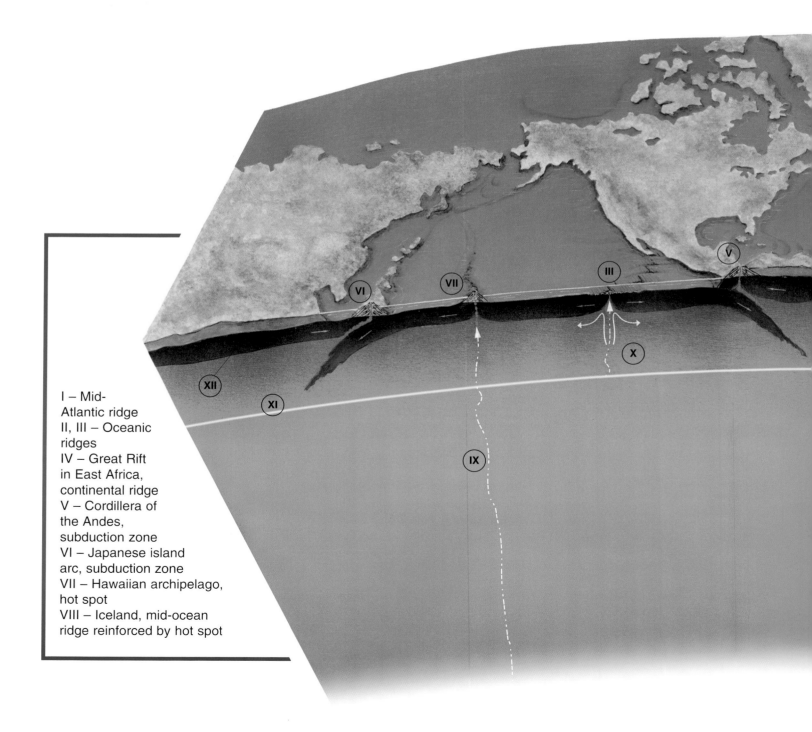

I – Mid-Atlantic ridge
II, III – Oceanic ridges
IV – Great Rift in East Africa, continental ridge
V – Cordillera of the Andes, subduction zone
VI – Japanese island arc, subduction zone
VII – Hawaiian archipelago, hot spot
VIII – Iceland, mid-ocean ridge reinforced by hot spot

(see page 71). As two plates move away from each other, they allow new ocean floor to be formed. Almost exactly halfway between the Americas in the west and Europe and Africa in the east, the mid-Atlantic ridge (I) is the best known. Most volcanic activity of this type takes place under water (II, III), but an extensional boundary can occur between two continental plates, as it does at the Great Rift in East Africa (IV).

Volcanic activity at the margins of converging plates

Where two lithospheric plates are converging, three types of situation can arise.

First, the plates may collide, and when this happens, a mountain chain forms.

For volcanoes to arise, though, one of the plates must go under the other, and this is called subduction. It can take two forms: the forced subduction of an oceanic plate encountering a continental one produces cordillera volcanoes, as in the case of the Andes (V), while spontaneous subduction gives rise to island arcs, like the islands of Japan (VI).

Volcanoes in the middle of plates

Volcanoes found far from plate margins (mid-plate volcanoes) are thought to be connected with material rising from very deep down, at the core/mantle boundary. These centers of activity are known as "hot spots," and they give rise to strings of volcanoes, like those of the Hawaiian archipelago (VII). The mid-Atlantic ridge comes above the surface of the sea at Iceland (VIII) because a hot spot at that point coincides with the extensional plate boundary. ∎

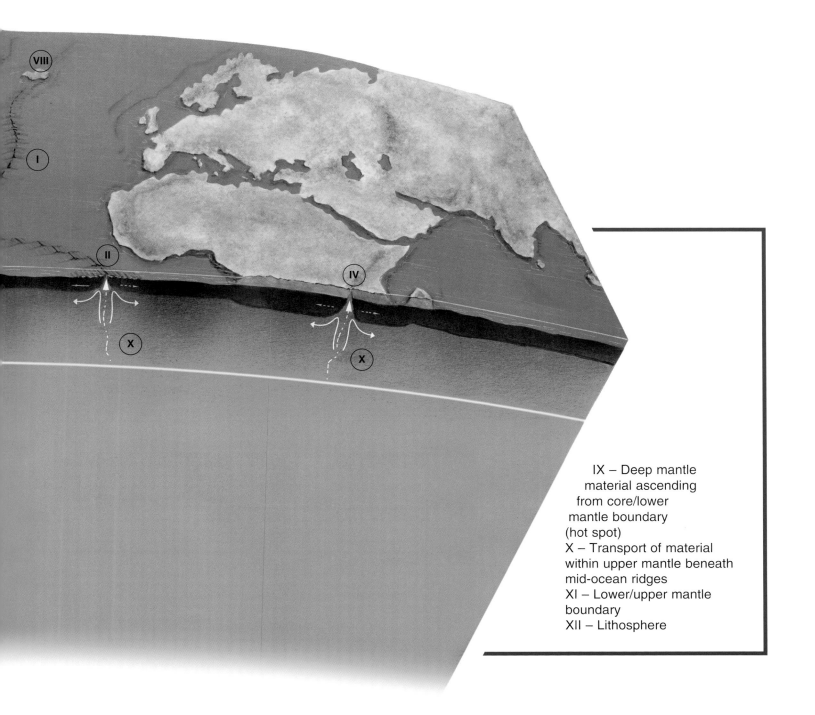

IX – Deep mantle material ascending from core/lower mantle boundary (hot spot)
X – Transport of material within upper mantle beneath mid-ocean ridges
XI – Lower/upper mantle boundary
XII – Lithosphere

VOLCANOES IN SUBDUCTION ZONES

Krakatau (Indonesia, 1883), Santa María (Guatemala, 1902), Katmai (Alaska, 1912), Cerro Azul (Chile, 1932), Agung (Indonesia, 1963), Mount Saint Helens (USA, 1980), El Chichón (Mexico, 1982), Pinatubo (Philippines, 1991), and Rabaul (Papua New Guinea, 1994): all of these have a number of features in common. These nine volcanoes are responsible for the most violent eruptions that have occurred in the last century and a half. Between them, they threw out so much magma that it is measured in cubic kilometers, and the greatest eruption of all, at Katmai or Novarupta, hurled between 10 and 16 cubic kilometers (2.5 to 3.8 cubic miles) of material into the atmosphere. These huge aerosols of dust and gas are sometimes driven as high as 30 kilometers (100,000 feet), well into the stratosphere, where they are carried away on the jet stream and spread over vast areas of the globe.

All of these colossal eruptions were produced by volcanoes in subduction zones. There are two forms of subduction, but in both the volcanic activity is connected with the downward movement of part of the oceanic crust. As descending material from the lithosphere is subjected to high temperature and pressure, it releases substances in a liquid state, producing magma, at a depth of about 100 to 150 kilometers (60 to 100 miles).

When this type of magma returns to the surface, it forms andesite, which accounts for some 70% of all lava. It is found in cordilleras such as the Andes (hence the name), but also in the island chains, such as Japan and Indonesia, which go by the name of "island arcs." Andesitic volcanoes have a strong tendency to explode and are the most common volcanoes on the face of the planet, if underwater ones are discounted.

Island arcs

Island arcs form in subduction zones where what some scientific authors call "spontaneous subduction" takes place. Lithospheric material that has drifted for some 150 or 200 million years since it was first formed has had time to cool, and as it does so it grows denser, until it is heavier than the asthenosphere on which it rides. It therefore starts to sink of its own accord toward the center of the planet. This kind of descending plate is always oceanic, but the neighboring plate may be either another oceanic one, or continental. In the first case, the older of the two oceanic plates heads downward, opening up an oceanic trench that may be as much as 10,000 meters (33,000 feet) deep, like the

Augustine in Alaska (above) and Stromboli in Sicily (left) are both typical island-arc volcanoes, but each also has unique features of its own. One of the extraordinary things about Stromboli is that it has been erupting almost without a break for nearly 4000 years.

The most famous cordillera volcanoes are probably those of the Andes, including Cotopaxi (left) in Ecuador and the hundreds of Guatemalan volcanoes (above). All the way from Mexico to Tierra del Fuego, these magnificent giants rear their unmistakable cone-shaped summits to heights challenged only by the solitary condor.

Marianas Trench in the western Pacific.

The trenches fill with water-saturated sediments, and some of these sediments are dragged down in the subduction process and swallowed up in the asthenosphere. At a depth of around 150 kilometers (100 miles), both the sediments and the oceanic crust release fluids, leading to melting of the upper mantle and giving rise to andesitic magmas. It is directly above these magma sources that island arcs form, volcanic islands strewn like a string of pearls along the edge of the plate, with their characteristic pattern tracing out an elegant curve.

There are some of these arcs in the western Atlantic (including the Lesser Antilles), as well as in the northern and western Pacific (the Marianas, Kuriles, Aleutians, etc.), but other types of island arc are formed where oceanic and continental plates meet, as in southeast Asia. The Indonesian archipelago is an example: it is in a particularly complex region, where oceanic and continental crust are juxtaposed in a jigsaw of microplates, some of them bordered by island arcs that, to varying extents, diverge from the classic model (the Sunda Islands, Sangihe, the Moluccas, the Banda islands, etc.).

Cordillera volcanoes

The great cordilleras, crowned with the majestic cones of their andesitic stratovolcanoes, are fewer in number than the island arcs. The textbook instance is of course the cordillera of the Andes along the west coast of South America, but the Cascade range straddling the US/Canadian border can also be regarded as typical. Both of these mountain ranges are in fact located on the eastern shore of the Pacific, in subduction zones where plates of two different kinds (oceanic and continental) meet.

The oceanic crust here is too close to the ocean ridge where it originated, less than 30 or 40 million years ago, and too young, warm, and in consequence light, to sink of its own accord. It is only because it has encountered a continental mass that is far thicker but even less dense, and moving in the opposite direction, that the ocean floor has been forced to bend downward here and form a subduction zone. The clash of these two plates is accompanied by folding, crumpling, and in some cases overlapping, all of which go to form the mountain chain eventually presided over by the great volcanic structures.

As in the case of the island arcs, the andesitic magma typical of the cordilleras comes from a region 100 to 150 kilometers (60 to 100 miles) deep, at the base of the lithosphere of which the continental crust is part. However, as the magma rises, some material from the continental crust becomes mingled with it, producing andesites which petrographers can distinguish from those of the island arc volcanoes.

It takes several tens of millions of years for the lithosphere and its oceanic crust to be completely swallowed up. As it heads down beneath the continental plate, friction between the two plates causes earthquakes, some of which originate as far as 700 kilometers (435 miles) beneath the surface. At this depth, the whole of the lithospheric material finally becomes amalgamated into the mantle; meanwhile, up on the surface, the volcanic activity associated with subduction ceases. ∎

VOLCANOES ON THE MID-OCEAN RIDGES

Our earth is not called the Blue Planet for nothing: 70% of its surface is covered by oceans. It is not surprising, then, that the greatest volcanic range of all – 60,000 kilometers or 37,000 miles long – was the last to be discovered, or that it remained unknown for so long: it is under water!

The mid-ocean ridge is a great "wound" which encircles the whole earth, dividing in places. So far, it seems to have similar features throughout its length, but of course our deep-sea explorations have only recently begun (with Famous, the French–American Mid-Ocean Undersea Survey, in 1973), and our detailed knowledge comes almost exclusively from mapping ventures undertaken by the USA, the European Union, and Japan only in the two decades.

The ridge rises on average some 2500 to 3000 meters (8000 to 10,000 feet) above the abyssal plains, but its "peaks" are still (on average) the same distance again beneath the surface. The mountain slopes extend for a distance of 1000 to 3000 kilometers (620 to 1860 miles) on each side of the ridge crest, occupying nearly a third of the whole ocean floor. Magma is produced almost constantly along the axis of the ridge, amounting to some 21 cubic kilometers (5 cubic miles) of new oceanic crust each year. This is the largest-scale volcanic activity anywhere on the planet in terms of volume produced.

However, not every part of the mid-ocean ridge is erupting at any one time. The pattern of activity varies, depending on how the ocean floor is extending and reforming along the center line of the ridge. This zone can be regarded as a deep rift in

Thanks to state-of-the-art technologies such as made the pocket submersible Cyana possible, the ocean ridges can now be explored in detail.

the earth's crust between two plates which are moving apart, while the space left by their divergence is being filled with basalt that originates in the upper mantle by a process of partial melting.

Differing mid-ocean ridge profiles

During the last decade or more, scientists have compiled enough topographical data to distinguish three types of ridge profile. These appear to correspond to different rates of extension of the ocean floor. There are "slow-spreading" ridges, where the ocean floor is growing at a rate of 1 to 5 centimeters (fi inch to 2 inches) per year. These typically have median valleys, also known as rift valleys or axial rifts, which are wide (30 kilometers, or 20 miles) and deep (1–2 kilometers, or 3000–6000 feet). The mountainous slopes on both sides are known as rift mountains.

Then there are "intermediate" ridges, where the divergence is of the order of 5 to 9 centimeters (2 to 3fi inches) per year. Their central zone is a plateau that is not particularly high.

Finally, there are "fast-spreading" ridges, where the plates are moving apart most rapidly, at a rate of 9 to 18 centimeters (3fi to 7 inches) per year. The central zone here is not depressed, but forms a roll, or "dome."

These should not be regarded as the only possible ridge types: like most attempts to classify natural phenomena, this system has to make allowance for a great many exceptions. The profile of the ridge is often altered by the presence of a hot spot nearby, or by other causes, some of which are as yet unknown.

Indeed, our exploration and observation of the mid-ocean ridges has only begun very recently and has so far been on a very small scale, compared with the immense length of the fissure itself. The Famous mission, which began in 1973, involved making direct observations from the bathyscaphe *Archimède* and the submersibles *Cyana* and *Alvin*. These proved for the first time the existence of the mid-Atlantic ridge in the neighborhood of the Azores.

Five years later the *Cyana*, which could reach depths of 3000 meters (10,000 feet), was used in the Cyamex (*Cyana* Mexico) project to explore the eastern Pacific ridge off the Gulf of California. The observations made on these two voyages of discovery provided volcanologists with a great deal of data on deep-ocean volcanic behavior, their knowledge of which had been entirely theoretical up to that point.

Eruptions "Twenty Thousand Leagues Under the Sea"

The mid-ocean ridges lie beneath an enormous amount of water (2500 meters or 8000 feet deep on average), and the pressures at such depths prevent the gases trapped in magma from escaping and causing eruptions like those that occur on surface volcanoes. Undersea eruptions consequently take the form of material welling up quietly. In recent years, detailed investigation of some stretches of the mid-ocean ridge has revealed that the eruptions in the central zone of the ridge produce three main types of outflow: lava lakes, flows, and pillow lava.

This last phenomenon was seen for the first time at a mid-ocean ridge in 1973, by the members of the Famous expedition, though it had long been familiar from specimens now on dry land: the curious, bolster-shaped lava formations had been intriguing geologists since the beginning of the 20th century. The first examples of pillow lava to be described were some very ancient formations in Cornwall, UK, and similar ones were

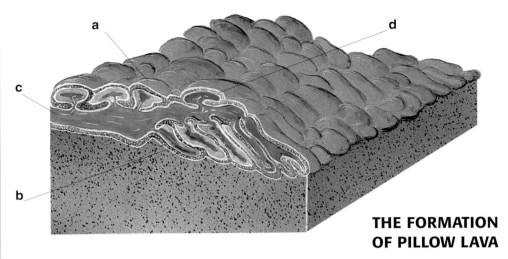

THE FORMATION OF PILLOW LAVA

Pillow lava is formed by flows that keep producing "buds" (a) or "fingers" (b) for as long as the supply (c) continues and their internal pressure remains high enough to break through the glassy crust (d) formed by contact with the cooler seawater.

Bathyscaphe divers have found many formations similar to these, both on the mid-ocean ridges and on seamounts (or underwater volcanoes) like this one at Teahitia.

subsequently reported from low-volume basalt eruptions under shallow water, in lakes for instance. They have also been found in Iceland, where they are created by eruptions taking place under ice, and in the ophiolitic rock types characteristic of deep-sea environments (see page 91).

These underwater flows all proceed in the same manner: as soon as the lava comes into contact with the water, provided it is being produced at only a moderate rate, its surface cools very rapidly and a glassy shell is formed. A crust of solid, glassy rock just 1 to 2 centimeters (fi to 1 inch) thick is enough to stop the flow spreading, and it can only continue by flowing along finger-shaped tubes.

The internal pressure of the lava trapped in these tubes causes them to crack, enabling the molten material to escape and create new tubes here and there – but their surface glazes over even as they form. So long as lava continues to be produced, the flow progresses in the same way, leaving behind it the jumble of pillows and bolsters (tubes) after which it is named.

At the mid-ocean ridges, where this type of lava accumulates above the fissures supplying the material, it builds up structures with very steep sides: the slope may be as steep as 17%. These heaps, effectively volcanoes 50 to 80 meters (150 to 250 feet) high and several hundred meters in diameter, extend parallel to the line of the ridge. Larger structures form on slow-spreading ridges, growing to a height of 300 meters (1000 feet), perhaps because 80% of the volcanic material produced by this type of ridge takes the form of pillow lava.

Lava lakes, on the other hand, arise where the lava is produced at a greater rate, which more often occurs on fast-spreading ridges. The structures associated with these lakes were first seen at the Galapagos ridge in 1977, using cameras dragged along the

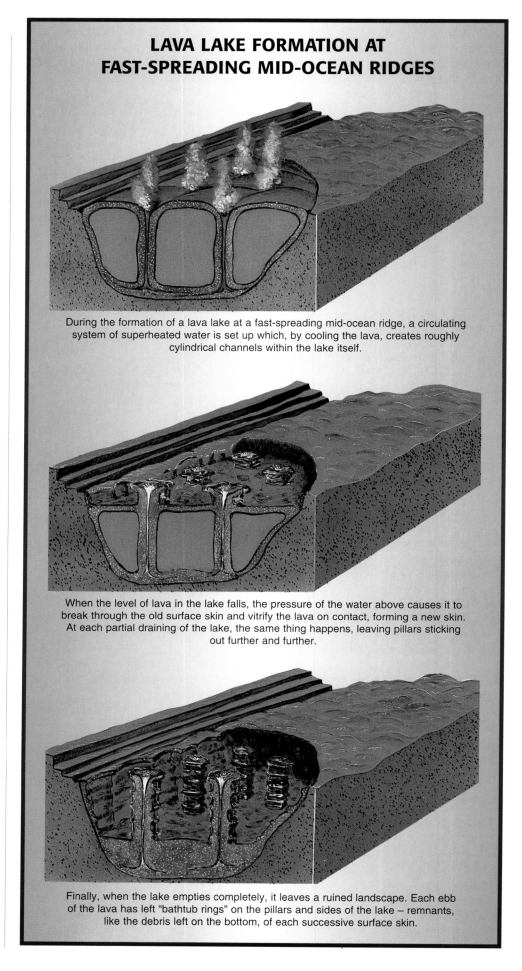

LAVA LAKE FORMATION AT FAST-SPREADING MID-OCEAN RIDGES

During the formation of a lava lake at a fast-spreading mid-ocean ridge, a circulating system of superheated water is set up which, by cooling the lava, creates roughly cylindrical channels within the lake itself.

When the level of lava in the lake falls, the pressure of the water above causes it to break through the old surface skin and vitrify the lava on contact, forming a new skin. At each partial draining of the lake, the same thing happens, leaving pillars sticking out further and further.

Finally, when the lake empties completely, it leaves a ruined landscape. Each ebb of the lava has left "bathtub rings" on the pillars and sides of the lake – remnants, like the debris left on the bottom, of each successive surface skin.

ocean floor. In 1978, the *Cyana* team came across the same phenomenon in the Rita zone, on the eastern Pacific ridge.

What happens is that enormous volumes of lava are produced at a great rate by wide fissures. The rapidly-flowing lava cannot cool quickly and spreads over an area of many square kilometers, filling depressions in the terrain and so forming huge lava lakes under the sea. A lake will gradually drain, ebbing in many stages before it finally dries up completely. The pressure of the water

A lava lake as the deep-sea explorers see it, some 2500 meters (8000 ft) beneath the ocean surface.

above then causes the hardened surface skin to give way. In the middle of the lake, a forest of pillars remains standing, the remnants of a drowned Atlantis that owes nothing to human ingenuity.

The columns of this natural temple of Poseidon are, in sober fact, the result of currents of water circulating within the lava lake itself. Each pillar turns out to be a pipe, a channel for a "geyser" of hot water. Though heated to over 400°C (750°F), this water remains liquid. As it circulates, it forms a layer of solid lava around itself, building a

sleeve of rock which is gradually left sticking further and further out of the lava lake as its level drops.

Outflows of the third type, "lava flows," arise when the volume of lava produced and the rate of supply fall somewhere between those that produce pillow lava and those of the lava lakes. These flows sometimes harden into prismatic shapes, but they most often resemble the pahoehoe flows seen on land, forming the folded lava strands known as "ropy lava."

The volcano-tectonic cycle of mid-ocean ridges

The processes that play the most important role in the formation of mid-ocean ridges are of two types. Tectonic activity, with its associated forces, causes the axial zone of the ridge to spread, a process known as extension. Volcanic activity, on the other hand, causes material to accumulate at more or less the same location.

The two types of activity cannot be separated, but the extension of the ocean floor is regarded as a continuous process, while the volcanic activity that takes place

along the great axial rift is, by contrast, sporadic.

It is therefore possible to distinguish phases of two different types in the life of a mid-ocean ridge: in one, tectonic activity predominates, while the other is a phase of profuse volcanic production. This gives rise to the concept of a volcano-tectonic cycle: during a so-called eruptive phase, fluid products accumulate in the central zone, compensating for the pulling apart of the plates, and a kind of roll with a dome-like profile appears above the deep mid-ridge rift. This "dome" continues to grow until the eruptive phase comes to an end, giving way to the second, tectonic phase.

The tectonic phase is a dormant or "resting" period for the ridge's volcanoes. The two sides of the rift continue to move apart, but since no material is being produced to compensate for the movement, the space between the two plates tends to collapse and form a graben, or subsidence valley. This continues until a new eruptive phase begins and material starts to accumulate once more, completing the cycle, which repeats for as long as the ridge remains.

This is a fairly recent hypothesis which accounts quite well for the profiles of the various kinds of mid-ocean ridge. It seems, moreover, that some stretches of ridge, characterized by different rates of extension and bounded by the larger transform faults that lie at right angles to the line of the ridge, follow a volcano-tectonic cycle of their own. The cycles repeat at intervals that vary from 0.7 to 1 million years in the case of the mid-Atlantic ridge; shorter intervals of about 50,000 to 70,000 years apply to the eastern Pacific ridge. There have been some observations, though not enough yet to be conclusive, which suggest that the cycle of each of the stretches making up the ridge is not synchronized with that of the adjoining stretches. ∎

VOLCANOES AT HOT SPOTS

The existence of volcanoes at plate margins accords very well with the overall theory of plate tectonics: subduction zones and rifts fit entirely logically into the established model.

Mid-plate volcanoes, though, are somewhat trickier to explain, since they are located far from any zone of magma production. The concept of hot spots has been evoked to account for them.

Hot spots

Scientists think that mid-plate volcanoes are caused by ascending heat within the mantle. The existence of such hot plumes, or "surges," is not really in doubt, but there has been some debate about the depth at which they originate. It is generally accepted nowadays that they are created about 2900 kilometers (1800 miles) deep, at the lower mantle/core boundary. The plumes, lighter than the surrounding mantle because they are hotter, "float" slowly up toward the surface like surreal underground balloons and are trapped beneath the lithosphere. They flatten themselves against this ceiling and begin to work their way through it, acting on the lithospheric plate like a blowtorch on sheet metal: the base of the plate melts, and it is pierced right through to the surface, where a volcano forms.

Starting with undersea releases of gases and culminating in outflows of liquid lava, hot-spot shield volcanoes build up gradually until they break through the surface, towering above the ocean floor far below.

THE WANDERINGS OF PELE

Hot spots probably have their origin more than 2900 kilometers (1800 miles) deep within the earth. The volcanoes they produce, however, rest on plates of lithosphere (a) which change their position (b). Volcanoes form above the hot spot and then move away as they continue to grow, eventually getting cut off from their deep magma source (c). While the volcano that has moved away from the hot spot ceases to be active, another is already being built up. Hence, the younger the volcanoes are, the nearer they are to the hot spot. The direction in which the lithospheric plate is moving determines the alignment of the chain of volcanoes (I, II, III). The Hawaiian islands are a good example, but in their case there are two different alignments, because the direction of the plate's drift has changed over time (b'). In this way, a second alignment has formed (III, IV, V, VI). The ancient people of Hawaii had a different explanation for these chains of volcanoes. It was said that Pele, goddess of the Earth and of Fire, was expelled from Tahiti by her sister and fled toward what is today the Big Island of Hawaii, leaving behind her a string of craters and smoking volcanoes. It just so happens that the direction of Pele's flight corresponds with the diminishing age of the archipelago's volcanoes – which only goes to show that sometimes science and legend can trace out the same path.

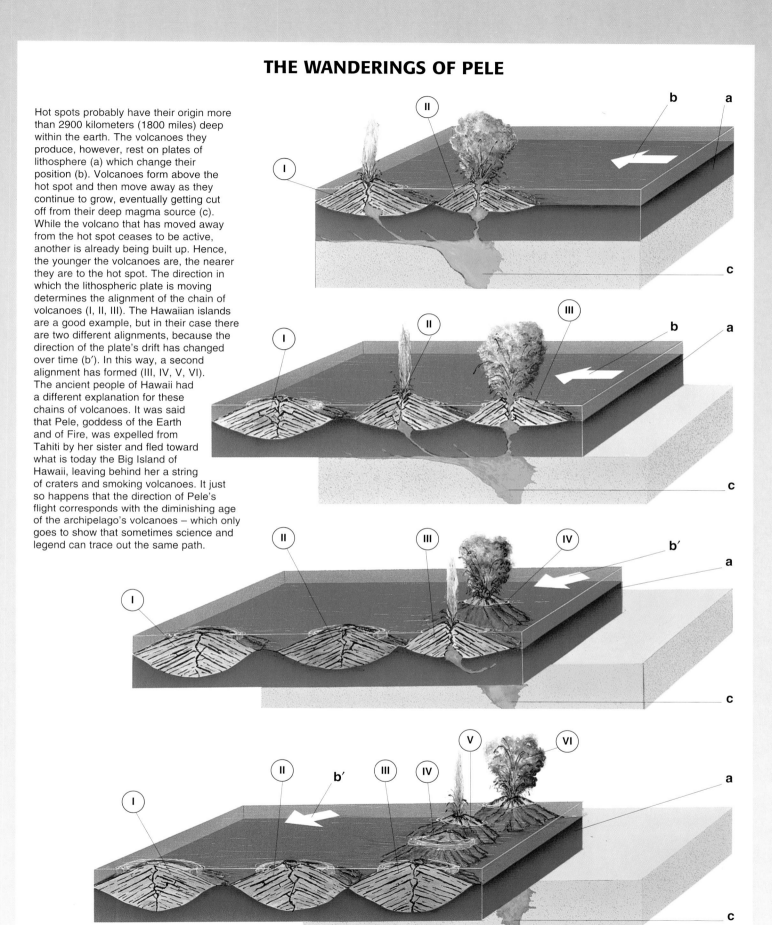

Two types of hot-spot volcano

The position of these hot spots is regarded by almost all scientists as fixed, and they can occur in both oceanic and continental plates.

Although hot-spot shield volcanoes are not common on continents, there are some spectacular examples, such as Mount Cameroon. The greater thickness of the continental crust (30 kilometers, or 20 miles, on average) readily explains their rarity: it takes far longer for the plume of heat to pierce through the lithosphere where this is thickened by an enormous mass of granite, than to traverse the oceanic lithosphere, where the crust consists only of a skin of basalt roughly 10 kilometers (6 miles) thick.

For the magma to work through to the surface, a continent has to remain stationary above a hot spot for a very long time, probably several million years. But the continents are moving: there are few fixed spots on the surface of the globe, and the great continental shield volcanoes are therefore only found in stable regions, where there is no continental drift (Africa) or almost none (Yellowstone, USA). They differ from their ocean-floor "cousins" in containing rhyolites, lavas that are chemically equivalent to granites and probably originate in the melting of some of the continental crust beneath the volcano.

However, hot spots proliferate in the middle of oceanic plates, where they produce the greatest heaping up of minerals anywhere on the planet. Mauna Loa, a total of 9000 meters (30,000 feet) from base to peak, is thus the largest active volcano in the world, and also the earth's highest mountain, even though its summit rises only 4171 meters (13,681 feet) above sea level.

The birth of these monsters goes totally unnoticed, for it always takes place in the depths of the ocean. In 1982, it was discovered that the undersea volcano Teahitia, 40 kilometers (25 miles) from Tahiti, was experiencing tremors, regular seismic vibrations which are the telltale signs of magma rising. Until then, volcanologists had thought that Teahitia was inactive and the hot spot was extinct, but underwater exploration of this volcano, whose summit is 1500 meters (5000 feet) beneath the surface, revealed recently-formed pillow lava and intense hydrothermal activity. Like many underwater volcanoes, Teahitia had been active behind the scenes.

Even Mount MacDonald, which comes much closer to the surface of the Pacific, was only recognized as an active volcano in 1967, and twenty years later the research vessel *Melville* was given the task of investigating it. The volcanologists arriving at the spot believed that the top of the cone was some 50 meters (165 feet) down. But just as an intriguing coloration of the water drew them directly over the site of the volcano ... it began to erupt! The erupting vent was in fact some 150 meters (495 feet) below them.

Each of these great volcanoes, sitting on the drifting ocean floor, gradually moves away from its hot spot, and before long it is cut off from its deep supply of magma. Meanwhile, a virgin portion of plate arrives over the hot spot to replace it, and a new volcano begins to form. For as long as the hot spot remains active, this sequence of events is repeated, and the resulting volcanoes stretch out in a line, forming an island chain at the ocean's surface.

Hawaii is the longest chain of volcanic islands of this type: the archipelago, consisting of some fifteen islands and strung out over a distance of more than 2500 kilometers (1550 miles), has taken about 65 million years to form. For the first 22.5 million of those years, the volcanoes were aligned more or less north–south, indicating that the plate was moving north during this period. But 42.5 million years ago, the lateral forces acting on the Pacific plate altered, and the islands began to move along a southeast to northwest alignment. The youngest of the volcanoes on these islands, Kilauea and Mauna Loa, are still extremely active: these two volcanoes are still close to the hot spot in the southeast, but they are already moving away toward the northwest in the wake of their "ancestors."

Mount MacDonald, also standing on the Pacific plate, belongs to another line of volcanoes that runs parallel to the more recent Hawaiian islands. Piton de La Fournaise, in the Indian Ocean, has already (in theory) moved more than 400 kilometers (250 miles) away from its hot spot. However, it is still supplied from magma reserves near the surface, which have moved with it and its migrating plate. Once these magma chambers are empty, the volcano's activity will cease – but that will not happen for many more thousands or even millions of years.

The island of Réunion is not the first volcanic structure to have risen over its particular hot spot. Mauritius, the whole Mascarene island plateau, and even the Deccan in India all owe their existence to passing over this natural blowtorch. The Deccan is sited on continental crust, the Mascarenes (Mauritius and Réunion) on oceanic crust: clearly, some hot spots last long enough to pierce through first one and then another of these drifting plates, even when one is continental and therefore thicker.

It is rarer to find a hot spot located at a plate boundary, but this is the situation that has created Iceland, on the mid-Atlantic ridge. Here, ocean-ridge volcanic activity and hot-spot activity have joined forces to raise the ocean floor up into the light of day. ∎

THE ORIGIN OF MAGMA

From Plato's river of fire, Pyriphlegethon, to modern theories of the origin of magma, the road has been long and tortuous, with many dead ends. But scientists through the ages have always been fascinated by the strange molten masses that rise up from so far beneath their feet.

FROM MAGMA TO LAVA:
VOYAGE FROM THE CENTER OF THE EARTH

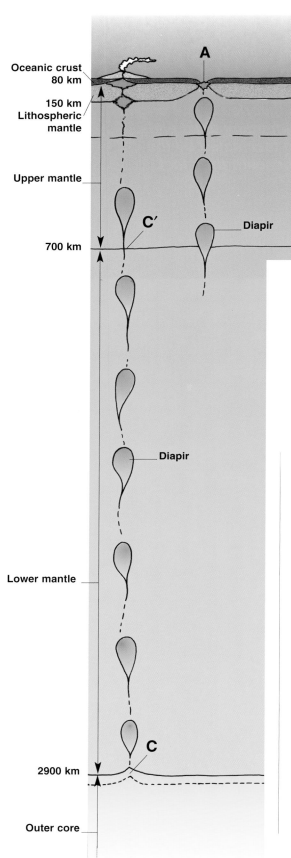

Oceanic crust
80 km

150 km
Lithospheric
mantle

Upper mantle

700 km

Lower mantle

2900 km

Outer core

A

B

Lithosphere

Asthenosphere

C'

Diapir

Diapir

C

A – Region of tholeiitic magma formation: depth approx. 80 km (mid-ocean ridges)

B – Region of calc-alkaline magma formation: depth 100–150 km (subduction zones)

C – Region of alkaline magma formation: depth 2900 km (hot spots and continental Great Rift)

C' – Suggested alternative region of alkaline magma formation: depth approx. 700 km

Humankind long ago conceived the notion that there was a "fire" burning within the earth. Even today, most people picture our planet as a sphere with a hot, molten center. This is a false picture, but it is one that was long shared by scientists. In fact, it seems that only the outer core, from 2900 to 5100 kilometers (1800 to 3160 miles) deep, is made of material that reacts to transverse seismic waves as if it were something akin to a liquid. The earth's inner core is solid, as is the mantle.

Magmas and magmatic series
The term "magma" comes from the Greek word for "something kneaded." Volcanologists distinguish three states of magma:
– Liquid magma, usually a mixture (known as a "bath") that consists mostly of silicates.

– Magma containing gas. Deep down in the earth, where it is under great pressure, gas is dissolved in the silicate liquid. As the magma approaches the surface and the pressure reduces, the gas forms bubbles.
– Magma containing solid material, consisting of crystals in suspension.
On reaching the surface and losing their gas content, magmas become lavas. It is not uncommon to find lavas poor in silicates (basalts) together with other, silicate-rich ones (rhyolites) in the same volcanic range. Usually, rocks of intermediate composition are also present, and it can easily be demonstrated that they all originated in the same primary magma. In this way, petrographers and geochemists have identified groups of lavas which they call "magmatic series."
On a world scale, it can be seen that these series are distributed according to geodynamic conditions, and it is possible to distinguish three magmatic series arising out of three different types of primary magma:
– tholeiitic magmas, associated with extension zones (the mid-ocean ridges and rifts);
– calc-alkaline magmas, formed in subduction zones (the island arcs and cordilleras);
– alkaline magmas, characteristic of volcanic activity in the middle of plates (above hot spots) and at the continental Great Rift.
Each series has its own distinctive features, but contains a range of lava types with varying silica content. Those poorest in silica are known as "basic" or "less differentiated," while at the other extreme are the silica-rich "acidic" or "differentiated" lavas. What happens is that, as the

primary magma moves toward the surface, its composition is altered by a number of physical and chemical processes. All of these changes are collectively referred to as "magmatic differentiation."

From magma to volcanic rock

What can be seen of a volcano at the earth's surface is just, so to speak, the "tip of the iceberg," and its eruptions are only the final stage of a journey that began thousands, if not many millions, of years before, as magmas worked their way through the earth's crust. Due to their viscosity, some of these magmas never make it to the surface: they form immense, bubble-shaped bodies known as "plutons" that gradually solidify, still at great depths. As these huge bodies of magma cool very slowly, large crystals can form, giving rise to coarse-grained rocks. The best known of these is granite. Both volcanic (or extrusive) and plutonic (or intrusive) rocks are classified as "igneous" (from the Latin *ignis*, "fire"), but only volcanic rocks have their origin in lavas, which end their molten journey at the earth's surface.

The magma's progress

Magma progresses through four main stages. The first is the formation stage. How magma is formed depends on tectonic conditions in the part of the earth where it originates: oceanic ridge, subduction zone, or hot spot. The zone determines the form the magma takes and where it will emerge. Depending on the zone, material from deep within the mantle or crustal material may be incorporated into the magma, affecting its composition.

During the transport stage, magma travels in the form of a fluid which, on its arrival in the lithosphere, is subjected to pressure from the earth's tectonic movements. The resulting forces determine the route taken by the magma, and the rate at which it travels depends on its viscosity.

Thirdly, there are "halts," or storage phases. Magma may stagnate in huge pockets known as "magma chambers," and it is here that most of the changes in its composition take place.

Finally, how it erupts depends on the magma's chemical composition and gas content, which in turn are determined by the differentiation that has occurred in the parent magma as it passed through various levels during its transport and storage stages.

This final stage is the only one that is seen on the surface, but eruption is just the last chapter of a long and eventful story. By studying what happens in eruptions, and the materials produced by them, we can reconstruct the magma's journey from the center of the earth.

Where and how is magma formed?

Scientists now universally agree that magma is created when all or part of a solid precursor passes into a liquid state. The formation of magma can therefore be thought of as a melting, or partial melting, of solid material. The magmas poorest in silica (basic magmas) are created by partial melting: they are the direct result of this process and are therefore known as primary or primitive magmas.

During the transport and storage stages, these basic liquids are altered by magmatic differentiation to produce liquids with a higher silica content, known as differentiated magmas.

Extension zones (oceanic ridges) and subduction zones, both of which occur at plate boundaries, are the principal points where magma is produced. At extension zones, rising currents in the mantle break through the lithosphere, bringing a mixture of crystals and liquid – mainly silicates – into contact with the oceanic crust. This ascending current is initially composed entirely of crystals, but as it rises and comes under less pressure, fluid appears and gradually forms a larger and larger proportion in relation to the solids. It is only this fluid component, arising from the partial melting of the mantle material, that finds its way into magma chambers beneath the oceanic ridges: the solid component is left behind at the upper boundary of the earth's mantle.

The process that takes place at subduction zones is rather different. Here, the lithosphere (complete with its oceanic crust, overlaid by sediments saturated with water) is dragged down into the asthenosphere, a region of high temperature and pressure, where it partially melts. The magma so produced is lighter than the mantle and rises toward the surface. As it does so, the upper part of the mantle through which it travels partially melts in its turn, and mixes with the primary liquid. The now-altered magma continues to move upward and is further enriched by the other liquids (molten oceanic or continental crust) through which it passes before emerging at the surface.

These two processes of magma production are quite distinct. But, although different materials are involved in each process, similarities do exist between them, since in both cases the magma is formed in the upper mantle.

Where magma is created in the middle of a plate, different mechanisms altogether are at work. The magmas that well up at hot spots must originate very deep down in the lower mantle. The production of these mid-plate magmas can only be explained by enormous movements on a planetary scale: scientists have concluded that immense convection currents bring huge amounts of material at very high temperatures all the way up from the mantle's lower boundary, where it meets the earth's outer core. ∎

OCEANIC BASALTS (THOLEIITIC SERIES)

Before the great undersea exploration ventures of the 1960s, it was thought that the ocean floor was composed of alkaline basalts like those of the great volcanic islands, such as Hawaii, that lie in the middle of the ocean. But the first samples collected from mid-ocean ridges across the world proved to have a tholeiitic composition, and on comparison these basalts were found to be so similar to one another that scientists gave them the name Mid-Ocean Ridge Basalts (MORB).

As the rising material reaches the upper limits of the convection cells, at depths of 20 kilometers (12 miles) or so beneath the ocean ridges, it comes under considerably less pressure. This causes the peridotite of the upper mantle to melt – but not completely, and only a small proportion of this material is destined to form the primary, tholeiitic silicaceous liquid that supplies the magma chambers. Peridotite is composed almost entirely of olivines, deep green minerals that are occasionally found as a residue in some basalts. Trapped nodules of peridotite dragged up to the surface along with the liquid magma give scientists an opportunity to study the make-up of the upper mantle: their composition is very similar, except that a few components have got left behind on the journey. Thus we can now form a good idea of what the upper mantle is made of, though some details remain rather hazy.

The tholeiitic primary liquid, on the other hand, is very well understood. It is poor in silica (50%) and has a low potassium content. It may develop into other, more differentiated liquids if it remains stored for a long enough period in one or more large magma chambers.

Along the ocean ridges, rock strata alternate in a highly characteristic pattern. The earth's oceanic crust, here 6 to 8 kilometers (3.7 to 5 miles) in thickness, consists of the following layers, from top to bottom. First, there are the oceanic basalts, some 2 kilometers (1.25 miles) thick, taking the form of pillow lava at the surface but riddled lower down with a network of veins, which act as channels feeding volcanic activity on the surface.

Then come 4 kilometers (2.5 miles) of gabbros, coarse-grained

Black smokers are among the most spectacular sights undersea explorers have come across. These little chimneys just a few inches in diameter spew out superheated water, at around 350°C (660°F), which is rich in metallic sulfides. The plumes shoot up to heights of 150 meters (500 feet) above the chimneys, which are capable of ejecting more than 10 liters (2fi gallons) of liquid every second.

OCEANIC BASALT FORMATION AT FAST-SPREADING RIDGES

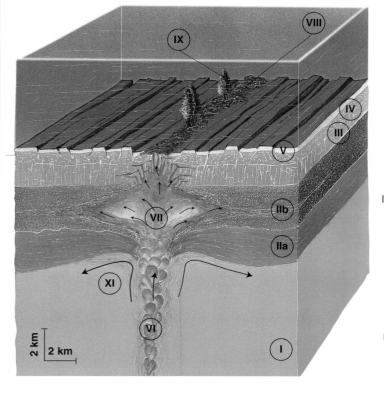

I – Upper mantle
II – "Mixture" of gabbros and peridotites
IIa – Layered gabbros and peridotites
IIb – Gabbro blocks
III – Network of veined basalt
IV – Basalt as pillow lava
V – Sediments
VI – Supply of magma to chambers by rising diapirs
VII – Longitudinal magma chamber

rocks chemically the same as basalt, but which have had time to cool more slowly, thus allowing large mineral crystals to form. Below these is a layer of peridotite, deformed and in part transformed by the high pressure and temperature into a rock made up of minerals known as serpentines, because they are mottled and streaked like a snake's skin. All of this is sometimes overlaid by layers of sedimentary material.

The most ancient examples of this layered structure in the ocean floor today are some 170 million years old. Strangely enough, in order to understand the processes involved in forming the seabed, we have to look high in the mountains: the same rock sequence that is characteristic of the ocean floor, the ophiolite sequence (from the Greek *ophis*, meaning "serpent"), is often found in mountain ranges like the Alps. Much distorted by

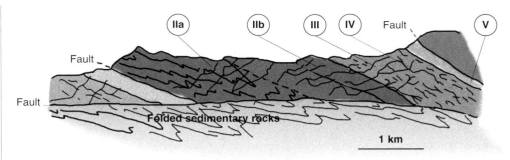

The numbers refer to the descriptions in the diagrams below and opposite.

mountain-building and other tectonic processes, these ophiolites are the remains of "fossil" oceanic crust caught in the collision between two plates. Tens of millions of years later (between 60 and 180 million years in the case of the Alps), they enable geologists to study the ocean floor on dry land!

Three types of mid-ocean ridge behavior have been distinguished: slow spreading (a low rate of extension of the ocean floor), fast spreading (a high extension rate), and a third type

Schematic diagram of an ophiolite sequence

In mountain ranges such as the Alps, geologists have found, tucked between two faults, sequences of rocks similar to those that form at the mid-ocean ridges.
These rocks once formed the floor of an ancient ocean, which was crumpled into folds as two plates collided.

intermediate between these two. In all three cases, melting takes place as a result of the reduction in pressure that occurs in these zones, though probably only 5 to 20% of the total volume of mantle material that reaches the zone actually melts. The liquid so formed moves upward through channels (veins) and eventually wells out on the ocean floor. While this is happening, large crystals are accumulating in the magma reservoirs at a depth of about 5 kilometers (3 miles). First to arrive are crystals of olivine, which form peridotite, though of a slightly different composition from the peridotite in the mantle. Then other minerals (pyroxene and plagioclase feldspars) are added to the olivine, creating a mixture that, on cooling, produces gabbros by fractional crystallization (see pages 94–95).

At the slow-spreading ridges, flows of varying composition often arrive at the surface simultaneously. Since seismic data gives no indication of great volumes of liquid beneath these ridges, what is probably happening here is that there are a number of small magma reservoirs, each with its separate channels to the surface, of which now one, then another is active. ∎

OCEANIC BASALT FORMATION AT SLOW-SPREADING RIDGES

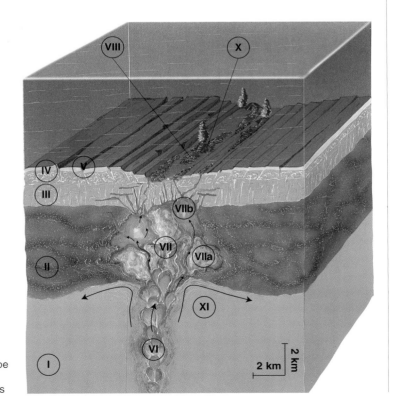

VIIa – Inactive magma chamber
VIIb – Active magma chamber
VIII – Flows of pillow lava
IX – Black smokers (not to scale)
X – Volcano formed by accumulation of lava flows
XI – Movement within mantle, causing lithospheric mantle to be pulled away from area under mid-ocean ridges

Andesitic stratovolcano

Continental crust

80 km

Lithospheric mantle

Deep magma chamber (within crust)

Deep magma chamber (at mantle/crust boundary)

Magma rising in the form of diapirs

Zone of partial melting of upper mantle

c.120 km

Liquids (mostly water) expelled from oceanic crust

Oceanic lithosphere

SUBDUCTION-ZONE BASALTS
(CALC-ALKALINE SERIES)

The oceanic crust which sinks downward along with the rest of the lithospheric plate at a subduction zone contributes to the formation of magmas in these zones, but there is still some divergence of views about the exact process by which primary magmas of the calc-alkaline (or andesitic) series are formed.

The lavas produced by arc volcanoes, whether on ocean-island arcs or continental cordilleras, tend to be saturated or even supersaturated in silica. They are composed largely of andesites with a silica content of between 53 and 62%. Differentiation products such as dacites and rhyolites are quite often found on arc volcanoes, while calc-alkaline basalts are more common on the ocean-island arcs.

These primary magmas vary to a considerable extent, depending on the type of plate involved, and specialists distinguish four categories of magma, which might be called "subseries," classified principally according to the silica and potassium content of the primary magmas. Some magmas from different subseries can be found side by side in the same island arc.

The processes by which all these magmas are formed, however, have certain points in common. The magmatic liquids start to

Basalt shield volcano

30 km

Upper mantle

Deep magma chamber

c.120 km

Zone of partial melting of upper mantle

c.670 km

There is an alternative theory which holds that the diapirs start from a zone 670 km deep. Possibly both theories are correct, and a combination of the two processes would explain why hot spots last so long.

Lower mantle

2900 km

Core

Formation of diapirs

MID-PLATE BASALTS
(ALKALINE SERIES)

The concept of hot spots, which emerged at the end of the 1960s, relied fundamentally on the hypothesis that a deep thermal imbalance existed in the mantle. The scientific community readily accepted that these hot spots persist for an extremely long time (measured in tens of millions of years), and that throughout their active life their positions relative to one another remain fixed. In the oceanic context, hot-spot basalts, also known as ocean-island basalts (OIB), have a measurably different chemical composition from that of the ocean-ridge basalts, or MORB (see page 90). This difference can be explained by supposing that they have a very deep origin, 2900 kilometers (1800 miles) below the surface, at the core/mantle boundary.

It has been shown by experiment that the boundary between two bodies of fluid of different viscosity and density is a likely site for the generating of excrescences known as plumes. Such a process occurring right at the upper limit of the outer core is apparently what causes bodies of hot material to ascend through the mantle. When they reach the upper mantle, the heat of these plumes causes partial melting of the peridotite, and the fluids in the plume itself then mingle with those of the mantle, creating the primary magma characteristic of the oceanic islands. The upward form at a depth of around 120 kilometers (75 miles), where the pressure is at least 30 kilobars (0.4 million pounds per square inch). The material that enters into the melt is lithospheric, consisting of the rigid upper part of the mantle and the oceanic crust that overlays it. The basalts and gabbros in the crust are transformed by the high pressure and temperature at these depths. The mantle peridotite cannot melt, even partially, at pressures around 30 kilobars if the temperature is only a little over 1000°C (1800°F). However, the introduction of liquids, especially water, which are present in the oceanic crust does enable partial melting of the mantle material to occur under these physical conditions. Once it is established that pressure (due to the depth), temperature, material for melting, and water are all present, models can be developed to explain how the calc-alkaline magmas arise.

The model favored by earth scientists is a three-stage process. First, at around 100 kilometers (60 miles) down, the descending oceanic crust, which has already begun to be metamorphosed (chemically transformed by huge increases in pressure and temperature), now encounters conditions where its transformation entails the expulsion of water and other liquids. These liquids, released under high pressure, are probably loaded with silica and many other compounds.

In the second stage, the resulting fluid moves from the crust into the mantle material immediately below, and by mingling with the mantle peridotite it causes this to melt partially, creating a body of liquid surrounded by solid material. A bubble of magma has been formed, and it starts its upward journey through the mantle, working its way through the rigid lithosphere above to reach the crust directly over the melting site. In the third stage,

the magmatic fluids are altered during their passage through the crust. An exchange of fluids takes place between the magma and part of the crust, and some of the crustal material itself (especially if it is continental) is also assimilated: these processes, which both take place during prolonged halts of the magma in magma chambers, are the mechanisms by which the primary magma becomes differentiated into what is known as the andesitic series. Where the differentiated magma, stored in near-surface magma reservoirs, is expelled is determined by the faults in the overlying rock, which provide the magma's final pathways to the surface.

It should be pointed out, however, that many scientists believe that sedimentary material, dragged down in the course of subduction, plays an important part in the creation of calc-alkaline magmas. The question is by no means finally resolved. ■

motion continues, and enormous bubbles or diapirs arrive at the base of the rigid lithosphere. They flatten themselves against it, forming vast mushrooms hot enough to have a blowtorch effect that wears away the lithosphere at that spot. Faults and other fragile structures allow this primary magma through to feed near-surface magma reservoirs, and from there to reach the surface: it is in this last zone that they become differentiated.

However, while the volcano is directly over the plume, the primary magma is not of this type. The magma of origin is tholeiitic, and the early, undersea stages of volcano formation involve tholeiitic basalt emission; but as soon as the drift of the plate takes the volcano out of direct reach of the hot spot, the primary magma becomes alkaline and gives rise to lavas of the alkaline series. This transition from the tholeiitic to the alkaline

series has been observed only in the context of the Hawaiian volcanoes: so far, no other hot-spot volcano has yielded any lava from the tholeiitic series. The transition can probably be accounted for by a reduction in the time it takes for the deep material of the plume to reach the surface.

This model provides a satisfactory explanation for the origins of the Hawaiian archipelago's range of magmas, but it fails to account properly for all instances of mid-plate volcanic activity. Although the theory is very attractive, it is in fact restricted to contexts where three conditions apply:

– First, the volcanoes must be aligned in the direction of movement of the plate on which they sit.

– Second, their age must be greater the further away they are from the active volcanoes.

– Third, the lavas produced by the volcanoes must be chemically

different from those of the ocean floor.

Mid-plate volcanoes are indeed frequently arranged in a line, but their ages do not always increase from one end to the other of the archipelago (for instance, in the Cook Islands and the Austral Islands). This creates difficulties for the theory of fixed hot spots (fixed at least on a human time scale).

There are other models that are capable of explaining alignments like those of the Cook Islands and the Austral Islands, where the problem of age arises. One of these models suggests small-scale convection currents, rolls of convection just beneath the lithosphere, at right angles to the oceanic ridges. It is a controversial theory, to be sure, but such controversies are the living proof that the matter is not settled, and that mid-plate volcanic activity has not yet given up all its secrets. ■

MAGMA TRANSPORT AND STORAGE

Between the time of its creation and the instant when it emerges in an eruption, magma undergoes a slow process of change. Its progress toward the surface is straightforward so long as it is passing through the asthenospheric mantle, but when it arrives at the rigid lithosphere the process becomes more complicated. The enormous bubbles of magma, or diapirs, can go no further: they are halted by what is in effect a "ceiling," and the only way out for the magma is to thread its way through fissures. It is in these fractured and fragile zones of the lithosphere that the primary magmas undergo most of their transformation.

Magma transport within the lithosphere

Whether in the crust or in the mantle, the force driving the magmatic fluids upward arises from differences in density, which create buoyancy. The magma is not only lighter than the peridotite of the mantle, it is also less dense – at least initially – than the rocks of the crust; it therefore tends to press upward toward the surface, progressing by displacement, as demonstrated by Archimedes. In the solid but ductile part of the mantle, such movement is perfectly possible, but in the rigid lithosphere displacement is not the only force affecting the transport of these fluids. The magma has to work its way through the fissures that form in this zone, and it can only progress if they are open. Whether the magma finds a path to the surface therefore depends on the chance opening and closing of these fissures, large and small, and this in turn is subject to two main factors: local tectonics (or geological deformation), and what is known as lithostatic pressure.

Both large and small fissures open up and close again under the ebb and flow of local tectonic forces, and the magma finds its way through by seeping into the fissures that are expanding. Most volcanoes are in zones where there is a great deal of tectonic activity. We may reasonably imagine the magma thrusting its way toward the surface along constantly-changing routes: a great labyrinth, as it were, with corridors that become blocked or unblocked as their walls move.

However, there comes a point at which the magma finds itself surrounded by rocks whose density is close to its own, and this means that the effect of Archimedes' force dwindles, eventually ceasing altogether. The magma can rise no further. This close to the surface, the lithostatic pressure is insufficient to force shut all the little crevices (fissures, vacuoles, vesicles, etc.) naturally present in a surface rock, so a given mass of rock occupies a much greater volume than might be expected, making its density far lower. In the case of basaltic magmas, the ones associated with the great oceanic shield volcanoes, which have an average density of 2.6 to 2.7, the equilibrium depth is somewhere between 2 and 7 kilometers (1.25 to 4.35 miles). So it is probably at this depth that the magma reservoirs form under the Hawaiian shield volcanoes, such as Kilauea and Piton de la Fournaise.

Reservoirs or magma chambers

The existence of large reservoirs has been posited to account for the immense diversity of volcanic phenomena that we observe on the surface of the earth. These are the melting pots where the primary magmas are transformed, as if by alchemy, into a multitude of differentiated magmatic liquids.

In more prosaic terms, geologists have concluded that three major processes give rise to and explain magmatic differentiation.

Fractional crystallization

This phenomenon arises from the fact that different rocks crystallize at different temperatures. Some of the special steels developed during World War II made it possible to conduct experiments in the postwar years in which artificial magmas were cooled in autoclaves. The experiments demonstrated that the crystals found in volcanic rocks do not all form at the same time. Olivines and pyroxenes crystallize at the highest temperatures, then amphiboles, and finally micas: these minerals therefore together constitute a temperature series within the silicate family. They are rich in iron and magnesium, and are accordingly known as ferromagnesian minerals.

A quite different crystallization sequence occurs in the case of the plagioclase feldspars, which are silicates rich in calcium and sodium. Here, it is the plagioclase richest in calcium, called anorthite, that crystallizes while still very hot, whereas its sodium-rich cousin, albite, requires a lower temperature for crystallization. Thus the first crystals to form in a magma chamber, at high temperature, are the olivines (known in gem form as peridots), pyroxenes, and anorthite.

THEORETICAL CROSS-SECTION OF A MAGMA CHAMBER

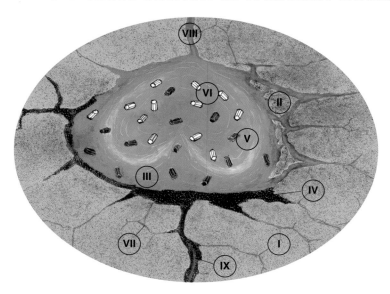

I – The rock surround within which the magma chamber has formed.

II – A fragment of the surrounding rock breaks off and "contaminates" the magma, altering its composition: for example, silica-rich granite may make a magma more acid.

III – The magma is stirred by heat currents, as convection cells (shown by the two yellow arrows) form within the magma reservoir.

IV, V, VI – Denser crystals (V, shown in black) accumulate in a heap at the bottom

or on the sides of the magma chamber; the heap may then solidify, on contact with the cooler surrounding rocks. Other, lighter crystals (VI, shown in white) will rise and form a skin at the top of the chamber.

VII – Fractures form in the rock surround.

VIII – A channel (volcanic chimney) allows magma out of the chamber.

IX – A supply channel for the chamber: fresh supplies of magma can arrive at any time, renewing the volcano's potential to erupt.

The crystals formed in this way are often heavier than the liquid surrounding them, so they sink to the bottom of the magma chamber, where a heap of crystals accumulates: in this instance, a heap of olivines, pyroxenes, and anorthites, in which most of the iron, magnesium, and calcium is concentrated.

The remaining liquid has thus become differentiated by the removal of the elements that have crystallized out: this is what is meant by "fractional crystallization." In some cases, the plagioclases are less dense than the liquid in which they form: these therefore become separated from the (heavier) ferromagnesian silicate crystals, and rise to form a floating, inverse "heap" on the ceiling of the magma reservoir.

Mixing of magmas

The existence of a number of magma chambers, at least one of which is deep down near the crust/mantle boundary, offers a possible explanation of the fact that some magma arrives, already differentiated, in a chamber relatively near the surface. But a near-surface chamber can at the same time be supplied directly with primary magma, and the resultant mixing of magmas will usually produce a mixture that is more homogeneous in its chemistry, although it sometimes creates a liquid at the silica-rich end of the spectrum.

Contamination from the crust

Lastly, differentiation can arise directly from contact between the magma and the walls of the magma chamber. These walls are not always very stable, and moreover they are subjected both to extremely high pressures and, because they are so close to the magmatic fluids, to very high temperatures. It is therefore not unusual for whole sections of the rock surrounding the chamber to break off and be swallowed up and "digested" by the magma.

These sometimes very large quantities of rock enrich the magma in the chamber with their load of chemical elements: for example, the incorporation of a block of granite containing around 70% silica (SiO_2) will "contaminate" a basaltic primary magma with siliceous material, making it more differentiated.

The physical and chemical processes taking place in these reservoirs are in fact considerably more complex than described here, but it is this layering or stratification of magmas in the chamber by density that accounts for the different forms taken by successive eruptions, as the various types of magma are expelled one by one.

Just before the final stage of magma transport (eruption) occurs, the near-surface magma chamber may become enlarged due to the pressure of gases, volatile components dissolved in the liquid silicates. This pressure causes the ground surface to be pushed out of shape to a measurable extent, giving observers forewarning that an eruption is due, sooner or later. The warning signs are relatively well understood in the case of basalt shield volcanoes: their magma is not highly differentiated and therefore tends not to display explosive behavior. But things are very different in the case of the andesitic stratovolcanoes. Their magma is more differentiated, and their eruptions are both more violent and rarer, which limits the opportunities for observation and consequently our understanding of how their magma chambers work. ∎

THE CARBONATITES OF OL DOINYO LENGAI

The East African Great Rift is known for its alkaline volcanoes. Nyiragongo, Nyamlagira, and Erta Ale are only three of the many famous volcanoes here that owe their spectacular eruptions to the extremely fluid alkaline magma producing them. But they have a curious neighbor in Ol Doinyo Lengai, the only volcano in the region that is fed by carbonate-rich magma.

One of the factors determining the nature of volcanic activity at the surface is the silica content of the magma involved. This is rarely lower than 49%, but there are exceptions, and carbonate-rich magmas with only 3% of silica do come to the surface in a few places. Their principal component is calcium (they contain around 30–45% CaO), which combines with carbon dioxide (CO_2) to produce the calcium carbonates (in the form of calcite or dolomite) that give these lavas the name of carbonatites.

Magmatic liquids of this type are always associated with the alkaline series (see pages 88–89), but exactly how they form is still a matter of dispute. Three hypotheses have been proposed: partial melting in the upper mantle (see pages 88–89), differentiation as a result of fractional crystallization (pages 94–95), and a tendency to remain separate when different magmas mix (pages 94–95). The fact remains that these carbonatites appear only sporadically and, so far as extinct volcanoes are concerned, in only a few places on earth, including Canada and South America.

Only one active volcano currently produces this type of lava: it is Ol Doinyo Lengai, located on the East African Great Rift in Tanzania. Carbonatites are very free-flowing, although their temperature is low (around 300°C/570°F). Because they are not hot, they do not glow brightly, and appear black as they emerge. Curiously, though, as they cool they whiten and eventually turn as white as calcium carbonates of sedimentary origin, such as chalk. ■

Lava lakes, flows, and fountains (shown here at Nyamlagira in the Republic of Congo) are characteristic of the East African Great Rift volcanoes, which produce alkaline magmas rich in silicates.

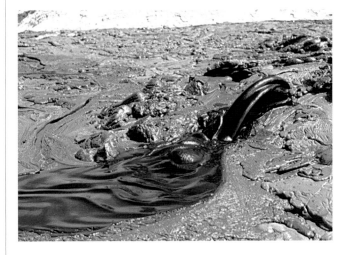

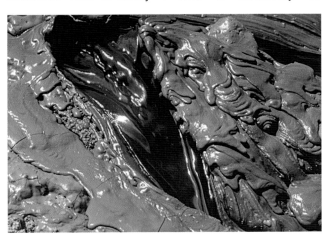

Molten carbonatites (left and above) flow from the summit of Ol Doinyo Lengai, Tanzania, in streams as black as slicks of crude oil. These lavas are extremely fluid, and produce flows that resemble pahoehoe lava. But as they cool, in the short space of a few days or weeks, the dark flows turn as white as chalk.

THE MECHANICS OF
VOLCANIC ERUPTIONS

*A volcano is given life by its eruptive activity, which follows a cyclic pattern,
from the murmuring of fumaroles to the terrifying roar of an explosion. If we understand this,
we can listen to its heartbeat – and be prepared for its changes of mood.*

ERUPTION MECHANISMS

Volcanologists use the term "eruption" to refer to two very different kinds of event: explosive activity and effusive activity. An eruption is caused by the arrival of magma at the surface, and this magma, as we have seen, consists of a bath of molten silicates (a sort of rocky paste) with gases dissolved in it. These two components determine the way eruption mechanisms work.

The part played by the gases

While it is stored in a deep reservoir (see pages 94–95), magma comes under enormous pressure from the walls of the chamber. This pressure, due to the weight of the rocks, is known as lithostatic pressure. It decreases, of course, as the magma rises through the channels that bring it closer to the surface. When it reaches a comparatively shallow depth (about 500 meters, or 1600 feet, for a magma like that involved in the Pinatubo eruption of 1991), the gases begin to form bubbles, which increase in number and grow bigger and bigger as the magma continues to rise. At the same time, the pressure within the bubbles mounts, and as they approach the craters it becomes sufficient to burst the lava apart and hurl it out in fragments, causing an explosion. Volcanologists are familiar with the idea that it is gases which are responsible for explosive eruptions, but the on-site study of eruptions shows that explosions come in a great diversity of forms.

The mere presence of gases is not enough to account for the difference between the red lava fountains of

The familiar plume towering over an active volcano, like the one (above) that followed the eruption on February 10, 1990, of Kelut in central Java (Indonesia), consists mainly of water (60–90%). The other major ingredients are, in descending order, carbon dioxide (CO_2) and sulfur dioxide (SO_2), and in addition more than twenty other chemical compounds are present in lesser proportions. Exhaust gases from Merapi, also in central Java (left), amount to some 8.7 million tonnes (9.6 million short tons) of volatile materials each year: in fact, most of the material produced by volcanoes takes this form. Mount Etna, in Sicily, is capable of emitting as much as 70 million tonnes (77 million short tons) of gases per year.

Volcanic eruptions often begin with an explosive phase, but they may continue – once the surplus gas has been released from the magma – by emitting lava flows, such as this one, photographed on the slopes of Mount Etna during the 1991–92 eruption (right). Flows of particularly free-running basalt can travel dozens of miles from their source, and have been known to attain speeds of over 80 kilometers (50 miles) per hour. In the end, though, the cooling process always brings even the fastest and most abundant flow to a halt (inset, below).

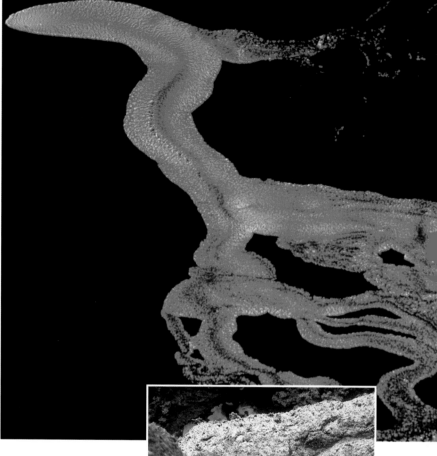

Hawaii and the huge Plinian cloud columns that rise to more than 40 kilometers (25 miles) above their craters, as on Pinatubo. To understand the action of gases better, a simple experiment can be made, demonstrating the "champagne bottle" effect. Any carbonated drink, in fact, if over-warm or too recently shaken, has an unfortunate tendency to blow its top, followed by a good part of its contents. This "eruption" mechanism in a champagne bottle is similar to that of a volcano – but the analogy goes no further, because champagne is of course extremely free-flowing, far more so than any magma, let alone the more viscous kinds. How easy it is for the gases to escape also depends partly on the viscosity of the silicate bath in which they are held.

The part played by the silicate bath

This is the component that will become known as "lava" when it has lost its surplus gases. It consists predominantly of silica, and it is the proportion of silica that largely determines its viscosity: lava could be compared to a syrup, in which the sugar content plays the same role as that of the silica in the lava. Increasing the proportion of sugar in a syrup makes it thicker and more viscous; in the same way, the richer lavas are in silica, the less easily they flow, or the higher their viscosity. So basaltic magmas, containing little silica (around 50%) and emerging at high temperatures (around 1000°C / 1800°F) are comparatively free-flowing.

By contrast, rhyolitic magmas, which are rich in silica (sometimes over 70%) and emerge "cooler" (around 700°C / 1300°F), will be more viscous, hardly flowing at all. Gases will stay trapped within such silica-rich magma, and the bubbles that form cannot rise to the surface as they do in a glass of champagne: only a big increase in their internal pressure can enable these gases to escape, by literally blowing the lava to bits. This is what causes the impressively tall columns of gray "smoke" that rise over some volcanoes.

Where the magma contains little silica, on the other hand, its viscosity is lower and the bubbles of gas can rise and break on the surface. The escaping gas spatters the ground around the volcano with lava so hot that it glows, and in extreme cases fountains of lava several meters high may be formed.

Magmas can be found representing every stage in between, from the most fluid to the most viscous, or from the least to the most explosive, which comes to the same thing. Once the magma has lost its surplus gases, explosions of any kind cease and give way to effusive forms of eruption. But even then, the lava cannot flow unless it is runny enough. If it is viscous, a dome or spine of thick lava will form and plug the volcano's supply pipe or crater.

So effusive activity, too, has its two extreme forms, which again depend on the viscosity of the parent magma, and between the extremes is a continuous range of intermediate types. ∎

THE RANGE OF ERUPTION TYPES

Water-driven eruptions

In underwater eruptions near the surface, like that of Surtsey (1963), water coming into contact with magma plays a dominant role.
The water is superheated and vaporizes; the energy of this process increases the explosive potential of the eruption. The water can be supplied by the sea, or it may be phreatic (groundwater), or simply lake or river water. All of these eruption types in which the explosive force is solely provided by the meeting of water and magma are grouped together under the name "hydrovolcanic."

◀ The term **Surtseyan eruption** is restricted to those underwater eruptions which take place just a few meters below the ocean surface. They take the form of explosions producing tall, tapering plumes full of steam and fragments of lava soaked by contact with the water. The type is named after the eruption of Surtsey in Iceland, where it was properly studied for the first time. It typically leaves behind cones of tuff, which eventually cut off the magma from the water source, after which the continuing eruption takes one of the purely magma-based forms.

Gas-driven eruptions

Terms such as Hawaiian, Strombolian, Plinian, and Pelean have become everyday words. They were first used in the early 20th century in the classification drawn up by Alfred Lacroix, the famous French volcanologist who, to top his other achievements, made a remarkable study of the eruption of Mount Pelée in 1902. He coined these terms to describe classes of volcanoes whose eruptions ranged in increasing violence from the Hawaiian to the Plinian. They are still used today, but are applied to types of explosive eruption which can be defined in terms of magma fragmentation and magma dispersion, the area over which the tephra (the volcanic projectiles) are scattered. The effect of the magmatic gases, the type of lava, and the amount of energy released in an eruption can all be quantified in terms of these two parameters.

The **Vulcanian eruption** type is perhaps the least well defined of all. It takes its name from Vulcano in Sicily, and is characterized by a series of regular, violent explosions from a blocked volcanic pipe. The magmas involved are moderately viscous and tend to throw out "breadcrust" lava bombs. These projectiles are formed by the bursting of a solidified shell of lava under pressure from gas in the still-molten interior of a lava lump. It was long believed that the lumps form a shell because of the comparatively viscous – taken to mean cooler – nature of the lava, but their crusts always have a shiny, glassy appearance. It is now thought that Vulcanian eruptions can only be explained by some sort of interaction with water.

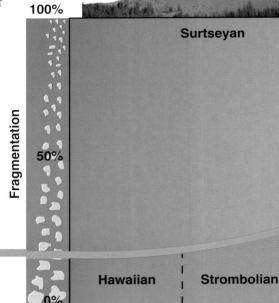

100%	**Surtseyan**
Fragmentation	
50%	
0%	**Hawaiian** ¦ **Strombolian**

0.05 km²

Dispersion

The **Hawaiian eruption** type features continuous emissions (often from cracks) of lava and of gases, which can make the lava spurt out in a fountain. Fragmentation and dispersion are both low; the spurting lava falls back, still hot, around the vents and forms cones of fused cinders (scoria). Effusive activity is also associated with this eruption type, taking the form of great streams of free-flowing lava like the frequent pahoehoe flows on the slopes of Kilauea and Mauna Loa in Hawaii. Lava may also be retained in craters, forming spectacular lakes of molten lava, though these are very rare.

The **phreatomagmatic eruption** type, characteristic of the (extinct) Puys volcanic range in central France, occurs where water is present, either on the surface or under ground. Phreatomagmatic explosions are violent, because the contact between magma and water takes place hundreds or even thousands of meters below the surface. Large funnel-shaped vents (diatremes) are formed, cutting a hole through the rocks like a pastry-cutter all the way up to the surface, where they leave a wide crater with a ring or crescent of tuff round the edge, known as a maar. ▶

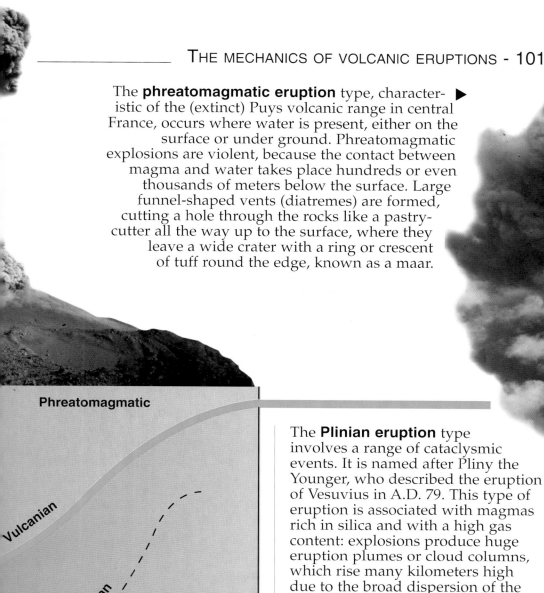

Phreatomagmatic

Vulcanian

Plinian

Pelean

500 km²   5000 km²

The **Plinian eruption** type involves a range of cataclysmic events. It is named after Pliny the Younger, who described the eruption of Vesuvius in A.D. 79. This type of eruption is associated with magmas rich in silica and with a high gas content: explosions produce huge eruption plumes or cloud columns, which rise many kilometers high due to the broad dispersion of the finer particles, and then spread in a characteristic "mushroom" shape, as was seen at Mount Saint Helens (USA, 1980), Pinatubo (Philippines, 1991), and Rabaul (Papua New Guinea, 1994).

A **Pelean eruption** occurs when rising viscous magma accumulates just below the surface, forming domes or protrusions. When these eventually break apart, they can give rise to the unique phenomenon known as a "nuée ardente" (glowing cloud). The most famous example was the one that destroyed the town of Saint-Pierre on Martinique in 1902. Nuées ardentes belong to a family of very fast flows known as pyroclastic flows (from the Greek words meaning "fire" and "broken"). They consist of a mixture of gases and solid particles, cinders and blistered lumps, which behaves like a gigantic aerosol. Moving at 75–300 kilometers (45–200 miles) per hour, the flows are immensely destructive and sweep away everything in their path. ▼

The **Strombolian eruption** type takes its name from the universally-known volcano Stromboli in Sicily, where it is the most frequent type of activity. It is characterized by regular explosions. This is the most common type of volcanic activity on earth, and the resulting cones of cinders are accordingly the most frequently-seen volcanic structure. These cones are formed by the accumulation of fragments of liquid lava that harden as they fly through the air. They are sometimes accompanied by flows of a type of clinker lava known as "aa."

THE PRO-DUCTS OF ERUPTIONS

The wide range of eruption products is a consequence of the different viscosities of lavas and the varying gas content of magmas. Volcanic structures produced in the course of a single event, with just one eruption type, have the shapes characteristic of their eruption type. It is impossible to list all eruption products here, and the distinctions between them are not always perfectly clear-cut: where does one draw the line, for instance, between two types of cone? But in principle, the classification depends on silica content, except in the two cases of hydrovolcanic and undersea eruptions.

Explosive

Effusive

Very fluid

Spatter cone (Hawaiian eruption type)

Spurts of hot, liquid lava fall back and heap up around the vent, forming a cone of fused cinders (pyroclastic fragments) known as a spatter cone (a). The shapes of the fragments thrown out result from their low viscosity. If their trajectory is short, they plop down flatly on the ground as largish lava "packets" (hence they are also known as "cowpat" bombs!). A longer trajectory produces a drawn-out strip of solidified lava known as a "ribbon" bomb (b). Huge lava fountains of the Hawaiian type hurl lava droplets hundreds of meters into the air, each trailing behind it a fine stream of basalt. These streams cool and harden to form glassy threads known as "Pele's tears" and "Pele's hair."

Moderately fluid

Cinder cone (Strombolian eruption type)

A cinder cone (a) is an accumulation of lava blocks, scoria, bombs, and lapilli the size of gravel, around a crater. This is the most commonly-found volcanic structure (on land). Cinder cones, also called Strombolian cones, are often associated with complex volcanoes, as parasitic, lateral, or adventive cones. Sometimes, the fragments thrown out are rotating rapidly; they then acquire the characteristic shape of a "rotational bomb" (b).

Pahoehoe flows

The word "pahoehoe" comes from the Hawaiian language and is used for great smooth-surfaced streams of lava with a consistency like that of caramel, but on a grand scale. These flows may acquire a solid skin which sometimes wrinkles, producing ropy lava (above). They can also advance in other ways, such as by budding or branching. Each form of motion gives rise to its own typical shapes, with names like "pudding lava."

Aa flows

The term "aa" is applied to flows that have a rough surface, consisting of blocks of cinders varying in size from one centimeter (fi inch) to many meters (yards) across. These flows move forward in the same way as a caterpillar track, and they are often found in association with pahoehoe flows: in fact, a flow may change during an eruption from the one type into the other.

Very fluid   **Moderately fluid**

Explosion crater (Vulcanian eruption type)

The relative viscosity of these magmas, in conjunction with the presence of water, produces fairly violent explosions that form great cup-shaped craters, much wider than they are deep.

The projectiles typically produced by Vulcanian explosions are glassy-shelled bombs with an interior of foamed rock. After the bomb's impact, the gases in this foam expand, and the shell splits under the internal pressure: the result (pictured above) looks like crusty bread and hence is known as a "breadcrust bomb."

Composite stratovolcano (Plinian/Pelean eruption type)

a

b

Viscous magmas are always associated with structures built up over long periods, known as composite or stratovolcanoes. These produce great Plinian cloud columns, whose cindery fallout (a) can cover vast areas. They also throw out blocks of pumice. Where the crater is blocked by a dome, a directional eruption occurs, only affecting one area of the volcano (b).

Surtseyan/Vulcanian/ phreatomagmatic eruptions

a

b

Encounters between magma and water produce violent explosions. If the two meet deep down, the structure typically produced is a maar (a) on top of a wide, round pipe (diatreme) that goes very deep indeed. If the water is quite near the surface and the explosions take place beneath fairly shallow water, a cone of hyaloclastic or aquagene tuff is formed.

In either case, the magma fragments in contact with water become soaked and take on the characteristic pimply shape of "cauliflower" bombs (b).

Lava-block flows

Lava-block flows are quite similar to aa flows, except that in this case the lava is not clinker-like, but consists of jagged, often glassy fragments. Obsidians in particular tend to form this kind of flow.

Domes and spines

Domes and spines are what is known as extrusive phenomena: they form from slow-moving magma. There are three types of extrusion, classified according to how free-flowing they are. The flow dome is shaped like a flattish cake; the Pelean dome is more viscous and therefore spreads out less; and the third type, quite the most spectacular, is the spine. One of these (pictured left) was thrust up in the Mount Pelée eruption of 1902.

Pillow lava

Flows emerging under deep water may form pillow lava. This is so called because of its shapes, which result from the way it advances (see pages 80–82). Pillows form when the lava's surface cools on contact with the water. Under pressure from the lava within, a crack appears in the pillow's surface and another oozes out, joined to its parent "bulb." This in turn produces others, so that the whole flow advances by a succession of such extrusions.

THE LIFE STORY
OF AN ANDESITIC STRATOVOLCANO

The visible part of a volcano is the culmination of lengthy physical and chemical evolution of the magma deep below. The shape of the volcanic edifice is determined by the eruption type, itself the result of this slow transformation, which began long before the volcano was born and continues for most of its active life.

Unlike those homogeneous volcanoes that are formed in the course of just a few hours or a few years, by a single event involving only one eruption type, andesitic stratovolcanoes are "composite" volcanoes: structures built up over a long period, between ten thousand and many millions of years.

During their long lifetime, composite volcanoes may produce eruptions of various types, depending on the nature of the magma that arrives at the surface. They may grow to a height of several thousand meters, and their shapes are often more complex than simple cones, with bases that cover hundreds or even thousands of square kilometers. This is the most common type of volcano on the surface of the earth.

Andesitic stratovolcanoes are associated with subduction zones. In theory, if a stratovolcano is periodically resupplied with magma, its development will follow the five-stage sequence shown here.

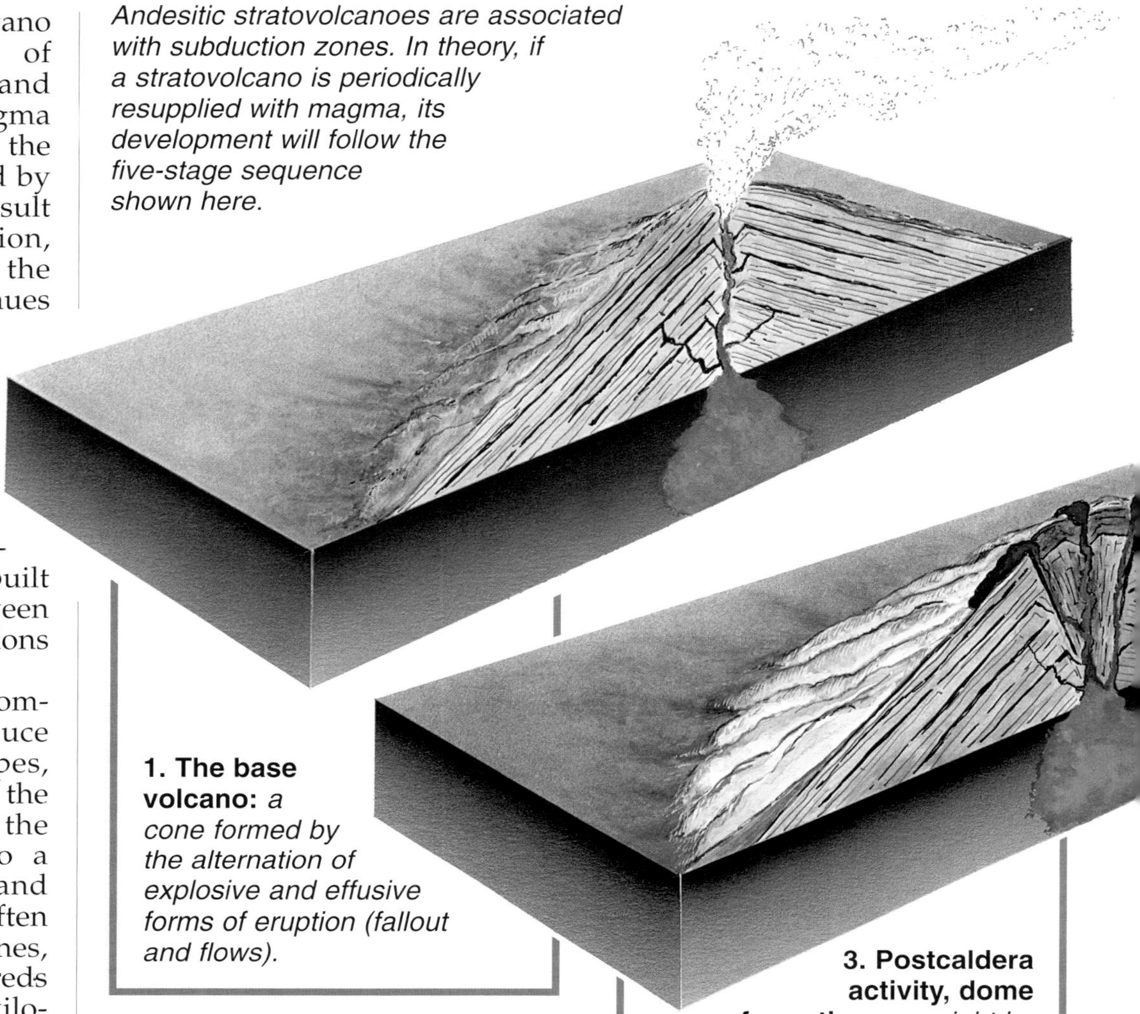

1. The base volcano: *a cone formed by the alternation of explosive and effusive forms of eruption (fallout and flows).*

3. Postcaldera activity, dome formation: *as might be expected, an effusive stage follows the explosion, and leads to the formation of domes and/or viscous flows (lava-block flows).*

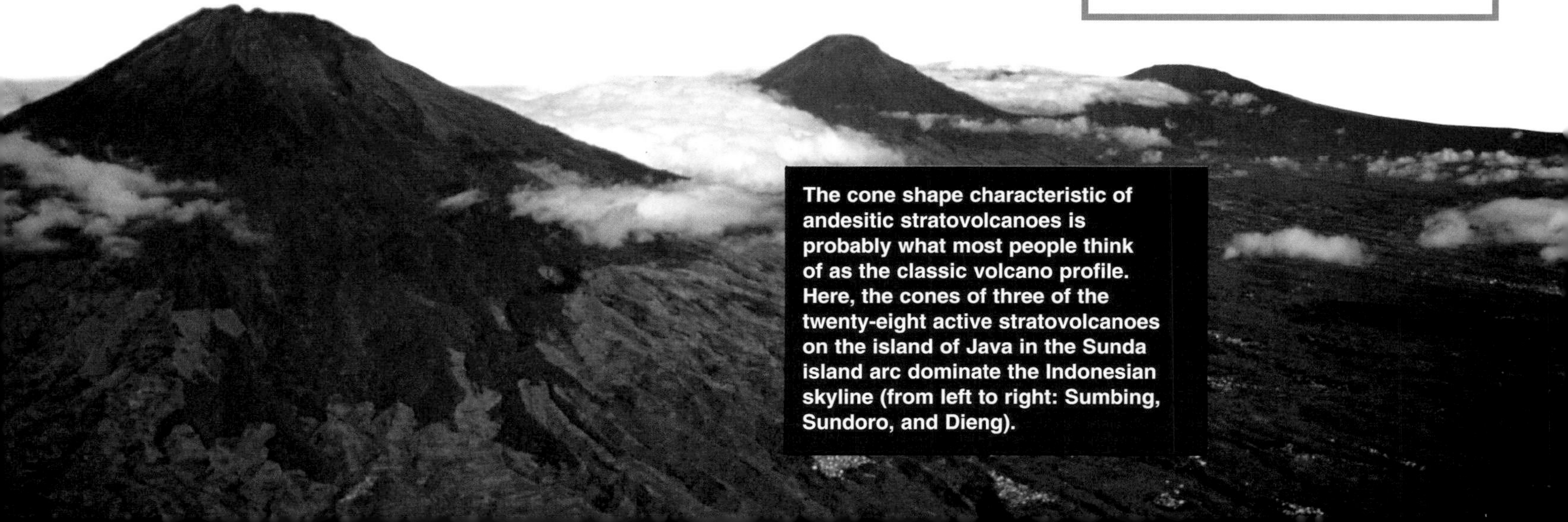

The cone shape characteristic of andesitic stratovolcanoes is probably what most people think of as the classic volcano profile. Here, the cones of three of the twenty-eight active stratovolcanoes on the island of Java in the Sunda island arc dominate the Indonesian skyline (from left to right: Sumbing, Sundoro, and Dieng).

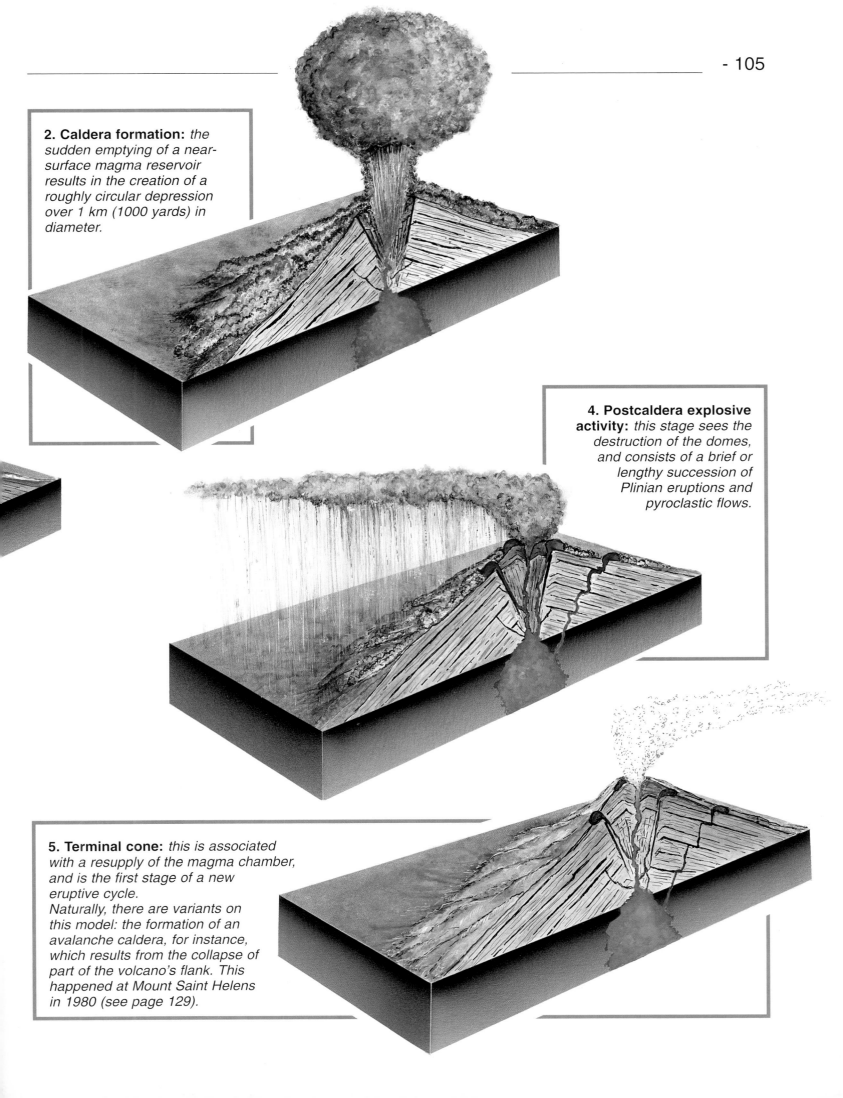

2. Caldera formation: *the sudden emptying of a near-surface magma reservoir results in the creation of a roughly circular depression over 1 km (1000 yards) in diameter.*

4. Postcaldera explosive activity: *this stage sees the destruction of the domes, and consists of a brief or lengthy succession of Plinian eruptions and pyroclastic flows.*

5. Terminal cone: *this is associated with a resupply of the magma chamber, and is the first stage of a new eruptive cycle.*
Naturally, there are variants on this model: the formation of an avalanche caldera, for instance, which results from the collapse of part of the volcano's flank. This happened at Mount Saint Helens in 1980 (see page 129).

THE LIFE STORY
OF A SHIELD VOLCANO
(Hawaiian pattern)

Shield volcanoes are also built up over a long period. They are formed almost entirely from very free-flowing lavas (tholeiitic or alkaline basalts: see pages 88–93), and their slopes are never steeper than 10°. Most, like those of Hawaii, are sited over oceanic hot spots, but there are other shield volcanoes: both on continents, like those of the East African Great Rift (Erta Ale, Nyamlagira, etc.), and in other ocean contexts (Iceland).

The largest of these volcanoes, though, are the ones sited over oceanic hot spots, such as Mauna Loa, which has grown to a height (above its base on the ocean floor) of almost 9000 meters (30,000 feet) and a volume of 42,500 cubic kilometers (10,200 cubic miles). This enormous mass actually makes the ocean floor bend under the weight of the volcano (an effect known as subsidence, and deliberately exaggerated in the diagrams opposite): the development of the volcano itself is affected by this. During the first four stages, the rate of subsidence increases and the volcano sinks down into the ocean floor; then, as the shield is built up, the subsidence slows but does not stop completely. There are old shield volcanoes which can still be seen above the surface, but will soon sink below the waves: these are the paradise islands we know as "atolls."

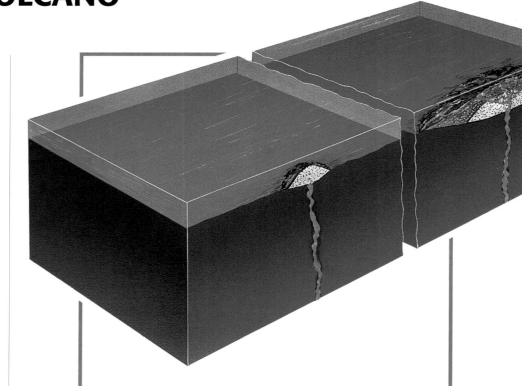

1. First stage, the birth of the volcano: *we know little about this stage, which takes place under the ocean, but it probably involves the welling up of alkaline lava.*

2. Shield building, underwater stage: *before long, the type of magma emitted changes into the typical ocean-floor tholeiitic basalt. Eruption is still taking place underwater, and the volcano starts to form, mostly through the accumulation of dense, glassy pillow lava, or the debris from such pillows. There may be pahoehoe flows, occasionally even flows of aa. Throughout the underwater stage, the great downward pressure of the mass of water above the volcano prevents any kind of explosion from occurring.*

In these diagrams the vertical scale is greatly exaggerated, and the subsidence therefore looks deeper than in fact it is.

Very gently-sloping sides and an extremely broad base are the features characteristic of shield volcanoes like Kilauea in Hawaii, shown here in typically low profile against the horizon.

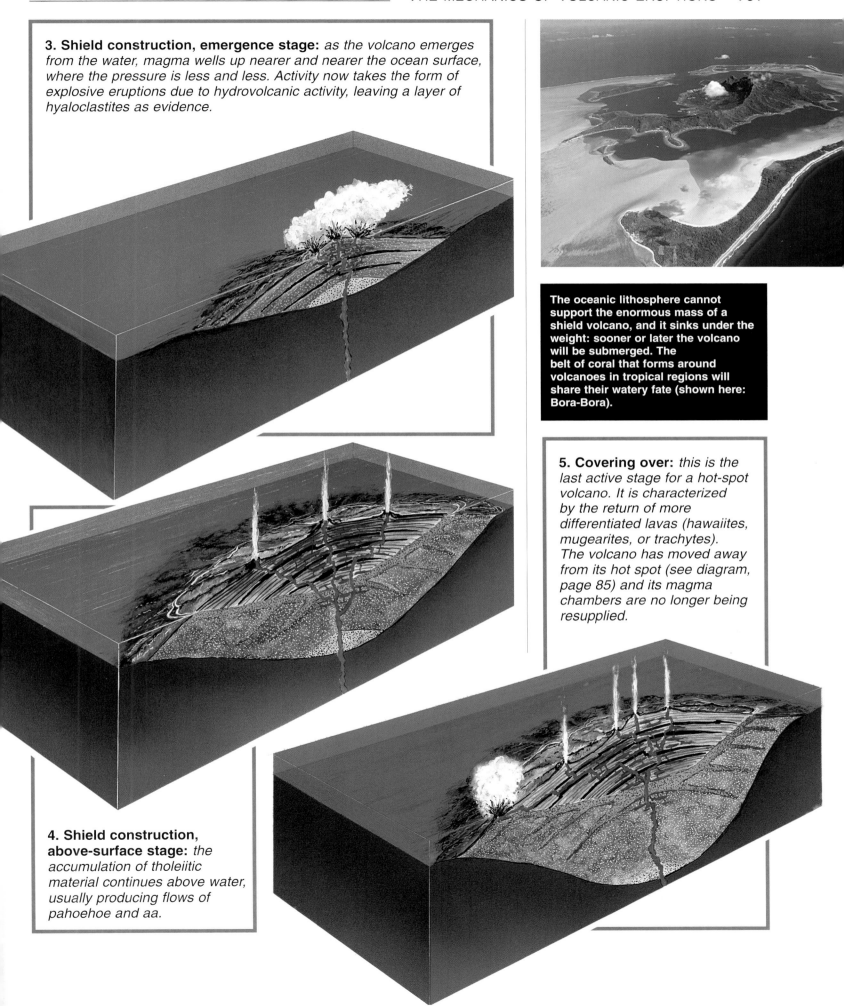

3. Shield construction, emergence stage: *as the volcano emerges from the water, magma wells up nearer and nearer the ocean surface, where the pressure is less and less. Activity now takes the form of explosive eruptions due to hydrovolcanic activity, leaving a layer of hyaloclastites as evidence.*

The oceanic lithosphere cannot support the enormous mass of a shield volcano, and it sinks under the weight: sooner or later the volcano will be submerged. The belt of coral that forms around volcanoes in tropical regions will share their watery fate (shown here: Bora-Bora).

5. Covering over: *this is the last active stage for a hot-spot volcano. It is characterized by the return of more differentiated lavas (hawaiites, mugearites, or trachytes). The volcano has moved away from its hot spot (see diagram, page 85) and its magma chambers are no longer being resupplied.*

4. Shield construction, above-surface stage: *the accumulation of tholeiitic material continues above water, usually producing flows of pahoehoe and aa.*

SECONDARY VOLCANIC PHENOMENA

Eruptions are of course the most spectacular volcanic events, but there are others that also form part of what we commonly think of as volcanic activity.

Fumaroles and solfataras

Between two periods of eruptive activity, areas appear from which "fumes" escape, often made visible by the large amount of steam they contain. These zones of "fumaroles" may remain active from one eruption to the next. Fumaroles often arise in heavily fissured areas, and they are very closely watched, for the arrival of fresh magma always alters the composition of their gases, raises their temperature, and gives other clues about the eruption to come. Accordingly, many fumarole zones are equipped with monitoring apparatus, but it is not easy to measure the emissions continuously. In most cases the equipment cannot long withstand the corrosive effects of the fumaroles, many of which emit considerable quantities of sulfur dioxide (SO_2). This combines with water to produce sulfuric acid, which is harmful to both instrument and volcanologist. Where sulfur is present in large quantities, it is sometimes deposited in the pure elemental form, either colloidal or crystalline: its color, and the shapes of any crystals formed, depend on the temperature of the fumaroles. These sulfur-rich fumarole zones are known as solfataras.

Geysers and hot springs

When water circulates in areas that are heated by nearby magma, it can give rise to strange phenomena called "geysers," from the Icelandic word *gjosà* meaning "to spurt forth."
Geysers tend to spout at very regular intervals, since it is the heating of a column of water at its base that creates enough steam pressure to shoot the cloud of droplets into the air. A height of 460 meters (1500 feet) was achieved by the Waimanger geyser in New Zealand between 1899 and 1904.

Yellowstone National Park in the western USA is famous for its geysers, which perform so regularly that tourists arrive at set times to watch the spouting jets.

Hot springs are less spectacular than geysers and not always associated directly with active volcanoes, but with the geothermal anomalies that often occur in volcanic regions. Such geothermal fields are sometimes used as energy sources, for instance in Iceland and at Larderello, near Pisa in Italy.

Crater lakes

Like immense funnels upturned to the sky, volcano craters are ideal containers for storing rainwater. Yet crater lakes occur only quite rarely, and sometimes last only a short while. Just a few cracks will prevent a crater from filling, or will cause it to empty rapidly: to make the crater watertight, any such cracks in its floor or walls have to be stopped with clay.
In tropical regions, the vitreous ash from volcanoes breaks down into clay quite quickly, within a matter of three months, and this –

At 120°C (250°F), sulfur melts: shaped by escaping gases, it hardens again into strange forms (above). At Kawah Idjen in Java (below), men collect the sulfur and carry it over 20 km (12 miles) on their backs.

A scene of destruction in the town of Santa Rita Concepción (Philippines), caused by the lahars from Pinatubo.

saturated with carbon dioxide. On August 26, 1986, for reasons still unknown, the carbon dioxide dissolved in the depths of Lake Nyos was released, killing nearly 1800 people from the villages around the volcano by asphyxiation (see pages 132–3).

Mud flows (lahars)

The word *lahar* is an Indonesian one, meaning simply "flow." Volcanologists use it in a narrower sense to refer to flows in which fragmented volcanic products (including ash) are mixed with water (see also pages 128–9). Lahars are not a feature of the eruption itself, but are closely connected with it.

Before an eruption occurs, a frozen lake or a covering of snow may melt and become a muddy flow, but lahars most commonly happen after a major eruption, when ash that has accumulated on the slopes of the volcano becomes saturated with rainwater. This enormous quantity of material can very easily turn into a fluid mass that rushes down the valleys around the mountain, destroying everything in its path. Lahars like these may recur over and over again in the years following an eruption: they continued for five years, for instance, after the eruption of Mount Saint Helens. ∎

along with the heavy rainfall – may explain why crater lakes are a little more common in such latitudes.

Any accumulation of water (and sometimes these lakes hold considerable amounts, even millions of cubic meters) on an active volcano creates a serious risk of a hydrovolcanic explosion. The waters of crater lakes may also feed mud slides, or primary lahars, in the early stages of an eruption, as they did in 1919 at Kelut (in central Java, Indonesia), where lahars swept away seven villages, killing over 5000 people. Crater lakes are useful sources of information for volcanologists: between eruptions, the crater is often the scene of intense activity, of earth tremors on a small scale and of fumaroles. Active fumaroles at the bottom of a

crater lake will release thousands of bubbles, which in turn produce a riot of infrasound. The intensity of the infrasound varies with the rate of gas release, which increases as an eruption draws nearer. Electronic ears (hydrophones) have been placed at strategic points: on Kelut, for instance, where the crater lake was able to warn scientists for the first time, in 1990, that the mood of the volcano was turning ugly.

Fumaroles also play another role in the crater lakes: many of the chemical compounds in the gases they emit are dissolved in the water, in particular oxides of sulfur and carbon. Some lakes, like Kawah Idjen (which means "green crater"), become lakes of acid (sulfuric, hydrochloric, etc.), while others, like Lake Nyos in Cameroon, have their waters

Active fumaroles at the bottom of a crater lake acidify its waters, as here at the summit of Poas in Costa Rica (right). The crater of the famous Kawah Idjen in Java (below) currently holds the largest natural reservoir of sulfuric acid in the world.

LARGE-SCALE VOLCANIC STRUCTURES

In the course of its long life, a stratovolcano has only short periods of destructive fury. Many human generations can come and go, and many people live and multiply on the generous slopes of these sleeping monsters. For five hundred years, no sign of volcanic activity was seen around Pinatubo, and the local population had never before witnessed the unleashing of such power. They were totally unprepared, not even having tales to keep alive their collective memory of such an event. But how many people, anywhere in the world, would be able to give an account of what was happening in their area so long ago, when the European continent was only just emerging from medieval times, and when Columbus was still planning his first voyage across the Atlantic?

Andesitic stratovolcano calderas

These quiescent episodes only apply to the surface: far below and deep inside, the volcano remains active. In reservoirs, near the surface or deeper down, the magmas are growing richer in silica and so, as we have seen (pages 98–99), more viscous, with a higher dissolved gas content. The longer they stagnate there, the greater the differentiation is likely to be and the more violent the awakening when it finally comes.

On andesitic stratovolcanoes, cataclysmic eruptions recur in cycles, at intervals which can be as short as a few hundred years or as long as several thousand (see pages 104–5). These major eruptions throw up enormous Plinian cloud columns and emit pyroclastic flows which can spread into sheets, covering almost the whole of the volcano's sides with pumice to a depth of many tens of meters (at least a hundred feet). The volumes produced are immense: over 5 cubic kilometers (1.2 cubic miles) of material was thrown out by Pinatubo in 1991, and around

The summit of Mount Mazama collapsed 7000 years ago, leaving a depression 10 kilometers 6 miles) in diameter: Crater Lake was born!

18 cubic kilometers (4.3 cubic miles) by Krakatau in the Sunda Strait (Indonesia) in 1883. The Valley of Ten Thousand Smokes in Alaska was created by the explosion of Katmai in 1912, which threw out 25 cubic kilometers (6 cubic miles) of material. Each of these eruptions left a large, more or less circular depression where the mountain had been, even in cases like Krakatau where it had stood many hundreds of feet above sea level. These enormous depressions, never less than a kilometer (1000 yards) in diameter, are known as calderas: the word is Spanish and means "cauldron," but it has long been used in the Canary Isles in this topographical sense.

Some seven thousand years ago, Mount Mazama in Oregon, USA, blew its top off, leaving an almost perfectly circular caldera 10 kilometers (6 miles) in diameter. Researchers have estimated that

THEORETICAL DIAGRAM OF THE FORMATION OF AN IGNIMBRITIC CALDERA

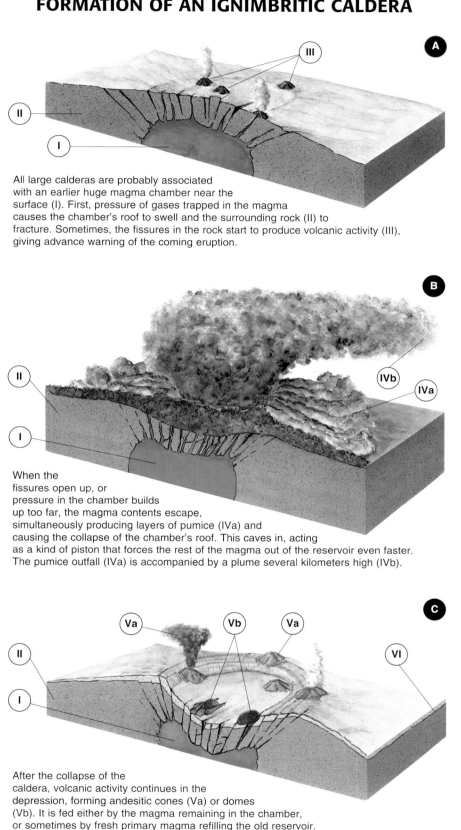

All large calderas are probably associated with an earlier huge magma chamber near the surface (I). First, pressure of gases trapped in the magma causes the chamber's roof to swell and the surrounding rock (II) to fracture. Sometimes, the fissures in the rock start to produce volcanic activity (III), giving advance warning of the coming eruption.

When the fissures open up, or pressure in the chamber builds up too far, the magma contents escape, simultaneously producing layers of pumice (IVa) and causing the collapse of the chamber's roof. This caves in, acting as a kind of piston that forces the rest of the magma out of the reservoir even faster. The pumice outfall (IVa) is accompanied by a plume several kilometers high (IVb).

After the collapse of the caldera, volcanic activity continues in the depression, forming andesitic cones (Va) or domes (Vb). It is fed either by the magma remaining in the chamber, or sometimes by fresh primary magma refilling the old reservoir. The only traces that remain of the violent eruptive events are the caldera itself (typically over 10 km or 6 miles in diameter) and the layers of pumice deposits (VI), which can be tens or even hundreds of meters thick.

this depression, filled at present by a lake 600 meters (2000 feet) deep, has a volume of some 60 cubic kilometers (14.5 cubic miles), a figure that roughly corresponds with the amount of magma thrown out during the eruption. Deposits from the explosion have been found covering an area of more than 1.2 million square kilometers (460,000 square miles) around the Crater Lake caldera.

What happens is that the magma chamber is suddenly emptied, and the roof caves in. The correspondence between the volume of material emitted and the volume of the resulting depression supports this model of caldera formation by collapse, which solves the conundrum that was posed when two-thirds of the island of Krakatau disappeared in 1883. That spectacular event was accompanied by a sound blast heard more than 5000 kilometers (3100 miles) away, and by a tsunami 30 meters (100 feet) high which ravaged the coasts of Java, Sumatra and Malaya (see page 130). Geologists of the time were puzzled: had the island subsided beneath the waves, or had it been blown to bits by the explosion?

It is now agreed that these huge features many kilometers wide are not formed by the explosion of a volcano. If they were, the eruption deposits would contain a great many fragments of pulverized cone, but in fact few of the eruption products associated with caldera formation have the right characteristics for this. What is more, the correlation between the amount of magma ejected and the volume of the depression that remains is fairly close, in the best cases accurate to within 10 or 20%, which is quite acceptable given the imprecision of all such measurements.

Some calderas, like the Crater Lake one, are associated with a single volcano (in this case, Mount Mazama), while others, usually bigger, are linked to a group of volcanoes in close proximity: this is the case at Santorini (Greece), Krakatau, and elsewhere. It is also possible for many calderas to form from the same reservoir without the injection of any fresh magma; they then take the form of nested depressions resulting from successive collapses. This is what happened at Batur, on Bali in Indonesia.

At Krakatau in 1883, and again at Mount Saint Helens in 1980, part of the stratovolcano slid away sideways as the structure swelled (see page 129). These enormous landslides are not so frequent or typical as calderas like Crater Lake, but they do have a particularly devastating effect. They leave behind a characteristic scar in the shape of a horseshoe, open in the direction of the debris avalanche. The deposits typically consist of whole slabs of the former mountainside, mixed with material from the magma chamber. They are found spread over a very wide area, which is also dotted with small hummocks. This phenomenon was actually witnessed for the first time in 1980, and it has become clear since then that, though there have been many such landslides on all the stratovolcanoes taken together, they do not occur often in the lifetime of any single one. All the same, they cause such damage that scientists cannot ignore this risk when it comes to making their forecasts and issuing warnings.

Shield volcano calderas or basaltic calderas

Calderas on basalt shield volcanoes form in a rather different way. These basaltic calderas do not mark the final stage in the life of the near-surface magma chamber, but are present right from the start of the volcano's formation. The long-term coexistence of caldera and volcano was discovered during exploration of the very young underwater volcano Loihi, which lies off the coast of the Hawaiian archipelago, near Kilauea.

These calderas are of moderate dimensions (on Loihi, 3.7 kilometers long by 2.8 kilometers wide, or 2.3 by 1.75 miles) and form in stages at times of major lava flows on the volcano's flanks, especially on rift-zone volcanoes (see Piton de la Fournaise, pages 30–35). However, it appears that some stages in their formation are associated with explosive events of hydrovolcanic origin. Some scientific authorities believe that these depressions probably reach their maximum extent when several successive pit-craters (craters associated with the emptying of small magma chambers) collapse into one, but this hypothesis is not generally accepted, and is not the only candidate. How calderas like these form remains a mystery on a number of counts, but it does seem that, as a general rule, the great depressions change position, grow, and refill during the growing phase of a shield volcano. Eventually, they are filled in by subsequent effusive activity, and this is what has happened at Mauna Kea in Hawaii.

The great calderas or ignimbritic calderas

The third type of caldera is typically very large (at least 10 kilometers or 6 miles wide, and often nearly twice this size), and is associated with an eruption throwing out truly colossal amounts of tephra. The ejecta smother the neighboring region with one or more layers of pumice (ignimbrites), often to an accumulated depth of over 100 meters (330 feet). The volume of magma involved in creating the largest structures can amount to between 100 and 1000 cubic kilometers (24 to 240 cubic miles). Sometimes, after forming, these large calderas acquire a marked bulge in their floor, known as a "resurgent dome."

Tarso Voôn in Chad is a caldera of

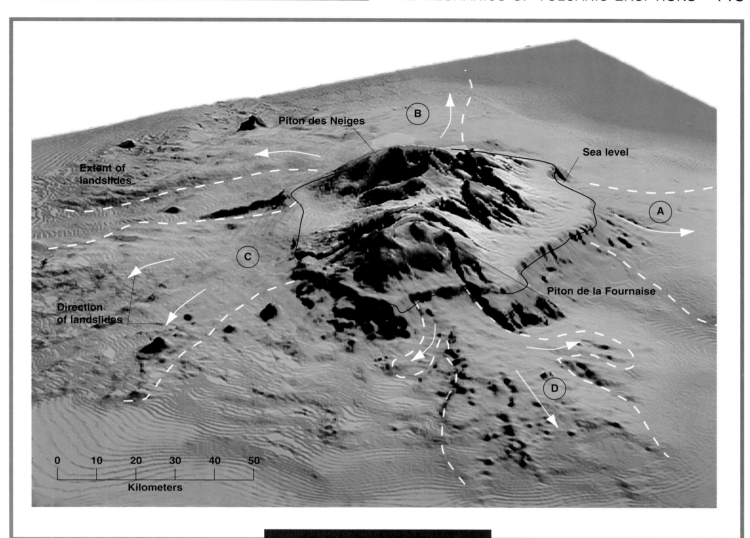

Piton des Neiges

Sea level

B

Extent of landslides

A

C

Direction of landslides

Piton de la Fournaise

D

0   10   20   30   40   50
Kilometers

The flanks of shield volcanoes are sometimes marked by great landslides (A, B, C, D), as can be seen in this virtual image of the island of Réunion: land heights and ocean depths around the island have been plotted by computer to produce a model of the terrain. Piton de la Fournaise seems to have been the scene of one such event in the past (D): 3000 years ago, some 20–30 km³ (5–7 cu. miles) of material slid under the force of gravity into the sea, leaving an enormous scar on the south side of the island.

this kind. Its products are spread over an area of 2600 square kilometers (1000 square miles) and add up to a volume of 130 cubic kilometers (31 cubic miles). For such immense zones to collapse, huge magma chambers must have been present beforehand, but hardly detectable from volcanic activity on the surface, except perhaps for a few eruptions prefiguring the cataclysm to come.

The largest caldera in the world is a structure of this type, probably formed in a number of stages; it measures 90 by 30 kilometers (56 by 19 miles). This is the Toba caldera in Indonesia, created some 80,000 years ago. Its asymmetrical shape is due to the great transform fault which crosses Sumatra and influenced the way in which the caldera collapsed.

While calderas' shapes give some clues to the processes involved in their formation, comparatively little is known about these huge structures, and there are still great gaps in our understanding. We have a great deal to learn about the largest calderas, but unfortunately modern volca-

nologists have not had a single opportunity actually to watch one in process of formation. This makes them a very difficult subject to study.

Nevertheless, it is in our interest to investigate the forces at work here: the eruption of Pinatubo in 1991, which resulted in the formation of a caldera 1.5 kilometers (1 mile) in diameter, forced more than half a million people who had lived within a 40-kilometer (25-mile) radius of the volcano into exile. On a planet whose population continues to grow, what might be the effect when a caldera several kilometers wide collapses? It is almost impossible to imagine the consequences of such a devastating event, especially if it were to happen in or near a densely-populated region. ∎

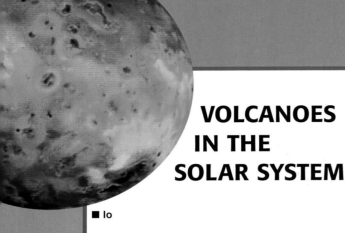

■ Io

VOLCANOES IN THE SOLAR SYSTEM

Exploration of the solar system by unmanned space probes during the last three decades has enabled geologists to join the astronauts in their headlong race to uncover the secrets of the universe. From the harvest of data gathered, a new science of comparative planetology has sprung up.

One of planetology's great discoveries has been the existence of extraterrestrial volcanoes. We now know that all the rocky planets in our solar system, and many of the planetary satellites, have been affected by volcanic events of various kinds, some unknown on earth. The existence of volcanic structures on a rocky planet seems to be conditional on three main factors. The first is the planet's size: by bringing out and dissipating some of a planet's internal heat, volcanic activity contributes to its natural cooling. The larger a planet is, the more slowly it cools, and the longer its volcanic activity will last. Second, there may or may not be processes that reform the planet's surface (building of volcanic structures, erosion and sedimentation, bombardment with meteorites, or – but only on earth – plate tectonics). On earth, erosion and plate tectonics have wiped out all trace of any volcanic structures more than 200 million years old, but on the solar system's other planets there is little or no erosion and plate tectonics do not operate. There, virtually all the features formed since the planet was created can still be seen. So there is not as much volcanic activity on Mars or Venus as their surfaces, compared with the earth's, would seem at first sight to indicate.

Finally, there may be a tidal effect from neighboring planets. Small satellites, like our moon and Io, would otherwise have cooled very quickly by simple conduction of heat out through their lithosphere, and would never have had any volcanic activity.

Venus

This is the planet that most resembles our own. It is about the same size (12,100 kilometers or 7500 miles in diameter), and, like the earth, it has an atmosphere. However, this atmosphere is dense (90 times the earth's atmospheric pressure, at ground level) and made up of carbon dioxide and various acids: it raises the surface temperature to over 450°C (850°F) by means of the greenhouse effect. What is more, it is opaque between 30 and 60 kilometers (18.5 and 37 miles) up, so that we have to rely on radar images of the planet.

The Soviet Venera probes landed on Venus as early as the 1960s, but although they were designed like fully-armored bathyscaphes their instruments were soon knocked out by the hellish conditions at ground level. From 1970 to 1975, probes Venera 7 through 10 analyzed the atmosphere and the composition of the ground, as well as sending back the first pictures of the surface. These revealed lava flows of tholeiitic basalt. At last, during the 1980s, Venera 15 and 16 were sent into orbit and compiled a complete radar map of the planet to a resolution of 1000–2000 meters (1100–2200 yards). In an initial survey of volcanic structures, over 50 shield volcanoes similar to the Hawaiian ones were counted, over 800 like Etna, and some 22,000 small ones "only" 5 to 20 kilometers (3 to 12.5 miles) in diameter. But it was Magellan, a US mission that mapped the whole planet at 300-meter (330-yard) resolution, which revealed Venus to be completely covered by volcanic plains (constituting 85% of the surface) dotted with millions of structures a kilometer (0.6 miles) or more wide. These are grouped in over 550 regions, some of which extend for around 100 kilometers (60 miles). The ones volcanologists are most interested in form five families quite unknown on any other planet:

– Coronas: huge concentric tectonic structures 500–1000 kilometers (300–600 miles) wide, encircling some volcanic regions.

– Novae: structures 50–300 kilometers (30–200 miles) wide, with "starburst" radial fractures.

– Arachnoids: structures with a central caldera fissured by a network of

Maat Mons (above): a perspective view compiled from Magellan's radar images (vertical scale magnified ˘ 10, artificial color). This is the largest of the shield volcanoes on Venus, 8 km (5 miles) high and some 400 km (250 miles) in diameter. Pancake domes (left) are shaped like a round farmhouse loaf with a flattened top. They are 20–30 km (12.5–18.5 miles) in diameter and 0.1–1 km (330–3300 ft) high, and are scored by radial cracks at their summits and concentric fractures at their bases.

faults that looks like a spider's web.

– Pancake domes: these resemble the silicaceous domes on earth formed by viscous lava. If this is the right interpretation, it will be the first discovery of differentiated volcanic activity elsewhere than on earth.

– Ticks: these owe their name to their shape, like an upturned bowl edged by peaks that resemble rows of tiny feet. They too appear to be the products of differentiated magma.

Though Venus is covered with tectonic structures that are still poorly understood, it seems unlikely that there is any plate tectonic activity on the planet. It therefore cools only by conduction, and the "convection" provided by volcanoes. Since Venus is almost as big as the earth, it is quite possible that some of its volcanoes are still active.

The moon

There are traces of volcanic activity on the moon: lunar basalt seas which appear as dark patches when seen from the earth. They are mainly concentrated on the visible side, indicating that they are due to the earth's tidal effect on the moon. Early in the solar system's history, this tidal effect slowed the moon's rotation and stabilized it so that it now rotates in time with its own revolution around the earth: as a result, the same side is always facing our planet. On this visible side, the earth's gravitational attraction is stronger than on the far side, and this is thought to have caused an asym-

metry in the moon's internal strata before it finished cooling. The denser layers would have been pulled off-center in the direction of the earth, thinning the crust on the visible side and making it easier for magma to reach the surface there.

Mars

Between 1976 and 1980, the probes Viking 1 and 2 revealed a variety of volcanic features on Mars similar to those on earth, although typically with less steep slopes. The principal structures are a few giant Hawaiian-type shield volcanoes, 350–550 kilometers (220–340 miles) in diameter and 16–24 kilometers (10–15 miles) high, the best known being Olympus Mons. Several domes have also been found, as well as paterae (a sort of extra-flat pancake dome) and hundreds of small cones.

Over 45% of Mars's surface is covered by fields of lava flows, some of which extend for 200 kilometers (125 miles). Using the number of impact craters to date these fields, it can be estimated that the most recent structures (including Olympus Mons) are between 60 million and 1000 million years old. As Mars has only half the volume of the earth, it is unlikely that any Martian volcanoes remain active.

Io, Jupiter's satellite

Io is astonishing. Scarcely larger than our moon, it should have cooled completely by now, and be geologically inert. However, early in the 1980s the

Voyager probes revealed that Io is the scene of constant and intense volcanic activity, featuring vast multicolored flows up to 200 kilometers (125 miles) long, from equally huge calderas 20–200 kilometers (12.5–125 miles) wide. These calderas are at ground level, and there are no built-up structures. Giant eruption plumes 70–300 kilometers (45–185 miles) tall and 1000 kilometers (620 miles) wide have also been seen. Io's low atmospheric pressure and weak gravitational pull help to explain their immense size. Still more surprising is the color of the magmas: the calderas themselves are brownish-black, and the flows are red, then orange, and then yellow as they move further from the eruption's source. These colors are reminiscent of the different states of oxidation of sulfur depending on its crystallization temperature. This, coupled with the fact that the thin atmosphere is mainly sulfur dioxide, suggests that the magma itself consists mainly of sulfur.

With such intense activity, the whole surface is being renewed in cycles of barely 10 million years – but why so much activity on so small a globe? It must be due to Io's position in space, surrounded by the giant Jupiter and its three other major

satellites, Europa, Ganymede, and Callisto. Jupiter exerts a powerful gravitational force on Io, pulling it into the shape of an American football. But when Io passes one of the other satellites, it is subjected to another gravity field which, though weaker, partially counteracts Jupiter's tidal effect, and the deformation is temporarily reduced. Thus Io is constantly being pulled out of shape, causing friction and consequent heating in its interior. ■

LIVING WITH VOLCANOES

THE HAZARDS OF VOLCANOES

At this dawn of the third millennium, it is estimated that some 500 million people live under threat from volcanoes. This number is equal to the total population of our planet at the beginning of the 17th century.
The hazards of volcanoes should be taken very seriously indeed.

Vesuvius has erupted many times, but its two best-known eruptions are probably the one of A.D. 79, which caused many deaths, and from which this casting of the imprint left by a human body comes (above), and the one that occurred in 1631 (see engraving, left), when people called on Saint Januarius for protection.

Volcanic hazards are linked, either directly or indirectly, to human activity. To some extent, they are obviously due to people settling in the neighborhood of active volcanoes, but this is not the whole story. As a result of the recent remarkable growth in civil aviation, many air routes now pass close to zones of volcanic activity, and this produces a new danger, one that could strike a long way from the original volcanic source. Of course, risks arising from settlement patterns primarily affect large conurbations, but there is also a vast number of villages and small towns near volcanoes.

Vesuvius, towering above the splendid Bay of Naples, is dormant at present. Recent studies by Italian volcanologists have shown that, in this instance, the interval of dormancy that precedes a new eruption is what determines the nature of that eruption when it comes: put in simple terms, a ten-year gap would herald a largely effusive eruption, like that of 1906 or 1944; a rest of one hundred years would produce an explosion with pyroclastic flows, like that of 1631; and a slumber of a thousand years would end in a Plinian eruption, like that of A.D. 79, which is notorious for having destroyed the towns of Herculaneum and Pompeii. At present, Vesuvius has been resting for fifty years or so, and we may therefore expect that when it

awakes there will be some kind of explosion.

If the eruption is similar to that of 1631, some 700,000 people will be directly at risk. The authorities responsible for civil defense are taking the risk very seriously, and have drawn up some extremely detailed plans to protect the public. Successful evacuation in the event of a major volcanic event depends on people being psychologically prepared, as well as on comprehensive emergency plans being in place.

In the Caribbean, a reawakening of Mount Pelée on Martinique would threaten between 22,000 and 65,000 people, depending on the nature of the eruption; La Soufrière on Guadeloupe likewise threatens 50,000 to 70,000.

In Colombia, the volcano Galeras stands just a few kilometers away from the town of Pasto, with its 400,000 inhabitants. In Ecuador, the Quito region is ringed by volcanoes capable of erupting explosively. In Indonesia, there are 1.5 million people living in and around Yogyakarta, at the foot of Merapi, while in Mexico the capital, Mexico City, is not far from Popocatépetl, and the city of Puebla (population 2 million) is only 25 kilometers (15 miles) from the summit: these two million people live at the very foot of the volcano, and are directly under threat.

There are very many similar situations: it is fortunate that the most deadly eruptions are fairly infrequent, at least by compar-

ison with other natural disasters such as earthquakes, cyclones and hurricanes, floods, or even the everyday carnage of road accidents.

Some 2000 corpses from the eruption of Vesuvius in A.D. 79, described by Pliny the Younger, have been found, and although archeological investigations are still going on and still turning up bodies, this death toll is small indeed compared with the 1815 eruption of Tambora in Indonesia. Tambora is practically unknown to the general public, despite claiming 92,000 victims.

The 20th century saw a number of disastrous eruptions: Mount Pelée (Martinique), La Soufrière de Saint-Vincent, Santa María (Guatemala), Kelut, Merapi, and Agung (Indonesia), Lamington (Papua New Guinea), Mount Saint Helens (USA), El Chichón (Mexico), Nevado del Ruiz (Colombia), Nyos (Cameroon), Unzen (Japan), Hibok-Hibok and Pinatubo (Philippines).

It can be assumed that we are aware of almost all the volcanic disasters that have occurred since about 1600, and it is estimated that some 300,000 people have been killed by volcanoes since that date. Major cataclysms that occurred before that time have been coming to light as volcanologists and archeologists continue their research: one of the most famous is Santorini, which erupted sixteen centuries before

Continued on page 122.

MAJOR VOLCANIC DISASTERS AND THEIR CAUSES

The more frequent a volcano's activity, the less dangerous it is for the people living nearby. Conversely, it is the infrequent eruptions that are the killers ...

There are two main reasons for this. The first is a human factor: those who live in a region of frequent – or even constant – volcanic activity learn to live with their volcano. They get to know its dangers and settle in areas a little further away, or at least a little more out of the way; they never forget that it is there, for memories remain fresh. On the other hand, a volcano which only shows its power once in a millennium is easily forgotten by the time a few generations have come and gone. Nature is peaceful, and the soil is fertile: the area becomes thickly populated, around what is no longer a volcano, just a mountain like any other. When such a volcano suddenly awakes it is not under surveillance, and a human catastrophe is inevitable. The 1982 eruption of El Chichón in Mexico is a good case in point.

The second reason is volcanological. Volcanoes can be divided into two broad groups: those that produce mostly free-flowing lava, the ones Maurice Krafft called "red volcanoes," and those whose activity is mainly explosive, and which smother the countryside with a gray blanket of eruption products. These he called "gray volcanoes."

Red volcanoes produce fluid basaltic lava. The gases in the magma can readily escape, so there is little or no explosive force. Their Volcanic Explosivity Index (see page 122) varies from 0 through 3, depending on the lava's chemical composition.

But gray volcanoes produce thick lava with a higher silica and gas content. Gases are trapped within this, and when their pressure rises high enough, they escape explosively. Some of these volcanoes, like Sakurajima in Japan, explode very frequently, but others, like Pinatubo in the Philippines, El Chichón in Mexico, and Arenal in Costa Rica, only experience the right conditions for an eruption once every few hundred years. Over such a time, considerable pressure builds up in the magma, and the decompression that takes place as it rises blows the whole top off the mountain, sending up fragments of more or less pulverized lava along with it.

Broadly speaking, the intervals between eruptions of a fluid basaltic lava volcano of low explosivity (0–3) are short (from one to a maximum of ten years), while the periods between major eruptions of explosivity index 4 or greater are much longer (measured in centuries or millennia).

WORST DEATH TOLLS IN ERUPTIONS SINCE 1700

Volcano	Year	Deaths	Cause(s)
Nevado del Ruiz (Colombia)	1985	25,000	Lahars
El Chichón (Mexico)	1982	2,500	Pyroclastic flows
Lamington (Papua New Guinea)	1951	2,900	Pyroclastic flows
Kelut (Indonesia)	1919	5,100	Lahars
Santa María (Guatemala)	1902	6,000	Pyroclastic flows
Mount Pelée (Martinique)	1902	28,000	Pyroclastic flows
La Soufrière (Saint-Vincent)	1902	1,560	Pyroclastic flows
Krakatau (Indonesia)	1883	36,400	Tsunami
Awu (Indonesia)	1856	3,000	Lahars
Galunggung (Indonesia)	1822	4,000	Lahars
Tambora (Indonesia)	1815	92,000	Famine and pyroclastic flows
Unzen (Japan)	1792	15,200	Tsunami
Laki/Lakagigar (Iceland)	1783	9,300	Famine
Papadajan (Indonesia)	1772	3,000	Pyroclastic flows
Makian (Indonesia)	1760	2,000	Lahars
Awu (Indonesia)	1711	3,200	Lahars

CAUSES OF DEATHS IN VOLCANIC ERUPTIONS

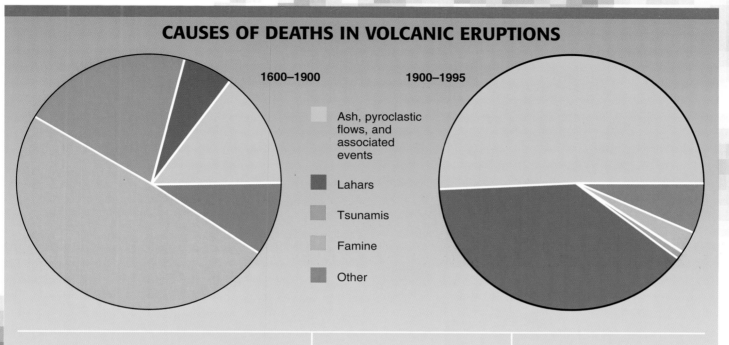

1600–1900   1900–1995

Ash, pyroclastic flows, and associated events

Lahars

Tsunamis

Famine

Other

Hazards	Deaths 1600–1900		Deaths 1900–1995	
Lava flows	1,185	(0.4%)	285	(0.3%)
Fallout of ash and lapilli	11,303	(4.3%)	3,369	(4.2%)
Pyroclastic flows and debris avalanches	55,055	(20.7%)	36,847	(46.3%)
Lahars	39,746	(14.9%)	31,438	(39.4%)
Seismic activity	89	(0.03%)	32	(0.04%)
Tsunamis	44,356	(16.6%)	407	(0.5%)
Atmospheric causes	63	(0.02%)	3	(0.004%)
Gases and acid rain	1,985	(0.7%)	1,983	(2.5%)
Famine	95,313	(35.8%)	3,163	(4.0%)
Other causes and cause unknown	17,182	(6.5%)	2,133	(2.7%)
TOTAL	266,277		79,660	

From the 16th century on, roughly half a dozen major eruptions have occurred in each century, though many more have left smaller traces in the records. The exact causes of the deaths attributable to volcanoes have changed over the course of time: the improvement in relief services during the 20th century has reduced the number of deaths from famine, which was very high in earlier centuries.

Urban development, on the other hand, and the increasing density of human settlement, have made pyroclastic flows and lahars even greater killers. In 1985, a mud slide set off by the eruption of Nevado del Ruiz killed 25,000 people, whereas an even bigger lahar in the same area had only killed 1000 in 1845. One single eruption from some volcanoes, like that of Mount Pelée in 1902, Nevado del Ruiz in 1985, or Unzen in 1792, can utterly skew the statistics for deaths from pyroclastic flows, lahars, or tsunamis.

A breakdown in communication between scientists and civil authorities, or a lack of mutual confidence, can also be catastrophic. This is what happened at Armero: the authorities had been warned that there was a high probability of a mud flow reaching the town, but gave no order to evacuate. The rest is history.

In 1995, scientific bodies worldwide jointly organized an international colloquium on relations between volcanologists, sociologists, civil authorities, and the media. The colloquium focused on how the message from scientists could be conveyed to the authorities and the general public, since it is vital to get the right information to the people affected. ∎

An active volcano is one that has erupted within recorded history – but how that is defined depends on when written records began, a development that did not happen simultaneously the world over! So a volcano may come to be recognized as active only when it begins erupting, like this one, Arenal in Costa Rica, in 1968, or Pinatubo in 1991. Which will be the next volcano to take us by surprise, and when?

the modern era, destroying the Minoan civilization and very probably giving rise to the legend of Atlantis (see page 59).

The Smithsonian Institution in Washington DC maintains a list of just over 1500 active or potentially active volcanoes. For many years, an "active" volcano was defined as one that had erupted within recorded times, or that showed fumarole activity: these number 550, but the limitation of using this definition was that it excluded many volcanoes in countries whose written records go back only four or five centuries.

Two volcanoes that were not counted as "active" were Arenal in Costa Rica, which erupted in 1968, and Pinatubo in the Philippines, which awakened in 1991. Detailed geological examination showed (after the event in the case of Arenal, and only just before it in the case of Pinatubo) that their last eruptions had happened some six centuries earlier. They were not, or were no longer, considered active: the memory of their eruptions had faded from collective awareness.

In the 17th century, the geographer Varenius counted 27 active volcanoes: in his time, virtually all the volcanoes in the Pacific Ring of Fire, some two-thirds of the world total, were unknown.

As exploration opened up new lands, and as written records became more widespread, the number of known volcanoes rose, and so did the number of recorded eruptions. Coming nearer to our own times, an important part has been played by the mass media in disseminating information. The press led the way, followed by radio and now television, which revels in spectacular images of volcanic eruptions.

The Smithsonian has compiled a list of all volcanoes on which information – historical, archeological, or geochronological – is available about their eruption history over the last ten thousand years. As our knowledge increases, this list may grow longer. Undersea volcanic activity, of which there is a great deal, hidden beneath thousands of meters of water, has not been taken into account: only a few undersea volcanoes whose effects are felt on the surface are listed, such as MacDonald, off the coast of Tahiti to the southeast.

A scale similar to the Richter scale for earthquakes has been established to classify volcanic eruptions: this is called the Volcanic Explosivity Index and goes from 0 to 8. It makes use of various criteria, such as the volume of tephra (volcanic fallout in particles of all sizes), plume height, etc. Each point on the scale represents ten times the explosive force of the point below it. Fortunately, as with earthquakes, the most frequent eruptions are those with a low explosivity index, and events of level 8 are few and far between. The formation of the Yellowstone caldera two million years ago was one such, in which 2500 cubic kilometers (600 cubic miles) of volcanic material was thrown out; it covered much of North America with fallout.

However, when a disaster occurs, the number of victims does not necessarily reflect the explosivity index of the eruption. This is partly because awareness among populations living close to dangerous volcanoes makes a significant contribution to reducing the risk. For this reason, the International Volcanology Association and Unesco have jointly issued a video cassette made by Maurice Krafft, intended for people living near volcanoes and illustrating the various hazards to which they may be exposed. Another aim of the video is to raise awareness of volcanic hazards among civil authorities, so that they can make the right decisions in good time. ∎

THE SEVEN PRINCIPAL VOLCANIC HAZARDS

Ash fallout

Ash consists of fine particles of solid material thrown out during an eruption. Both acidic magma and basic magma eruptions produce ash (see page 89), but it is generally the explosions of acidic (andesitic) volcanoes that cause the worst harm due to fallout. When a volcano of this type erupts, the countryside around is covered by a layer of volcanic ash, and the distribution of this material depends on weather conditions as well as the force of the explosion: it may extend for a few kilometers, or for tens or even hundreds of kilometers around. The thickness of the deposits is a function of the explosion's force and the distance the fallout has traveled, which also depends on the wind direction.

Before it falls back to earth, the ash rises in a hot plume, driven upward by the decompression of the trapped gases. Depending on the size of the explosion, the plume of gases and particles may pass through the tropopause, 10 kilometers (6 miles) high, and continue rising into the stratosphere, which extends from 10 to 50 kilometers (6 to 30 miles) in altitude. After several months, the finer ash particles will fall back out of the stratosphere; the sulfide gases given off by the volcano, on the other hand, combine in a photochemical reaction with the water vapor in the stratosphere to form aerosols of sulfuric acid, which remain circling the earth for a long time. These aerosols not only absorb some solar radiation, they reflect some of the rest back into space. Two months after Pinatubo exploded, the average temperature had dropped by several tenths of a degree, most markedly in latitudes between 20°N and 20°S. Some spectacular sunsets were seen after the explosions of Krakatau, Mount Saint Helens, El Chichón, and Pinatubo. It was Benjamin Franklin who first noted a connection between volcanic eruptions and climatic disturbance, when he sought to explain the hard winter of 1783/84 by reference to the eruption of Laki (or Lakagigar) in Iceland.

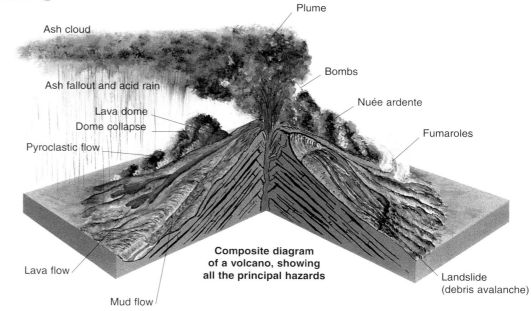

Composite diagram of a volcano, showing all the principal hazards

Plume
Ash cloud
Ash fallout and acid rain
Bombs
Lava dome
Dome collapse
Nuée ardente
Pyroclastic flow
Fumaroles
Lava flow
Landslide (debris avalanche)
Mud flow

Comparison of the volumes of ash emitted in various eruptions

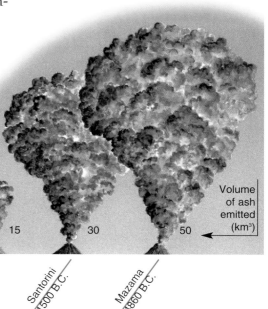

Volume of ash emitted (km³)

Laki 1783	0.2
Mount Pelée 1902	0.5
Mount St. Helens 1980	1
El Chichón 1982	1
Vesuvius 0079	3
Santa Maria 1912	5
Pinatubo 1991	6–10
Krakatau 1883	10
Katmai 1912	15
Santorini 1500 B.C.	30
Mazama 4860 B.C.	50

During the 1982 eruption of Galunggung in central Java (Indonesia), 90,000 people had to be evacuated from this mineral-caked landscape. It was in this eruption that ash from the volcano's 11-kilometer (7-mile) high plume was sucked into the jet intakes of a Boeing 747, causing a serious mid-air incident.

In andesitic eruptions, a large proportion of the explosion products falls back onto the slopes of the volcano and the area nearby, the larger fragments dropping closer to the erupting vent. Crops, homes, roads, and other communication routes are all coated with a thick blanket of volcanic ash. Unless the roofs of buildings are cleared regularly, they are likely to collapse, particularly if rain falls, making the ash wet and heavy.

Since the advent of international air travel, volcanic plumes and ash clouds have posed a frequent threat to air traffic. One widely publicized incident occurred when a Boeing 747 unwittingly flew through the eruption plume of Galunggung (Indonesia) in 1982: all four engine intakes became choked with ash at an altitude of 8000 meters (26,000 feet). Fortunately, one engine subsequently restarted, enabling the plane to make an emergency landing.

Ash thrown out by Pinatubo in June 1991 disrupted air traffic throughout the western Pacific for two weeks: airports were closed, and aircraft damaged both in the air and on the ground. This eruption of Pinatubo claimed comparatively few victims, since the population had been evacuated: 300 people died as a direct result, and 400 others in the evacuation camps succumbed to secondary hazards. A cyclone that coincided with the eruption, however, washed down a further ash fallout, which caused serious damage.

The eruptions of basic (or alkaline) volcanoes are generally less harmful. However, when lava fountains occur, basaltic magma can be ejected in the form of lapilli and Pele's hair. These ejecta may fall on pastureland where, together with gas emissions, they can cause serious problems.

In 1783, the eruption of Laki in Iceland had a devastating effect: almost all the cattle died after grazing on pasture contaminated by gases and Pele's hair, and the consequence was a major famine in which more than 10,000 people died. That was an extreme case, though, for a volcano of this type. In another incident in Iceland, when the volcano Eldfell erupted in 1973 near the town of Heimaey, black cinders of basalt completely buried about a hundred houses (see pages 26–27).

In the tropics, the combination of water and heat soon turns volcanic ash into extremely rich soil,

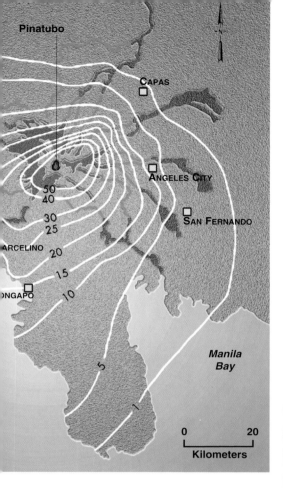

Zones affected by the Pinatubo eruption up to September 1, 1991

Isopach lines: each line joins points where the fallout is of equal thickness (unit: cm)

Extent of pyroclastic flows, June 12 through 15, 1991

Areas destroyed by lahars up to September 1, 1991

and provided the local inhabitants have not been wiped out, they soon return to cultivate their fields – until the next eruption drives them out again. They have nowhere else to go.

Hot ash flows

Hot ash flows, or pyroclastic flows, are produced by such events as explosions (Mount Pelée, 1902), dome collapse (Mount Unzen, 1991), and the fallout from pumice columns (El Chichón, 1982). The term covers a wide range of phenomena, including nuées ardentes, in which the flow is accompanied by a hot ash cloud. All types of pyroclastic flow consist of a mixture of hot gases, ash, and solid lumps of various sizes, and this whole mass can travel at speeds of several hundred miles per hour. For a while, the flow propels itself forward, at the same time expanding dramatically: the lumps of lava being carried along are hot and still full of gas, which expands and bursts the lava lumps apart, hurling ever smaller fragments into the mix.

Nothing can stand up to flows like this: they destroy everything in their path, and are

Continued on page 128.

Pyroclastic flows (top, from the volcano Augustine in Alaska) are among the most feared of all volcanic hazards – and rightly so. In the eruption of El Chichón in Mexico (above) they claimed 2000 human lives, as well as killing thousands of cattle that could not be evacuated.

The spread of the ash plume following the El Chichón eruption of 1982

By April 26, the plume had spread right round the globe.

On April 19, the plume reached Africa.

By April 9, the plume had been drifting westward for 5 days.

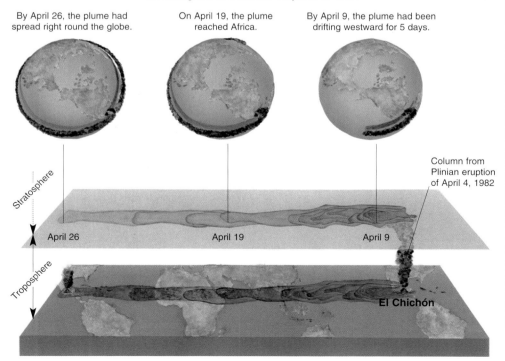

Column from Plinian eruption of April 4, 1982

Stratosphere

April 26   April 19   April 9

Troposphere

El Chichón

The spread of the volcanic ash cloud from the Rabaul eruption of September 19, 1994

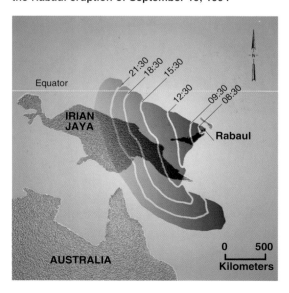

VOLCANOES AND AIR SAFETY

In the last few decades, several commercial flights have run without warning into clouds of volcanic ash. Very serious incidents occurred when planes flew into the eruption plumes from Galunggung (Indonesia, 1982), Redoubt (Alaska, 1989), and Pinatubo (Philippines, 1991).

When a volcano erupts explosively, an ash plume is hurled violently upward through the atmosphere. It may reach a height of 40 kilometers (25 miles) in the space of less than an hour. A great quantity of ash remains in the troposphere and the lower regions of the stratosphere, collecting at around 15,000 meters (50,000 feet), precisely the cruising altitude for commercial airline flights. As winds and other atmospheric conditions dictate, the ash spreads and forms clouds that can create difficulties for air traffic hundreds of kilometers from the original eruption site. Usually, these clouds return to earth as fallout over the next few days or weeks, but even this is long enough to cause serious problems.

The ash consists of volcanic rock debris, comprising jagged fragments – crystals – of rock or glass. Though most of the debris is very fine, the particle size can nevertheless be as much as a centimeter (half an inch). Worse still, this ash is mixed with volcanic gases. Jet engines suck in enormous quantities of air, and any ash drawn in with it gets right inside the engines, where it abrades moving parts such as the compressor and turbine blades. Half-molten aggregates form in the combustion chamber, leaving the rotating blades, which are cooler, encrusted with glassy deposits. All of this results in a loss of power, or even engine failure. The ash also abrades the fuselage, pits and scratches the cockpit windscreen, clogs the navigation instruments, and so on. During the period 1980 through 1995, eighty aircraft had the misfortune to fly into volcanic ash clouds, sustaining this kind of mid-air damage: seven of them suffered dramatic power loss and on occasion engine failure resulted. Nobody has yet been killed in this way, but the damage to equipment has been costly: it cost $80 million, for instance, to repair a Boeing 747-400 caught in the cloud from Redoubt, near Anchorage (Alaska), in 1989.

When Pinatubo erupted in June 1991, it damaged some twenty aircraft in the air and many more on the ground. All air traffic between Manila, Singapore, Hong Kong, and Ho Chi Minh City was interrupted, with airfields covered in ash, ground installations disabled or destroyed, and other damaging effects. A number of airports were closed (Manila, for instance, was out of action between June 15 and 19), and flights did not return to normal until July. In the USA, the Mount Saint Helens eruption of May 1980 had likewise badly affected Seattle airport.

The International Civil Aviation Organization has responded to volcanic hazards by setting up a

Ash fallout caused extensive damage at Rabaul airport in 1994. As well as destroying ground installations, it pinned many aircraft to the ground and rendered them useless.

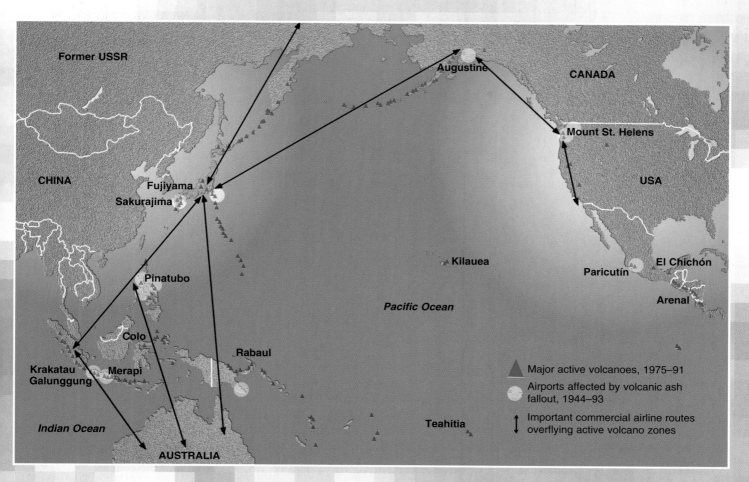

▲ Important airline routes in the vicinity of active volcano zones in the Pacific rim area

warning system in collaboration with the World Organization of Volcano Observatories (WOVO). As soon as an eruption occurs, the WOVO observatories issue instant warnings to designated control centers, which forward the information to airlines and aircraft in flight. Satellite images are used to follow the spread and drift of eruption clouds.

As a further precaution, the World Weather Organization (WWO) has set up centers running simulations that predict the behavior of the clouds on the basis of the location and intensity of the eruption and the current weather conditions. Simulations are also run for certain volcanoes even in the absence of an eruption, in order to assess the implications of various possible combinations of climate and eruptive force. Airline pilots now have precise instructions on what to do when alerted to the presence of an eruption cloud on their flight path; unfortunately, however, airborne radar is not yet capable of detecting these clouds. ■

The Pinatubo eruption
The spread of the ash cloud, shown at three-hourly intervals beginning June 15, 1991

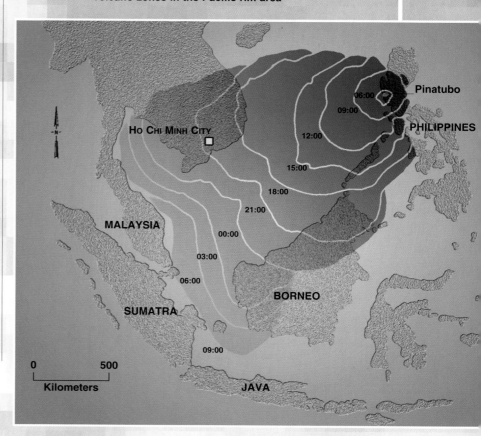

without question the most dangerous of all small- or medium-scale volcanic phenomena. Unfortunately, there is no effective defense against pyroclastic flows: if people have not been forewarned and evacuated from the area, a tragedy is inevitable. The most notorious instance, though there have been many others, was the eruption of Mount Pelée on Martinique in 1902, which destroyed the town of Saint-Pierre and the township of Morne-Rouge, killing 28,000 people (see pages 24–25). Could that disaster have been avoided? Although there was no volcanological observatory there – the only one in the world at the time was on Vesuvius – and the scientists of the day did not understand the phenomenon, the number of victims could still have been reduced considerably, because many warning signs had been recorded in the months, and even years, leading up to the explosion.

A more recent incident of this kind occurred at El Chichón in Mexico in 1982. The township of Francisco León was destroyed by a collapsing pumice column, causing 3500 deaths. In another eruption, at Mount Unzen in Japan in 1991, a pyroclastic flow more violent than the ones that had occurred previously swept

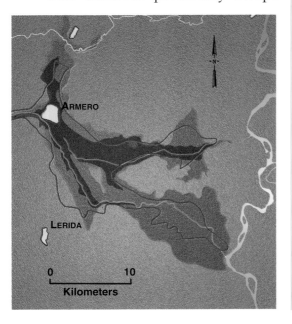

Actual and forecast extent of lahar deposits from Nevado del Ruiz in the Armero region of Colombia
- Gray: 1845 lahar deposits
- Red line: forecast of the extent of lahars from the predicted eruption of 1985
- Brown: the area actually affected by lahars in the 1985 eruption

along the bed of the River Mizunashi, which had 3500 people living on its banks. Fortunately, the inhabitants had been evacuated, but forty-three people who had stayed behind to observe the eruption were overtaken by the flow and killed. Among the dead were the volcanologists Maurice and Katia Krafft of France, and Harry Glicken of the USA, who had made Mount Unzen his particular study.

Mud flows (lahars)

"Lahar" is an Indonesian word, used to refer to a mixture of water, volcanic ash, lumps of rock, and even whole slabs of former mountainside that sweeps downslope, usually along riverbeds, at speeds often in excess of 50 kilometers (30 miles) per hour and with considerable destructive force. Lahars can arise in a number of ways. Rain falling on volcanic ash deposits during or just after an eruption, when the ash is still loose dust, can render a whole slope unstable and be enough to unleash a flow. This is

what happened at Pinatubo after the eruptions of June 1991, which occurred at a time when the region was being lashed by a typhoon. Every year since that eruption, the monsoon season has caused further lahars all around the mountain, and in fact 15,000 people had to be evacuated in July 1995: even all those years after the cataclysm, Pinatubo's destructive career had not ended.

Many eruptions are accompanied or preceded by continual earth tremors, which can vibrate waterlogged soil in such a way as to make it fluid. An eruption may also expel the water from a crater lake, as happened on Kelut in Java when it erupted in 1919. The crater lake overflowed and sent lahars of hot mud down several valleys, destroying many villages in less than an hour and leaving over 5000 people dead.

If large quantities of material are produced in the course of an eruption and find their way into a nearby lake, this also can create lahars. That is what occurred when the whole side of Mount Saint Helens slipped in May, 1980: lahars rushed down valleys at 100 kilometers (60 miles) per hour, sweeping all before them. Some of these mud flows were over 20 meters (65 feet) thick. Another way in which eruptions

Water-saturated ash deposits can turn into mud flows, set off by phreatic (steam-driven) explosions or by earthquakes. These flows are highly destructive: they sweep down the sides of volcanoes, causing havoc and permanently altering the landscape (left and above, Galunggung and Pinatubo).

MOUNT SAINT HELENS: A MOUNTAINSIDE GIVES WAY

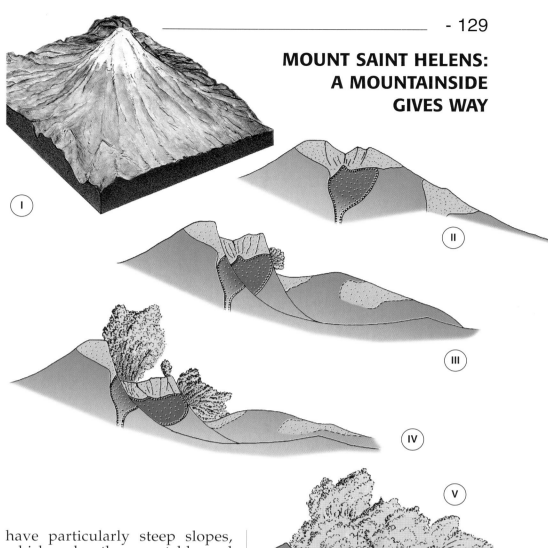

Before the fateful day of its eruption, Mount Saint Helens had the conical shape characteristic of andesitic volcanoes (I). At 8:32 a.m. on May 18, 1980, the volcano swelled (II) due to increasing pressure in the near-surface magma chamber inside the cone itself (the cryptodome). In the space of less than 15 seconds, one-third of the mountain slipped away, releasing the enormous pressure that had been contained within (III, IV, V). The avalanche of debris destroyed everything over a distance of 25 km (15 miles) to the north. When calm returned, the mountain was scarred by a horseshoe-shaped avalanche caldera (VI), 4 km (2.5 miles) wide. It was also 400 m (1300 ft) lower.

can generate a lahar is by melting snow and ice on the mountain-top. This happened at Nevado del Ruiz (Colombia) in 1985, where the town of Armero was destroyed in a few minutes by a lahar originating 50 kilometers (30 miles) away. This was only a small eruption, producing just 0.03 cubic kilometers (0.007 cubic miles) of magma, but its side-effect, the lahar, killed 25,000 people. The record distance covered by this kind of lahar is 240 kilometers (150 miles): that was the length of the one created by melting snow and ice on the summit of Cotopaxi in Ecuador, when it erupted in 1877.

Finally, there are lahars produced by eruptions taking place beneath glaciers, as happened at Katla in Iceland in 1918: the Myralsjökull glacier melted, forming a gigantic lahar that flowed into the sea on Iceland's southern coast.

Landslides and landslips

Volcanoes are formed by the accumulation of lava flows, ash, and various other eruption products. Explosive volcanoes have particularly steep slopes, which makes them unstable, and this instability is aggravated by changes within a mountain's structure due to the interaction of heat and water. As magma rises inside a volcano, the mountain may be forced considerably out of shape, and part of it may collapse. The best-known instance occurred at Mount Saint Helens in 1980: here the upthrust of magma formed a bulge on the northern side of the summit that swelled by more than 100 meters (330 feet) in barely two months. The whole slope then slid down into a valley, a distance of 25 kilometers (15 miles), generating a gigantic blast which knocked flat everything in the vicinity and was immediately followed by the magma eruption.

Detailed study of this eruption (see pages 16–21) has enabled volcanologists to recognize the evidence of similar past events on many other volcanoes of the

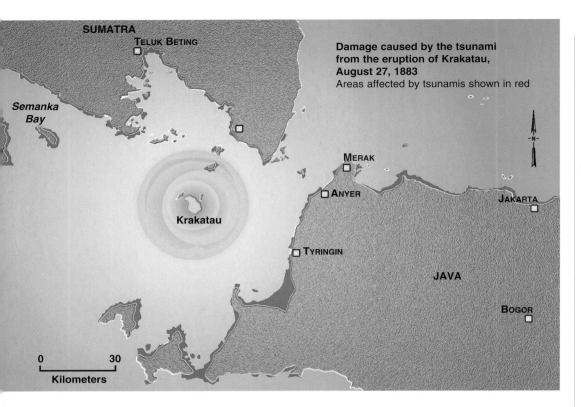

SUMATRA

TELUK BETING

Semanka Bay

Krakatau

Damage caused by the tsunami from the eruption of Krakatau, August 27, 1883
Areas affected by tsunamis shown in red

-N-

MERAK

ANYER

JAKARTA

TYRINGIN

JAVA

BOGOR

0   30
Kilometers

same type. At La Soufrière on Guadeloupe, for instance, a landslide like this happened three thousand years ago, burying the whole of the Saint-Claude area of Basse-Terre beneath an immense flow of debris.

Tsunamis

These are gigantic waves which can flood whole coastlines, still often referred to by the misleading name "tidal waves." They are associated with volcanic activity, and can be caused by the earthquakes that accompany eruptions, by undersea explosions in shallow water, by pyroclastic flows reaching and entering the sea, by the collapse of calderas, by landslides, or by phreatomagmatic eruptions. There have been two particularly tragic incidents. In 1792, a landslide caused by volcanic activity on Mayeyama (near Unzen) in the south of Japan unleashed a tsunami which destroyed the town of Shimbara, killing some 15,000 people. In the enormous eruption of Krakatau on August 27, 1883, the collapse of the mountainside (as at Mount Saint Helens) and large-volume pyroclastic flows produced a series of

tsunamis which ravaged the Java coast and left 36,000 dead. In both cases, the wave that broke on the coasts was several tens of meters (of the order of 100–200 feet) high. The eruption of Santorini generated a tsunami with 60-meter (200-foot) waves, and traces have been found in the Hawaiian islands of tsunamis 300 meters (1000 feet) high, caused by massive underwater landslides.

Lava flows

Free-flowing basaltic lava occasionally forms streams that race

This elephant was overtaken and smothered by a lava flow issuing at an incredible 100 kph (60 mph) from the fissuring of Nyiragongo (Republic of Congo). Only its skeleton remains, lying inside the mold formed by the animal's body in the solidified lava.

along at 100 kilometers (60 miles) per hour, though such speeds are rare. The speed at which lava flows depends on a number of factors: volume of flow, slope, the temperature and chemical composition of the lava, and whether tunnels are formed through which the lava can flow without exposure to the cooling air. Its speed therefore varies a great deal, ranging from only a few meters per hour to several kilometers per hour. Usually, lava flows present no immediate danger to humans, but they do destroy everything in their path: homes, crops, and vegetation. Land overrun by a lava flow will lie waste for many centuries before it becomes cultivable once more through the action of weathering. The slopes of Kilauea in Hawaii are ravaged by great fields of lava which have lain there since 1983, when two hundred homes, many roads, fields, and plantations were destroyed over an area of about 70 square kilometers (nearly 30 square miles). As if to compensate, the flows still add daily to the land area of the island.

In 1977, the southern side of the volcano Nyiragongo in the Republic of Congo split, probably as a consequence of an earthquake whose epicenter was nearby. The crater was filled almost to the brim with a lake of

In 1944, a flow of glowing lava like this one on Mount Etna (main picture) destroyed the village of San Juan, close to the volcano Paricutín in Mexico. Only the church (above) remains standing as a mute witness to the dramatic event. Fortunately, all 4000 inhabitants had been evacuated before the eruption, and nobody was killed.

Lava lakes themselves present no real danger, but sudden fracturing of the cones that contain them, as here at Nyiragongo in 1977, can release a flood of very fluid lava which moves surprisingly fast, with destructive and sometimes fatal results.

molten lava. As the crack opened, this highly fluid lava burst out, flowing at nearly 100 kilometers (60 miles) per hour. Birds were caught on the wing, vehicles moving at speed were submerged, and people fleeing from the torrent of lava were thrown to the ground and buried. In a herd of elephants, a male valiantly turned and faced the threat on behalf of females and young, but in vain: they were all smothered, and their skeletons were later found encased in molds of rock.

This particular flow traveled a distance of 15 kilometers (10 miles) in twenty minutes, coming to a halt just 500 meters (550 yards) north of the runway at Goma airport. After it had passed, tatters of lava could be seen hanging high up in the branches of trees. The official death toll was 200, but the actual figure was probably higher.

Following the eruption, the re-formed crater was 900 meters (3000 feet) deep, and in 1982 a new lava lake began to half-fill it. In late June and early July 1994, the lava lake rose again, as the nearby volcano Nyamlagira began to erupt. It was in mid-July that Rwandan refugees arrived, and the camps where a total of 800,000 people gathered were in the area immediately around the volcanoes: one of the largest was

actually standing on the 1977 flow. Given that the lava level in the crater was rising, it was felt that the very real danger of another event like that of 1977 could not be ignored, and the camp most at risk was moved. Fortunately, the level of the lake has remained stable since August 1995, and volcanic activity seems to be on hold.

Piton de la Fournaise (see pages 30–35) is also extremely active: many years see more than one eruption. These usually take place inside the Fouqué enclosure, a caldera open toward the sea, but in 1977 and again in 1986 eruptions occurred outside this enclosure. The first of these eruptions partially destroyed the village of Piton-Sainte-Rose, along with large areas of sugarcane plantation, while the second flattened houses in the small town of Saint-Philippe. On the other hand, both of these events actually enlarged the island, as happens on Hawaii.

Volcanic gases

When a volcano erupts, or sometimes even between eruptions, large volumes of gas are released into the atmosphere. A medium-sized eruption, for instance, may produce many millions of tons of sulfur dioxide every day; this can combine with water vapor in the atmosphere to form sulfuric acid. The quantity of sulfur dioxide emitted varies considerably, not only from volcano to volcano, but also for a single volcano at different times. It can be measured with a correlation spectrometer, or Cospec.

In January 1995, the volcano Galeras in Colombia vented some 300 tonnes of sulfur dioxide per day (one metric tonne is a little over one short ton); but in Mexico, at around the same time, Popocatépetl was producing 2000 to 3500 tonnes per day, and Colima around 500. In the Philippines, before the 1991 eruption, fumaroles on Pinatubo were producing 500 tonnes per day in mid-May, but the rate had risen to 5000 tonnes by the end of the month; it then dropped, just before the eruption began, to around 1500 tonnes per day. Immediately after the eruption, in early July, Pinatubo was producing between 1000 and 5000 tonnes per day, but by October only 20. It is estimated that during the paroxysm itself 50 to 100 million tonnes of sulfur dioxide were vented into the atmosphere, twice as much as at El Chichón (Mexico) in 1982.

Volcanic gases are rapidly diluted in the atmosphere, as a rule, and are seldom dangerous to people, though they can cause a tremendous amount of damage if winds or downdrafts bring them into contact with crops, or if they are washed out as acid rain. When this happens, the gases, often rich in fluorine or chlorine, can contaminate pastureland and kill livestock: this is what occurred in Iceland in 1783. More recently, when the volcano Lonquimay erupted in Chile in 1989, many animals were killed by fluorine poisoning.

Carbon dioxide (CO_2) emissions can be equally dangerous. Carbon dioxide may seep from volcanic fissures (as on the Dieng plateau on Java in 1979, where 142 people died), or the gas can build up more slowly in crater lakes. The incident at Lake Nyos in Cameroon, in 1986, was a terrible one: the waters of the lake, supersaturated with carbon dioxide, suddenly released the gas, and a layer of CO_2, heavier than air, spread across the valley floor. It asphyxiated nearly 1800 people, together with their livestock.

France's Massif Central also has several crater lakes, but studies have established that a similar occurrence is unlikely there for the present. ◼

Carbon dioxide gas, colorless and odorless, is heavier than air: it can be a great danger to humans and even more to animals (above, at Lake Nyos in 1986).
Vulcano (below) is a Sicilian volcano and a popular tourist attraction. It often releases large quantities of gas, and on some of these occasions clouds of carbon dioxide have been detected.

VOLCANO SURVEILLANCE AND THE FORECASTING OF ERUPTIONS

The global population explosion presents today's volcanologists with a new problem: an exponential growth in the risks arising from volcanic eruptions. As the 21st century begins, scientists are rising to a new challenge: to develop an applied science of protective volcanology in the service of humankind.

VOLCANOLOGICAL OBSERVATORIES: THEIR WORK AND DEVELOPMENT

By comparison with other natural hazards such as hurricanes, floods, and earthquakes, volcanoes have been responsible for relatively few major disasters. Because of the unevenness of population distribution, it is not always the largest eruptions that cause the most deaths. Even a minor eruption or its side-effects can lead to a full-scale disaster in a densely-populated area, if they are complicated by a lack of coordination (or even mutual incomprehension) between civil authorities, scientists, the media, and local people.

The November 1985 eruption of Nevado del Ruiz in Colombia, which destroyed the town of Armero and killed 25,000 people, was a striking case in point. There were warning signs (major fumarole activity and earth tremors that could be felt) as early as December of the previous year. Colombian scientists and their colleagues from UNDRO (the United Nations Disaster Relief Organization) tried to alert the government to the possibility that the volcano might be about to become active, and to suggest appropriate precautions – but in vain.

In August 1985, the United States Geological Service and UNDRO installed a seismic monitoring network around the mountain. The first eruption occurred on September 11, producing a lahar that flowed for 27 kilometers (17 miles). At last, the Colombian Ministry of Mines decided to draw up a volcanic risk map, but the map they produced (perfectly realistic, as events were soon to show) was received with hostility by the press, and the warnings it conveyed were contested for reasons that had to do with

local economic interests. The government was unable to make up its mind, and delayed taking action. In the second week of October, Franco Barberi, the Italian volcanologist sent to advise the Colombian authorities, presented a report containing specific recommendations for civil defense in view of the volcano's eruption record and the absence of reliable surveillance. But the provincial government of Tolima and the mayor of Armero were completely unprepared for such a critical situation: they lacked the time, the means, and the organization to handle it.

The crisis came at 3:06 p.m. on November 13, when an eruption hurled out pyroclastic products which melted the mountain's covering of snow and ice. A storm was raging at the time, and the eruption could not be seen: no radio link had been set up between the town of Armero and the observers positioned on the likely routes of any lahars. The Armero Red Cross is known to have appealed for the town to be evacuated on the afternoon of November 13, but nobody will ever know whether the evacuation order was in fact given.

As a consequence of this catastrophe and its heavy death toll, once things had quietened down the Colombian government ordered the national geological service (Ingeominas) to place the country's most hazardous volcanoes under surveillance, and Colombia now boasts three highly efficient volcanological observatories.

Every major volcanic disaster since the beginning of the 20th century has spurred a renewal of interest among scientists and civil authorities in the study and surveillance of volcanoes. As a

November 1985: Nevado del Ruiz comes back to life, and 25,000 people die in a mud flow that overwhelms the town of Armero.

result, significant advances and sometimes sudden leaps forward have been made in our understanding of the forces and mechanisms at work in eruptions. Although the very first volcanological observatory in the world, built on Vesuvius in 1841, was established primarily for scientific research (due to the interest of King Ferdinand II), most observatories since then have been set up in the wake of a catastrophe.

The deadly eruption of Mount Pelée in 1902, for instance, and others in the same year at La Soufrière de Saint-Vincent and Santa María in Guatemala, gave the French volcanologist Alfred Lacroix the opportunity to set up the Mount Pelée Observatory in 1903, at Morne des Cadets on

Less than 4 kilometers (2.5 miles) from the summit, the Mayon Resthouse and Observatory is the advance post of the two observatories maintained by PHIVOLCS (the Philippines Institute of Volcanology and Seismology) on the familiar but dangerous Mount Mayon.

Martinique. The sight of Saint-Pierre after the Mount Pelée disaster so affected the US volcanologist Thomas Jaggar that in 1912 he too founded a volcanological observatory, on the edge of the Kilauea crater in Hawaii. The Asama observatory in Japan was set up a few years later, and it was soon followed by others. Observations made at these facilities have helped to transform volcanology into a modern, multi-disciplinary science.

When the other Soufrière, on Guadeloupe, erupted in 1976, the French National Center for Scientific Research (CNRS) instituted a program of volcanological research which mobilized the relevant sector of the French scientific community for a decade. The research carried out contributed significantly to the advance of volcano science, and during the same period the National Institute for Sciences of the Universe (INSU) and the Paris Institute for Global Geophysics (IPGP), the bodies responsible for monitoring French volcanoes, upgraded the surveillance networks on La Soufrière and Mount Pelée into world-class research observatories. At Piton de la Fournaise on Réunion, the observatory Alfred Lacroix had asked for in 1936 was only built after the destruction of the village of Piton-Sainte-Rose by the eruption of 1977; today it is one of the best-equipped in the world. And it was the notorious eruption of Mount Saint Helens (see pages 16–21) that led to the construction in the USA of both the Cascades volcanological observatory and another in Alaska.

By the end of 1995, almost 60 observatories or research organizations were monitoring some 150 volcanoes by means of surveillance networks, and all of these belonged to the World Organization of Volcano Observatories (WOVO), a coordinating body which is a division of the International Association of Volcanology and Chemistry of the Earth's Interior. Not all of their networks are equally sophisticated, however: depending on the resources the various institutions have at their disposal, they range from simple visual observation posts to the most elaborate networks of telemetry stations, which take continuous measurements and relay them to centers where they are decoded in real time.

In the aftermath of a major volcanic event, governments tend to be receptive to the idea that volcanological research in general, and surveillance of the troublesome volcano in particular, are worthwhile: it makes good socioeconomic sense. But once the volcanic activity diminishes, or even ceases, researchers find that their support falters too. And there are always supposedly well-informed critics – sometimes even among the scientists themselves – who question or oppose the upkeep of observatories when volcanoes are quiet. Under such circumstances, it can be difficult to maintain uninterrupted observation. The first observatory on Mount Pelée, which as we have seen was established in 1903, was closed by the authorities after twenty years had passed without any sign of activity from the volcano. Four years after its closure, of course, the eruption of 1929 caught everybody by surprise. Volcanic activity on the mountain continued until 1932, happily without loss of life, and it was Alfred Lacroix once again who managed to get another observatory built, near the site of the original one. This has been functioning continuously ever since.

Volcanological observatories have two main purposes: research and surveillance. Research addresses the task of understanding the characteristics of a particular volcano, its present and past status, the eruption mechanisms at work, and the types of eruption they cause. The aim of surveillance is to observe and analyze eruptions, to identify warning signs, to process the data collected, and to relay all this information to both the supervising scientific authorities and the civil ones.

Observatories are in fact responsible for alerting the administrative authorities with all speed when there is a likelihood of the volcano becoming active, thereby giving them time to take the necessary measures – which may include evacuation. In 1991, information supplied by the Shimabara observatory in Japan meant that the local population had been evacuated by the time Mount Unzen released its pyroclastic flows and lahars. Apart from the forty-three people who remained at the foot of the mountain in order to carry out their work as journalists or scientific observers (including the

Continued on page 140.

THE VOLCANOLOGICAL OBSERVATORIES OF THE PARIS INSTITUTE FOR GLOBAL GEOPHYSICS

The Paris Institute for Global Geophysics (IPGP) has a statutory duty to "provide for continuous observation of various natural phenomena in France, in French territories overseas, and in other countries [...] these observations may contribute to the prevention and alleviation of hazards arising from earthquakes and volcanoes."

To carry out this duty, the IPGP operates seismological, magnetometric, and volcanological observatories. This last group consists of five establishments. Two of them are operated jointly with local research organizations in Djibouti and the Comoros, and three are in French Overseas Departments: one on Martinique to monitor Mount Pelée, one on Guadeloupe for La Soufrière, and one on Réunion for Piton de La Fournaise. Each of the last three is covered by a contract with the Departmental General Council and the National Institute for Sciences of the Universe (INSU) for the surveillance of the volcano.

On site, each observatory has a permanent staff of between seven and twelve to maintain the network, gather the data, and make an initial interpretation of it. They are in contact with the IPGP's various specialist teams, who cover the individual disciplines of seismology, ground deformation (inclinometry and geodesy), magnetic field measurement, gravitational measurement, geochemistry, and geology. In this way, around 60 people in all are involved, full- or part-time, in the functioning of these five volcanological observatories. They include engineers, technicians, researchers, and administrators. All the researchers and engineers take part in national, European, or international research programs, some involving fundamental research into eruption mechanisms and others concerning developments in surveillance network technology (for example, in the capture, transmission, and acquisition of data.) This organizational structure should ensure that all those who might have to take action in the event of a serious incident at one of the IPGP's volcanoes have the capacity to tackle the scientific and technical problems that could arise.

Regular colloquiums are held to discuss topics of interest to the observatories. Each researcher is kept informed of the work being done in all the observatories, both scientific and technical, so that nobody is working in isolation: true teamwork operates, in other words. Specifically, this means that each engineer is capable of taking over operational control of any observatory, as the need arises and at the drop of a hat.

The oldest of the IPGP's volcanological observatories is the one at Mount Pelée on Martinique, founded by Alfred Lacroix after the Saint-Pierre disaster of 1902. It is sited at Morne des Cadets, 9 kilometers (5.6 miles) from the volcano as the crow flies, and with a clear view of it. The observatory remained operational, still equipped with its original instruments, until 1925. During the eruption of 1929–32, again at Alfred Lacroix's prompting, it was decided to set up a more modern observatory, with seismographs, magnetic field recorders, apparatus for measuring electrical fields, a gravimeter, a chemical laboratory, and an observation telescope. This facility came into operation in 1935, at first managed by the Martinique Meteorological and Geophysical Service and then, when Martinique became a Department, under the IPGP. With only limited funds, modernization of the observatory proceeded piecemeal, and it was not until the early 1970s that the first seismic telemetry stations were set up.

When La Soufrière erupted on Guadeloupe, the IPGP's observatories were reorganized and, with resources made available by INSU and the CNRS (the National Center for Scientific Research), a modern monitoring network was installed on every volcano. Of course, there has been no shortage of critics who regard it as a waste of money to put sophisticated devices on top of dormant volcanoes – but they have no appreciation of the vital need to understand the sites where this surveillance equipment is installed, if the data is to be interpreted correctly. It was for lack of such background knowledge that serious errors of judgment were made at La Soufrière in 1976.

To give just one example, over the course of a year a tiltmeter station will record cycles of groundswell and subsidence that are connected with the rainy and dry seasons: saturation of the ground is followed by its drying out. If a baseline cannot be established, because regular measurements have not been carried out, a sizable swelling detected at a time when Mount Pelée, say, is beginning to stir will naturally be attributed to volcanic activity – and general panic will follow. Yet it may simply be the effect of heavy rain, or the result of strong sunshine on the rock where the station is sited. Conversely, the local site could be moving in a way that masks genuine volcanic activity, and the scientists will remain calm and complacent even as the magma is rising!

In either case, the reliability of the information passed to the authorities by the scientists, and their diagnosis of the situation, will be badly compromised. That is why it is so vital to keep an efficient network constantly watching over these volcanoes; in fact, for the people living in the area, it is literally a matter of life and death.

The second French observatory to be set up was the one at La Soufrière on Guadeloupe, instigated by the IPGP in 1950. It was not long before the seismic network they installed, although it would seem rudimentary today, showed its worth: it gave advance notice of the phreatic eruption of 1956. By the time of La Soufrière's next eruption in 1975, the network had been extended and modernized: it now had five seismic stations with telephone links to the observatory, 4 kilometers (2.5 miles) from the volcano's summit on the hills above Saint-Claude. The network sounded the alarm, and when the phreatic explosions began the observatory was moved (from its position too close to the front line in the event of a magma eruption) to Fort Saint-Charles at Basse-Terre. When the townspeople of Basse-Terre itself were evacuated, the "scientists up at the fort" were the only people left in the area. In 1993 – sixteen years after the volcano's last eruption – a new observatory built by the departmental administration of Guadeloupe, INSU, and the CNRS was inaugurated on the summit of Houëlmont, between Basse-Terre and Gourbeyre.

The surveillance networks here have been improved every year since 1976. Geophysical equipment naturally has pride of place, but the Soufrière observatory also boasts a modern geochemistry laboratory. There are permanent fumaroles on the dome of La Soufrière, as well as a number of springs on the mountainside, and samples of emissions from all of these are taken three times a month, for analysis at the observatory. Any change in their chemical composition will be pounced on by the geochemists, who can also trace the cyclical variations linked to the rainy and dry seasons. In this field, too, it is important to be thoroughly familiar with the "background noise," so as to take it into account when

necessary and not confuse normal variations with the changes caused by a volcanic event.

The third French volcanological observatory is located on Piton de la Fournaise, on the island of Réunion. After the Dolomieu Crater appeared in 1930 (no doubt due to the major flows of 1927 and 1929), and drawing on his close study of the volcano, Alfred Lacroix recommended in 1936 that a volcanological observatory should be built on Réunion; but it was more than 40 years before his recommendation was acted on. As noted above, it was the partial destruction of the village of Sainte-Rose in the eruption of 1977 that mobilized public opinion and enabled INSU, the CNRS, and the IPGP to raise the money required to build the observatory. Land was provided by the national weather service at Bourg-Murat, 15 kilometers (9 miles) from the volcano, in the center of the island. Construction of the observatory itself was com-

pleted in 1979, and the following year enough of the seismic network was operational to give warning of the 1981 eruptions.

These were frequent, and gave impetus to the rapid expansion of the observatory. By 1992, the IPGP regarded the volcano as a most useful research tool, and in that year it was designated a "laboratory volcano" by the European Commission's Volcano Risks Programme.

Intense scientific and technical activity is still carried on there, involving a great deal of international collaboration, and it is now an extremely well-equipped observatory, with a dense network of nearly 140 geophysical outstations. Half of these constitute a permanent network, continuously relaying data to the observatory itself, and the other half are devoted to specific research programs, their data being stored on site for later collection. These were intended to be temporary, but here as at many observatories the temporary became permanent, for what researcher will ever give up the prospect of gathering data on one more event? Especially when it is always the next event that will be the finest yet, and yield the fullest information.

Anybody familiar with Piton de la Fournaise will readily appreciate how much work the observatory staff must put in, just to maintain such a battery of apparatus – quite apart from coping with the

hurricanes, and the long and exhausting treks over "graton," the ribbed lava that makes getting around so difficult.

The other two French observatories, in Djibouti and the Comoros islands, are operated jointly with local research institutes. The Comoros observatory is concerned with Karthala, the volcano towering over the town of Moroni, some of whose more modern buildings are actually built on lava flows dating from the early 20th century. The last flow, in 1977, destroyed a whole village, and the volcano therefore poses a very real danger. This observatory already has a highly efficient seismic network, and other instruments are gradually being installed.

In Djibouti, the main task for the observatory is to study the region's seismic activity as the Carlsberg Ridge gradually spreads across the African continent; in addition, fundamental research is being carried out on the ridge itself. This is a desert region, so any volcanic eruptions that take place here, though interesting from the point of view of research, do not constitute a hazard to human life. The most recent eruption occurred in 1978.

Earthquakes, on the other hand, are a danger that cannot be ignored, and moderate-sized ones (registering between 5 and 6 on the Richter scale) have caused a great deal of damage in the past, especially those of 1961 and 1973. ∎

volcanologists Maurice and Katia Krafft and Harry Glicken), there were no fatalities, although severe damage was caused.

While the watch maintained by scientists in their observatories can and does assist the civil authorities in taking the appropriate steps to prevent loss of human life, in most cases it does little for the protection of land and property.

In recent decades, several countries have passed laws requiring compensation to be paid for losses due to natural disasters: France, for instance, made such a law in 1982, and in its first seven years over 25 billion francs (about $3.8 billion) were paid out in insurance. Hardly any of this compensation was on account of volcanic disasters, although the Saint-Philippe area on Réunion did suffer some damage in the 1986 eruption of Piton de la Fournaise.

Of course, the populations and economies of poorer countries are far more exposed to natural disasters than those of wealthier nations, which can afford to take preventive measures against certain kinds of catastrophe, for instance by imposing earthquake-resistant building regulations. Realizing this, the United Nations General Assembly passed a resolution proclaiming the decade starting on January 1, 1990, the International Decade for Natural Disaster Reduction.

The stated aim of this resolution was "to reduce through concerted international action, especially in developing countries, the loss of life, property damage, and social and economic disruption caused by natural disasters, such as earthquakes, windstorms, tsunamis, floods, landslides, volcanic eruption, ... and other calamities of natural origin."

Volcanological observatories have a crucial role to play in this endeavor, as an indispensable tool for reducing the risk from volcanic hazards. ∎

THE TECHNIQUES OF VOLCANO SURVEILLANCE AND ERUPTION FORECASTING

The monitoring of a volcano is founded on close geophysical and geochemical analysis of the phenomena associated with eruptions. As fresh magma arrives in a magma chamber, pressure builds up: the pressure of the rising magma itself combines with that of the gases bubbling out of it. This rise in pressure can be enough to force the mountain out of shape: parts of it, or the whole structure, may bulge and deform. Suitable detectors can record the resulting changes in ground profiles. Stresses in the rock caused by the increased pressure can split it in the direction of least lithostatic pressure, which is upward: this fracturing produces small earth tremors which can also be picked up by dedicated detectors. The formation of fissures leads to local decompression, and the magmatic gases then move toward the surface, contaminating the groundwater in aquifers within the rock. Consequent changes in the chemical composition of fumaroles and hot springs can be analyzed. The pressure gradients, or rather the resulting movements of fluid material, cause electrical changes that modify the local magnetic field, and there are devices to record these too.

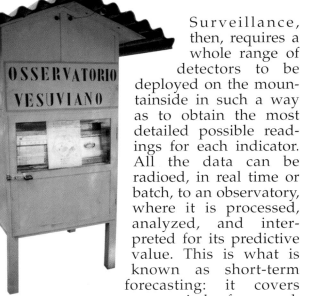

One of the tasks of the Vesuvius observatory near Naples, the first ever volcanological observatory in the world, is constantly monitoring the temperature of the fumaroles in the Solfatara Crater (Phlegrean Fields) at Pozzuoli.

Surveillance, then, requires a whole range of detectors to be deployed on the mountainside in such a way as to obtain the most detailed possible readings for each indicator. All the data can be radioed, in real time or batch, to an observatory, where it is processed, analyzed, and interpreted for its predictive value. This is what is known as short-term forecasting: it covers periods of one week to several months, or at the most a year. To read the information correctly necessitates a thorough understanding of the mechanisms involved in eruption, and that presupposes fundamental research. All the information accumulated by volcano observatories – particularly the Hawaiian one – since they were founded has contributed a great deal to improving basic understanding, which in turn has made it possible to develop better surveillance networks. Surveillance and research are thus interdependent, each supporting the other.

The short-term forecasts arising from geophysical and geochemical surveillance provide the basis for timely warnings to the authorities. In the case of effusive basaltic volcanoes, these predictions give fairly accurate answers to the questions Where, When, and How; but when it comes to the more dangerous explosive volcanoes, the answers are much less clear.

Once the warning signs have been detected, the volcano may be regarded as entering into an active phase, and the crisis can be monitored as it develops: when the various readings diverge from the norm as much as those registered in earlier similar eruptions, it can be said with some confidence that a major event is due in the near future – but then again, it may not happen at all! For example, intense seismic activity and ground swellings of up to 2 meters (6.5 feet) were recorded at the calderas in the Phlegrean Fields near Naples between 1980 and 1984, in Long Valley in the western USA during the same years, and again on Rabaul in Papua New Guinea between 1983 and 1985 – yet these crises all passed without an eruption.

If risks are to be reduced, it is essential to be able to answer the questions How will it happen? What kind of eruption will it be? What will its intensity be? What hazards will it present to the population? To answer those questions, fundamental research in specific fields is needed: studies of recent eruptions, reconstructions of ancient ones, modeling, and what-if simulations. The aim of such studies must be to compile a risk-evaluation map, and to draw up emergency plans on the basis of it. In terms of civil defense, this is what is referred to as "general" or "long-term" forecasting.

Seismic surveillance networks

Before El Chichón erupted in March 1982, the geophysicists of the National Geophysical Institute of Mexico already had records, going back almost a year, from a seismic network set up to monitor a dam some 80 kilometers (50 miles) from the volcano. Analysis of these records showed straight away that the focus of many of the shocks was located some distance from the dam, right under El Chichón. Most volcanic eruptions are preceded by seismic crises, and this one was no exception. In fact, fewer than 5% of eruptions have no attendant seismic activity – but not every seismovolcanic crisis results in an eruption.

The first time-recording seismograph was invented, and set up on Vesuvius, by Luigi Palmieri in 1855; soon afterward, he became the director of the observatory there. He was the first to detect volcanic earth shocks in this way,

Some seismic measurements are made by fixed stations; other equipment is portable and can be set up as required, like this seismograph being placed on Kilauea in Hawaii by an American geophysicist.

and with this equipment he was able to study the 1871–72 eruption of Vesuvius in a way never done before. A seismograph consists of a combined detector and recorder, and this is how the older apparatus was constructed. Modern instruments usually have separate detectors and are known as seismometers. Most seismometers used in volcanological observatories consist of a heavy weight suspended so that it can oscillate around a horizontal or vertical axis. This is held in a frame rigidly fixed to the ground: if the ground moves suddenly, so does the frame. Seismometers can detect both horizontal shocks (registering movement in two directions at right angles to one another) and vertical ones, so they produce a three-dimensional record of all ground movements.

The Quervain–Piccard seismograph, installed at the Morne des Cadets observatory following the 1929 eruption of Mount Pelée, consisted of a 20-tonne weight linked to a recording pen. This wrote to a drum that was fixed relative to the ground and wrapped in a smoke-blackened sheet of paper. As the drum turned, the pen traced a line

Setting up a seismic measuring station in the Comoros. The IPGP is working on such projects in collaboration with the Comoros government.

They look charmingly antique nowadays, but seismographs like this, which make a trace on a smoke-blackened sheet, can still be found working here and there.

known as a seismogram. Nowadays, the "weight" in a seismometer consists of a magnet suspended on springs and enclosed by a coil in rigid contact with the frame, which in turn is fixed to the ground. Ground movements thus produce an electrical current which is recorded either graphically or digitally – but the Mount Pelée instrument is a magnificent museum piece!

A seismic network for volcano surveillance consists, then, of seismometers deployed at suitable sites all over the terrain. When choosing the sites for seismic stations, their location around the volcano, the nature of the ground (sound rock rather than ashy rubble, so as to get a good response to any movements caused by a seismic shock), and the need to transmit the data must be taken into account. The number of such stations in a network varies: Piton de la Fournaise on Réunion currently has seventeen permanent stations, while Vesuvius has fifteen and the Hawaiian volcanoes between them have a total of fifty-one. Extra stations can be added temporarily if required.

Each station consists of a seismometer linked to a radio transmitter and antenna by

means of an electronic converter. Power is supplied by one or two solar panels, with a battery for buffer storage. The signals are radioed continuously to the observatory, where they are received, decoded, and analyzed. Depending on the sophistication of the equipment, the focus of each shock (in space and time) may be calculated either on or off line. In this way, changes in seismic activity can be followed over time, and its focus tracked upward as the magma rises: thus its time of possible arrival at the surface can be estimated.

Most eruptions are preceded by one or more seismic episodes featuring "seismic swarms." Each episode is separated from the others by periods of inactivity which vary greatly in length, from a few hours to several weeks. The number of shocks recorded also varies from one episode to another, and from volcano to volcano: it may be as low as a few dozen, or as high as several thousand.

There is no norm, then, and what is more, the shocks produced by internal cracking can be overlaid by another form of activity: low-frequency tremors. The cause of these tremors is not yet entirely clear, but the general view is that they are due to vibrations set up by movement in the magma and/or the resonating of gases in the channels. Before an eruption at Mauna Loa or Kilauea in Hawaii, tremors are usually recorded coming from a depth of several kilometers, but no such tremors occur at Piton de la Fournaise on Réunion. However, at the instant the magma arrives at the surface, tremors like these are recorded on virtually every volcano equipped with seismometers. So seismic networks allow volca-

nologists to hear, if not see, what is going on inside a volcano: they act as a sort of stethoscope. This is why seismology has long been regarded as the queen of the sciences so far as volcano surveillance is concerned. Indeed, on many volcanoes this is the only form of surveillance, and there is just a single seismic station that functions as a simple alarm.

A stethoscope enables doctors to make a limited number of diagnoses, but for many others they need access to other investigative techniques, including some that are still being developed. It is the same in volcanology: volcanologists have to take account of ground deformation, variations in the magnetic field, changes in the geochemistry of fluids, and so on.

Ground deformation surveillance networks

It is reasonable to assume that greatly increased pressure in magma chambers inside a volcanic structure, as well as movements of the magma itself, will cause the volcano, or parts of it, to change shape, and that this deformation will take the form of swelling.

Likewise, some kind of subsidence seems likely after an eruption: a sort of partial or total deflation. After the rapid expulsion of a large quantity of magma, in fact, the ground may be expected to collapse, and this is what happens when calderas are formed (see pages 110–13).

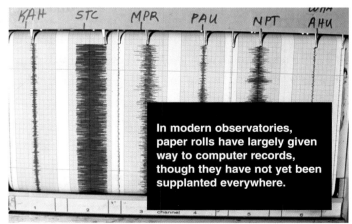

In modern observatories, paper rolls have largely given way to computer records, though they have not yet been supplanted everywhere.

SEISMIC ACTIVITY WARNS OF THE 1991 ERUPTION OF MOUNT UNZEN IN JAPAN

Mount Unzen, on the island of Kyushu in the far southwest of Japan, is part of the volcanic island-arc structure created (to simplify a little) by the subduction of the Pacific plate. The lava produced is known as dacite. Rich in silica (around 65%) and volatile components, it is very pasty. The volcano had erupted twice in historical times: in 1663 and again in 1792, when the eruption was followed by a landslide which caused a tsunami, killing 15,000 people in the Shimabara region. The catastrophe had not been forgotten, and a seismic surveillance network had been set up on the volcano, with stations forming a ring right round it.

In November 1989, a seismic episode began in the Bay of Chijiwa, at the western foot of the mountain. The earth shocks moved further and further east, and in July 1990 there was seismic activity directly underneath Mount Unzen; at the same time, the first tremors were recorded. Between August and early November, the network picked up larger and larger seismic shocks, and more and more tremors. The Japanese volcanologists were expecting an eruption, and the first phreatic eruptions (steam explosions throwing out pulverized rock) took place at the summit on November 17, forming two craters. After a lull during December, seismic activity picked up again in January 1991, and new fields of fumaroles appeared. There was also another major phreatic explosion on February 12, which formed a third crater. Fairly minor eruptions continued until March 29, growing more violent as the month went by. In mid-May, a marked increase in the strength of the seismic shocks and tremors under the volcano was recorded, and lahars swept down the bed of the River Mizunashi. On May 20, the first lava dome appeared on the summit, in the Jigokuato Crater; seismic activity intensified as it grew, a pattern that was to be repeated with the later domes. This first dome rapidly outgrew the crater and collapsed down the eastern slope in a succession of small pyroclastic flows.

On May 26, one of these flows traveled a distance of 2.5 kilometers (1.6 miles) from the crater. The lava continued to spill out of the crater, and on June 3 a larger pyroclastic flow, extending over 4 kilometers (2.5 miles), killed forty-three people, including the volcanologists Maurice and Katia Krafft and Harry Glicken. On June 8 there was another flow 5.5 kilometers (3.4 miles) long. The next day a new dome formed on the edge of the first, leading to further pyroclastic flows. There was a succession of eleven domes and flow domes in all, continuing until 1994, during which time the caldera at the mountain's summit filled with lava. Pyroclastic flows, which at first had been confined to the eastern side, subsequently swept down the north and south slopes: the whole mountainside was eventually covered by hundreds of flows. In mid-1994, the growth of the eleventh dome slowed dramatically, and one year  *later all surface activity had ceased, though dozens of seismic shocks and tremors were still being recorded each month. Four and a half years had elapsed between the first surface events and the last.*

As soon as the first tremors were recorded in July 1990, surveillance of Mount Unzen was stepped up, and immediately after the first phreatic explosion a committee was formed to manage the surveillance program and recommend measures to protect the inhabitants of the volcano's eastern and southeastern slopes. In February 1991, a plan to evacuate 16,000 people was drawn up, and this was implemented in stages: all the inhabitants of the high-risk zone were evacuated as soon as the first lahars occurred, between May 15 and June 7, and the last evacuation took place just one day before the biggest pyroclastic flow. On June 11, a dome explosion hurled pumice as far as the town of Shimabara, and the towns-people were advised to stay indoors. On June 17, following another major explosion, the town of Obama, more than 9 kilometers (5.6 miles) to the southwest, was covered with ash. In the entire course of the eruption, fewer than fifty people were killed, thanks to the precautions taken. However, hundreds of houses were destroyed and many square kilometers of crops ravaged; what is more, thousands of people were displaced and unable to return to their homes for many years.

As a volcano inflates, its sides become steeper, fissures appear, craters grow larger, and in some cases – especially on acid lava volcanoes (andesitic and dacitic) – there will be visible swellings. Early in the 20th century, the Japanese volcanologist F. Omori was the first to measure the deformations that appeared on the sides of volcanoes before eruptions and to correlate these with seismic crises. There have been two particularly famous instances of such swellings on mountains: one at Usu on Hokkaido (Japan's northern island), which inflated by 150 meters (500 feet) before the 1910 eruption, and one at Mount Saint Helens (USA), which measured nearly 200 meters (650 feet) when the eruption came in May 1980. As a rule, such bulges or

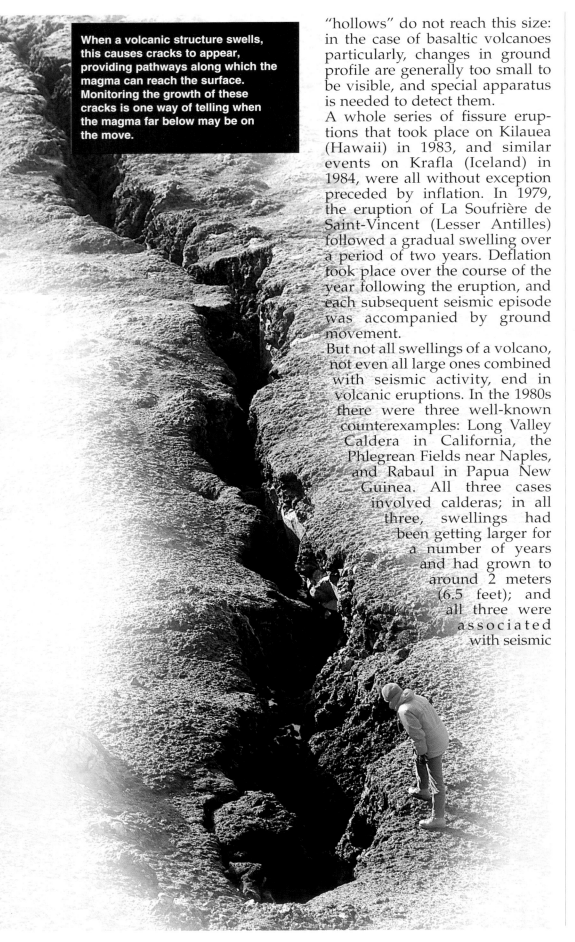

When a volcanic structure swells, this causes cracks to appear, providing pathways along which the magma can reach the surface. Monitoring the growth of these cracks is one way of telling when the magma far below may be on the move.

"hollows" do not reach this size: in the case of basaltic volcanoes particularly, changes in ground profile are generally too small to be visible, and special apparatus is needed to detect them.

A whole series of fissure eruptions that took place on Kilauea (Hawaii) in 1983, and similar events on Krafla (Iceland) in 1984, were all without exception preceded by inflation. In 1979, the eruption of La Soufrière de Saint-Vincent (Lesser Antilles) followed a gradual swelling over a period of two years. Deflation took place over the course of the year following the eruption, and each subsequent seismic episode was accompanied by ground movement.

But not all swellings of a volcano, not even all large ones combined with seismic activity, end in volcanic eruptions. In the 1980s there were three well-known counterexamples: Long Valley Caldera in California, the Phlegrean Fields near Naples, and Rabaul in Papua New Guinea. All three cases involved calderas; in all three, swellings had been getting larger for a number of years and had grown to around 2 meters (6.5 feet); and all three were associated with seismic activity. Evacuation plans were made, and the Italian town of Pozzuoli was in fact evacuated as a precaution: a number of houses had been cracked by earth movements and quakes, and there were fears of an eruption on the scale of Monte Nuovo in 1538. Apparently, other movements in the past had already altered the depth of the Pozzuoli caldera, or so it appeared from traces left by marine animals on the pillars of the famous temple of Serapis. These had long been attributed to changes in sea level; it now turned out that they were due, rather, to changes in ground level! But none of these developments was immediately followed by a volcanic eruption.

In the 1950s, the Japanese geophysicist K. Mogi developed some theoretical models of volcano deformation based on what was known at the time. He postulated a magma chamber of a given shape, volume, and depth within the volcano, and made certain assumptions about the pressures that would be operating on the walls of such a chamber. He then calculated the consequences of changes in pressure on the sides of the volcano in question. However, his calculations did not always match the observed facts very closely.

Of course, every volcano has its peculiarities: it is not possible to make a model that fits them all perfectly, and exactly what is happening on the ground needs to be established by measurement. But the great value of such models, those of Mogi and later, far more complicated ones developed with modern number-crunchers, is that they provide a general theoretical description of volcano deformation, which makes it possible to site tiltmeters and other instruments at the points where they are likely to register the most significant ground deformations.

It would be possible, in theory, to litter a mountainside with stations, so as to have the most complete picture possible of its deformation: but considerations of cost and practicality (maintenance requirements, for instance) make this unrealistic. So it is necessary to be selective and install a reasonable number of field stations.

Volcano deformation models, which by implication also model the movement of magma inside the mountain, are an essential element in predicting volcanic eruptions, and to build such models requires reliable sets of data. Deformation surveillance networks therefore carry out a whole range of measurements, each of which has its own theoretical basis and its own technical means of collection, to provide information about changes in the mountain's profile – on both the overall and the local scale. This is why we speak of "surveillance networks" rather than just one "surveillance network."

The networks that provide continuous measurement and real-time data transmission will be described first, as these are the most effective in surveillance, followed by brief descriptions of types of network that take one-off measurements (reiteration networks), and of the new technique of satellite-based deformation surveillance.

Tiltmeter networks

A network for measuring gradients comprises a number of stations (there are ten on Piton de la Fournaise, for instance), each of which has two tiltmeters: one in what is called the radial orientation (with its pendulum moving in a plane that passes through the summit of the volcano) and the other in the tangential orientation (at right angles to this). There are various types of tiltmeter: bubble tiltmeters (working on the same principle as a spirit level), water or other liquid tiltmeters (with two interconnected vessels), and pendulum ones.

THE ERUPTION OF PITON DE LA FOURNAISE ON APRIL 18, 1990

Activity giving advance warning of the eruption of April 18, 1990, was monitored as it happened by scientists at the Piton de la Fournaise observatory. If the weather had not been so bad, they might have been out there, watching, when the eruption itself began!

The eruption of Piton de la Fournaise (Réunion) on April 18, 1990, furnishes a textbook example of real-time data handling, which enabled the location of the erupting fissure to be predicted.

A fortnight before the eruption, the number of seismic shocks began to increase steadily. From fewer than ten events a day, more or less the usual "background noise," they rose to twenty or so, then to thirty. The seismic crisis proper began with forty shocks in twenty minutes, followed by continuous movement, shock after shock, lasting for thirty-four minutes. Tiltmeters sited near the summit reacted right at the start of this stage, registering alterations of 400 microradians. Stations elsewhere showed much smaller changes in gradient. Meanwhile, the observatory was tracking the seismic focus in real time, as well as processing all the information from the tiltmeter stations. Software specially designed by researchers at this observatory automatically collated all the distortion vectors to calculate where in the volcano the center of swelling was located. At the onset of the crisis, it was in the northeastern sector of the Dolomieu Crater. For the first fifteen minutes the swelling, caused by magma arriving near the surface, was fairly widespread; it then diminished overall, but became concentrated on a point in the southeast of the crater. For five minutes, observers watched on the screen as this focal point moved past the crater wall and away to the southeast. It was then soon lost, since the distortion was not large enough to be detectable outside the network.

What had happened? The most probable explanation was that an internal lateral fissure, or dike, had formed in one of the volcano's zones of weakness, and that the pressurized magma under the crater had drained into it: it was the movement of this magma that the observers had watched for several minutes on the computer monitor. As a result, the area where the surface fissure would open up could now be predicted. Three hours and seventeen minutes later, at 12:50 p.m., the ground split apart 4000 meters (13,000 feet) below the summit, and lava spurted out. If the weather that day had not been so appalling, they could have been right on the spot when the fissure appeared, ready to greet the lava as it erupted!

The fragility of this device makes a strange contrast with the forces unleashed by volcanoes. It is a pendulum tiltmeter, and can measure variations in the angle between the horizontal and the ground on which it is placed: the angle will change if the volcano is swelling, for instance under pressure of gases.

Iceland and France both use pendulum tiltmeters, though their equipment differs slightly, while other countries favor bubble tiltmeters; Japan uses both bubble and water types. The tiltmeter used in the French surveillance networks was invented and perfected by the French geophysicist P. A. Blum. It contains a horizontal pendulum consisting of a plate of silver suspended by two quartz threads, which oscillates around a near-vertical axis, its movements being damped by a magnetic field.

The detection system comprises an LED and a photoresistor: the voltage drop across the photo-resistor changes as a linear function of the position of the window through which the LED's light shines. In this way, the device records changes in the position of the pendulum caused by ground movements. It is of course linked to a GPS clock (see page 147). As in all field station equipment, electrical power is provided by solar cell arrays, with battery backup, and there is a system for transmitting the signals to the observatory.

These pieces of apparatus are extremely sensitive: they can detect variations of one micro-radian, which corresponds to a change in gradient of one milli-meter in one kilometer, or one inch in nearly sixteen miles. Point tiltmeters must be rigidly fixed to the ground, of course, and if their siting is unsuitable (for instance, if they are on unstable ground affected by the weather), the measurements will be meaning-less. The choice of site is therefore very important, and is made in strict accordance with geological criteria.

At the observatory, the tiltmeter signals are decoded and analyzed in real time. Radial and tangen-tial data (tilting in the direction of the mountain's slope and across it) are combined to give the orientation of the movement taking place at each point on the mountainside, as well as its extent in microradians: in this way, what is known as a defor-mation vector is calculated. Whether a movement affects only one tilt station or the whole network, it will be picked up immediately.

Stretched across a fissure on Piton de la Fournaise, this extensometer will register the slightest widening of the gap.

Extensometers, strainmeters, or fissurometers

All volcanoes, whether basaltic or andesitic, are riddled with fis-sures, ranging in size from a millimeter to many tens of meters across, caused by various kinds of eruption phenomena. When a volcano swells, not only do the gradients of its slopes change and new fissures appear, but the existing fissures can open further or close up. The movement of fissures is therefore a useful indicator of deformations con-nected with the rise of magma inside the volcanic structure. Measuring devices come in a number of different forms. One currently in use at some observa-tories works by electromagnetic induction: a stalk of quartz with a ferrite tip is fixed to one side of a crack, and coils mounted on another quartz stalk are attached to the other. When the sides move, the ferrite moves within the coils, inducing a voltage across them which is relayed to the observatory. The voltage varies in direct proportion to the movement, in other words the widening or narrowing of the gap across which the instrument is mounted.

This system is so sensitive that it can record changes in distance as small as a nanometer (40 billionths of an inch). However, it cannot be used for fissures more than a meter or so wide. To monitor larger cracks, wide-base extensometers or strainmeters have to be used. These typically function by measuring the tension over the length of an Invar rod which is strained between two pins set into the opposite sides of the crack. The device that records the measurement is incorporated into the unit, and measurements have to be taken manually – which is of course rather a disadvantage when a volcano has become active and the station is in a danger zone.

Automatic distancemeters

When a volcano is swelling, the distance between a given point on the volcano and a fixed external point will of course change. Optoelectronic (laser) distancemeters can measure distances of several kilometers with a precision of one unit per million (one millimeter in one kilometer). What they measure is the time taken by the laser beam to make the round trip between the device and a reflector sited at the chosen point on the mountain. By coupling a distancemeter with a motorized theodolite that is programmed to operate as required, it can be made to measure the distances between itself and a fairly large number of reflectors arrayed on the mountainside. Each reflector's coordinates are fed into the program, and as the laser beam passes through the theodolite's scope, the software seeks out each reflector in turn; when it detects the reflected beam, it takes several measurements over a period of a few seconds.

At Piton de la Fournaise, for instance, there are two automatic distancemeters, each with about ten reflectors in its field of view; half of these are common to both units. The combined data from the two devices gives a fairly complete picture of any swelling of the mountain that may be taking place. The measurements can also be transmitted to the observatory, providing a very powerful means of assessing the volcano's deformation under magma pressure.

Most observatories, however, have only one distancemeter, and measurements are taken manually from chosen sites around the volcano in turn, still by sighting the reflectors as described above. Depending on the volcano's activity type, the measurements may be repeated daily, weekly, or at longer intervals; this requires operators on the spot. Automatic or not, distancemeters need good visibility, because laser beams do not pass through cloud.

Satellite positioning

In the late 1970s, the US Department of Defense established a satellite navigation and positioning system known as GPS (Global Positioning System) that enables two facts to be known accurately and instantly at any point on the earth's surface: time and position. From these, velocity can also be calculated. The system now comprises 24 satellites located around the earth in orbits 20,000 kilometers (12,400 miles) up. Between four and eight satellites are visible from any point on the globe, and each satellite emits coded radio signals on two wavelengths, synchronized by highly stable atomic clocks. A purpose-built receiver or GPS set on the ground, equipped with a special antenna, receives these signals and performs the complex calculations needed to convert them into the precise, three-dimensional coordinates of the antenna itself: in other words, to give the set's position.

By applying a rather complicated relational or differential technique to the use of this system, measurements of relative ground movement can be taken that are precise to within a few millimeters. This is the most effective method of all for volcano surveillance, and theoretically a vast number of GPS sets could be dotted over the ground, transmitting their information to a processing center – but the cost of the sets, their high power consumption, and the difficulty of retrieving the information, are all factors that limit their number in practice.

However, this is without doubt the system of the future, and in view of the usefulness of the technique, volcanological observatory engineers are working hard to design a cheaper GPS set! The data collected is transmitted to the observatory, where it is collated with data from distancemeters, producing a combination of measurements that gives precise information about changes in the volcano's shape.

Gravimeters

Gravimeters are devices that measure the earth's gravitational field at a particular point. They are based on the principle of attraction between masses, and in essence consist of nothing more complicated than a spring balance, in which the spring extends as a result of movements of masses underground: simple in principle, but extremely complex to achieve in practice. At a given location, if nothing shifts or changes in the ground underneath, the gravity recorded will be constant; but any movement of magma within the volcano entails a transfer of mass, and since the hot mass of lava differs in density from the surrounding rocks, gravity as measured at that same location will change.

These gravity measurements are usually made at regular intervals at a number of predetermined points (see Reiterated measurement networks, page 150). At some observatories, however, readings are taken continuously, making it possible to trace the magma as it rises within the structure.

A gravimetric station consists of a recording gravimeter linked to a GPS set, since if the altitude changes the gravitational field measured will also change, and it would not otherwise be possible to dissociate this effect from the one being studied, the mass transfer. The GPS set makes it possible to compensate for this by reporting any change in the station's altitude, and a simple calculation gives the change in gravity that is due solely to the movement of magma. The station also incorporates circuitry for transmitting the data to the observatory.

Since recording gravimeters are costly items, just as GPS stations are, only a few of them can be deployed, and their siting has to follow careful studies of the terrain.

Magnetic field surveillance networks

The earth's magnetic field changes over time: this is quite normal, but these variations – as measured at the surface – are considerably distorted by the complex internal structure of volcanoes. Deep down, when the pressure of magma inside a chamber becomes excessive, stress variations are set up in the locality, and fissures form, large and small, through which gases circulate. All this activity gives rise to a series of processes which produce magnetic (sometimes known as volcanomagnetic) phenomena.

The magnetic orientation of the rocks may be altered by stress or heating, for example, or by ionized fluids circulating in cracks. These processes create what are known as induced magnetic fields. The magnetic field measured at the surface will be a composite of all these fields, including the magnetic field of the earth itself.

Preliminary studies are carried out in order to identify sites that have not yet been affected by other events, such as lightning strikes, and magnetic stations are then installed. Each station consists of a magnetometer (a kind of complex modern compass that registers the strength of the magnetic field) and associated circuitry for transmission of the data to the observatory.

The only measurements relevant to surveillance of the volcano are those of the volcanomagnetic field. To make it possible to strip out other components, another station is needed that lies outside the influence of the volcano-magnetic field: this is called the reference station. At the observatory, differences between the data received from each station and that from the reference station are recorded automatically. Both before and during an eruption, variations of up to 15 or 20 nanoteslas (the unit of magnetic flux density) are often recorded.

The processes involved are actually a little more complex, but this is a slightly simplified account of the way in which alterations in the magnetic field induced by eruption phenomena are isolated and monitored. At present, only the volcanoes in French territories, and a few in Japan and Italy, are equipped with magnetic surveillance networks as sophisticated as those described here.

Hydroacoustic surveillance networks

When lava and other fluids circulate, they cause vibrations; so do the minor earth shocks associated with small-scale fissuring (before the appearance of open cracks at the surface) in the neighborhood of magma chambers, and so does the propagation of dikes. All of these vibrations are quite muffled in the heterogeneous volcanic terrain, but much less so in a liquid medium. By placing very sensitive piezoelectric hydrophones in a crater lake, a well, or even a borehole filled with water, an excellent mechanical coupling is obtained between an acoustic transducer and the volcanic massif; sounds ranging from very low frequencies (0.1 hertz) up to ultrasonic ones (200 kHz) can be recorded by using this technique. A number of crater lakes are wired for sound in this way: Kelut in Indonesia is one of these, and Taal in the Philippines another. Similar installations are now being set up at Aoba in Vanuatu and elsewhere, and there was one at Ruapehu in New Zealand until 1995, when it was destroyed in an eruption.

In March 1994, a violent seismic crisis shook the volcano Taal, and there were major ground deformations. The island's four thousand inhabitants were evacuated as a precaution. In the event, no eruption took place, but the hydrophones in the crater lake had recorded ultrasound signals that began one month before the seismic events and then increased gradually in intensity. The signals were transmitted via the Argos satellite to the Manila volcanological observatory, and thence to Chambéry in France.

This is still a little-used technique, but it definitely has a promising future in volcano surveillance; it can be exploited wherever there are crater lakes or where suitably-placed boreholes can be drilled.

Disturbingly spider-like, perched on its long and slender metal legs, a magnetic field measurement station watches over the summit of Piton de la Fournaise.

Measuring devices placed in the fumaroles of Vulcano (Italy) are equipped with transmitters that radio the data directly to Pisa.

Geochemical surveillance networks

Magma is a bath of molten silicates containing dissolved gases and minerals. When the pressure of the magma is high enough to open or reopen fissures in the surrounding rock, the gases may reach the surface well before the magma itself, emerging either in existing fumarole fields or through the many small fissures or pores in the ground. This constitutes a diffuse release of gas. We do not at present have field geochemical detectors with low enough power consumption to undertake the continuous analysis of fumarole gases, but it is important, if data on geochemical changes in volcanic gases is to be compared with the simultaneously-collected data on geophysical changes, to have comparable sampling frequencies for both.

The most obvious thing to measure is the temperature of gases issuing from fumaroles or from groundwater springs that may have been heated by nearby magma; indeed, this is the oldest technique of all. Originally, measurements were taken at intervals, but temperatures are now recorded continuously, by means of thermometric probes placed in the fumaroles, crater lakes, or springs, or even in specially-drilled boreholes. The units incorporate circuitry to transmit the data to the observatory.

It all sounds simple, but in fact it is difficult to keep these probes functioning in environments which can be extremely hostile: in effect, they are often being asked to measure the temperature of neat acid at a minimum of 100°C (212°F) and often hundreds of degrees hotter than this. Corrosion presents enormous problems, and the equipment suffers badly, but the engineers are extremely skilled at keeping it working.

Radon surveillance networks

All volcanic rocks contain the isotope uranium-238. Basalts and andesites have one to two parts per million, and differentiated lavas contain higher proportions. Uranium is unstable and decays into a succession of other radioactive elements, including radium and its immediate derivative radon, before finally reaching a stable isotope of lead. The half-life of radon is 3.65 days; this means that every 3.65 days half the radon disappears by decay if it is not renewed from its "parent element" or precursor, which in this case is the radium contained in the magma. In principle, the magma inside a volcano will not contain any more radon than the lava that emerges above it, so long as both come from the same source; the consequence of this is that, if the magmatic gases take longer than a fortnight to reach the surface, what remains in them of the radon that was in the magma will by then be scarcely detectable.

So why do we measure radon? For four reasons: first, because being radioactive it is easy to measure with modern techniques; second, because it is everywhere in the ground; third, because water vapor and carbon dioxide escaping from the magma chamber bring it to the surface; and lastly because it is not possible with present-day techniques to take continuous measurements of the water vapor or carbon dioxide emissions themselves.

Some thirty years ago, Russian researchers demonstrated that the radon content of springs around the volcano Kirgurich, on the Kamchatka peninsula, increased before an eruption. For many years, scientists paid little attention to the potential of this method in the context of predicting volcanic eruptions, but a few teams in the Soviet Union made use of it, employing techniques that were simple enough in principle but fairly laborious in practice: a film sensitive to alpha particles, which are emitted by radon, was placed in the ground, and taken up and replaced every fortnight. When developed, this film was processed so that the number of alpha particle traces in a given surface area could be counted. This was an intermittent system of recording which measured the quantity of radon that had accumulated over a fortnight, a long period of time; it was nowhere near providing a method of real-time forecasting. It was, though, an extremely useful way of researching and validating the method itself.

Not until the early 1990s did the technology advance sufficiently to make available probes capable of monitoring radon continuously. These consist of a silicon diode that converts an arriving alpha particle into an electrical pulse which then goes through various stages of electronic amplification. The number of such pulses in a unit time (the choice of unit ranging from minutes to hours, depending on the degree of activity) is written to memory. At the end of a counting cycle, the memory's contents are transmitted to the observatory. The terrain has to be studied before sites for the probes are chosen: zones of maximum radon and carbon dioxide emission are sought out during periods of inactivity, and when the siting has been determined, the probe is sunk about one meter (40 inches) deep, in a plastic tube. These probes have peripheral equipment (solar panels and battery) similar to that of the geophysical field stations.

The finest ever example of a "radon peak" was recorded five days before the 1994 phreatic eruption of Irazú in Costa Rica. At Piton de la Fournaise in 1991, two stations also registered a peak four days before lava forced its way into a fracture. The radon/alpha particle count was between one thousand and one million times the "background level" for that location. Just as with other surveillance methods, the background level must be properly established in advance, and in this case it can be affected by atmospheric pressure, rainfall, storms, and so on.

Radon surveillance stations are relatively cheap, so a fairly large number of detectors can be deployed where the terrain is suitable. This not only gives a good overall picture of diffuse gas release, but also makes individual events easier to detect. A radon "surge" may not be uniform all over the mountain, and could be localized where the magma is moving, so it is important to be in the right place at the right time.

Reiterated measurement networks

All the types of network described above record data continuously and transmit it to the observatory either continuously or in frequeuent small batches. Reiterated measurement networks are quite different. Not long ago, all measurements carried out in the course of volcano surveillance used a reiterative procedure, because there was no alternative. Even now, not every observatory has the resources to install all the automatic networks described

here, and since in any case some measurements still have to be taken manually, reiteration networks remain with us today. There are two types: geophysical and geochemical.

Geophysical networks consist of markers (usually steel or brass bolts) set into the rock at sites chosen for their mechanical stability. All these sites together make up a network, or route. To measure ground deformation, for instance, each marker is precision leveled. The traditional surveying instruments are used: theodolite and leveling staff. Working from a reference point, two operators measure differences in level from one site to the next. Depending on the apparatus and methods used, and the skill of the operators, the precision of measurement can vary from one unit in a million to one in a hundred thousand. The measurements can be repeated as often as necessary, revealing the deformation that has taken place since the last survey, but since they are time-consuming and require specialist operators they are generally only carried out once or twice a year.

Measurements of magnetic field and gravity are similarly taken at each site in turn, once or twice a year during quiet periods and more frequently during periods of activity. In the case of gravimetry, the same sites are generally used as for altitude surveying, and if possible both sets of measurements are taken at the same time, so that precise corrections for any changes in altitude are available. Almost every volcano under surveillance has been marked out with "survey crosses," consisting of four points arranged around a fifth central one; from the center, using a theodolite and with leveling staffs at the ends of each branch of the cross, differences in level are measured over a distance of roughly 20 meters (22 yards). This creates a kind of tiltmeter which can reveal changes in gradient over fairly

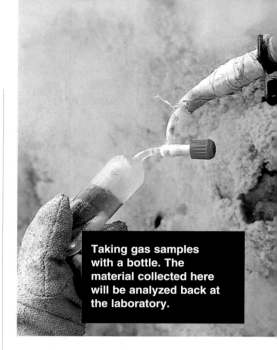

Taking gas samples with a bottle. The material collected here will be analyzed back at the laboratory.

long stretches of slope. During an eruption episode, the observatory staff wear themselves out running from one cross to another, trying to keep up with the swelling of the mountain! There are other methods, though they are less often used; volcano surveillance is a discipline rich in analytical techniques.

In geochemical surveillance, reiterated measurement (or sample-taking) is the norm, indeed universal apart from the radon networks. It has been explained that magma is a bath of molten silicates containing dissolved magmatic gases; how soluble these are depends on the gas in question and on the pressure in the magma. As magma rises and fissures open up at the top of the magma chamber, there is a gradual drop in pressure, and this decompression causes different gases to be released at different stages. This in turn leads to changes in the chemical composition of the gases issuing from fumaroles at the surface.

As these volatile substances (mainly carbon dioxide, hydrogen sulfide, hydrogen chloride, and alkaline halides) make their way through water-bearing layers above the magma, they contaminate the water. Geochemical surveillance is based on the regular analysis of fumaroles (where they are permanent) and the analysis of springs in the volcano's immediate neighborhood. Samples are taken from these at intervals that range from once to several times per month, depending on how active the volcano is. The samples are analyzed in the laboratory using traditional chemical techniques. Water vapor is of course the main ingredient of these volatile mixtures, often accounting for over 90%. Only some of this water comes from the magma itself: most of it is water that has filtered into the ground and then been driven upward again on contact with the magma.

Temperature variations at fumaroles and springs are also an extremely important indicator: obviously, if magmatic gases are arriving at the surface from deep down, where their temperature may have been around 1000°C (1850°F), the temperature of the fumaroles and springs is going to rise. Frequent temperature readings are therefore taken. Correlation spectrometers can also be used to measure the rate of sulfur dioxide emission at volcano craters. By analyzing all these indicators together, the volcano's activity can be monitored in detail.

Reconstructions of past eruption events

It has been seen that volcanoes that were once thought totally extinct, because not enough was known of their history, can unexpectedly return to life. This is why, in the case of a volcano that might prove dangerous, it is so important to have some idea – even a hazy one – of how long its earlier quiescent phases lasted. For volcanoes liable to explode, it is also vital to know what their most common eruption types have been, so that the likeliest scenarios in the event of renewed activity can be predicted: will there be pyroclastic flows, Plinian eruptions, dome formation with or without these forms of eruption ensuing, and what other warning signs will there be before a major explosion? To this end, geologists are painstakingly compiling volcanological maps, a task that involves laborious fieldwork followed by equally time-consuming laboratory work.

In order to assign a period to ancient eruptive events, existing rock formations have to be dated. There are many ways of doing this, the most frequently used being the so-called "carbon-14" dating method. In living plant tissue, the ratio between carbon-12 and carbon-14 isotopes is the same as that in the carbon component of atmospheric carbon dioxide. But carbon-12 is stable, while carbon-14 is radioactive and has a known half-life. When a tree is engulfed by a lava flow, its carbon-14 content will decrease by decay, at a fixed rate, from that moment on. Measurement of the amount of carbon-14 left in its remains (charcoal, for instance) will tell us when it died.

Finding material suitable for these dating studies requires a great deal of patience on the part of field volcanologists – and a bit of luck. It can take years of work to piece together just the last 20,000 or 30,000 years of a volcano's history, which is the period we can study by this method.

The most impressive recent reconstruction of a volcano's eruption history was the work done on Mount Saint Helens in the United States. In 1978, the US volcanologists Crandell and Mullineaux published the results of years of study on the mountain. They gathered information going back over the last five thousand years, and concluded that, in view of the pattern of eruption recurrence, Mount Saint Helens could be expected to erupt "within the next hundred years, and perhaps even before the end of this [20th] century." In fact the mountain blew on May 18, 1980: not bad for a long-term forecast!

When the first phreatic explosion took place at La Soufrière on Guadeloupe in 1976, nothing was known of the volcano's pre-Columbian history, but studies subsequently carried out by volcanologists from the Paris Institute for Global Geophysics, and from the Universities of Clermont-Ferrand and Grenoble, have made it possible to reconstruct La Soufrière's last major magma event, and to date it – to around 1440. We are gradually coming to know more of this volcano's story, though there is still much to be done. Because so many separate scientific

On remote volcanoes like Erta Ale in Ethiopia, continuous measurement is not possible, but the samples taken intermittently on expeditions to the volcano enhance our understanding of it.

disciplines are involved – geophysics, geochemistry, and geology, among others – volcanological observatories need to have specialists in many different fields among their staff, and individual team members require both skill and dedication, not to mention being fit enough to cope with difficult terrain, often in appalling weather.

Surveillance of a volcano entails getting as close as possible to its craters. Many advance posts for volcanological observatories, like this one on Sakurajima in Japan, are housed underground – an essential precaution for the protection of both staff and equipment.

Prospects for the future of surveillance

Volcanologists have made an all-out effort to achieve the objectives of the UN International Decade for Natural Disaster Reduction: to develop understanding of eruption mechanisms, since surveillance is only effective if the phenomena observed are understood, to develop surveillance techniques, and to transfer knowledge to developing countries. As we move into a new century, we can expect volcano surveillance to benefit from technical progress in four directions. Field networks will be increasingly automated, so as to gather continuous data on each of the relevant indicators. Emergency mobile networks will be set up internationally, to respond as needs arise. New devices for gathering geophysical and geochemical data will be designed and, lastly, satellite surveillance methods will be developed further.

In order to provide effective surveillance and make a rapid response when eruption activity begins, highly automated networks are needed on all the volcanoes that pose a threat to human populations; unfortunately, these are not yet in place everywhere. Automation would require a sufficiently large number of stations continuously recording and transmitting the data to observatories, where it could be processed automatically and presented in a user-friendly way. In the event of a crisis, a composite picture of all the indicators would then be available, making initial assessment of the events much easier.

To make this possible, what are known as "smart stations" would be needed, part-processing the data and forwarding it in the most efficient way, either by radio (with stations acting as relays for each other where necessary) or by telephone. Observatories would have dedicated mobile telephone networks, with two-way communication between the observatory and its stations supporting discretionary polling and even the remote maintenance of equipment.

In the observatories themselves, the development of software to handle the incoming data automatically is essential. Not all observatories will be able to do all their processing on site, so Internet links will be needed for effective collaboration between centers. This is one of the aims of the International Association of Volcanology and Chemistry of the Earth's Interior.

But some countries with a large number of dangerous volcanoes do not have the necessary resources in either people or equipment, and many volcanoes are equipped with nothing more than a simple alarm system. This is why the development of mobile networks is one of the objectives of the international community of volcano scientists. Until recently, there was only one such network in existence, belonging to the US Geological Service, but European volcanologists are also working toward the establishment of an effective emergency network.

The modernization of existing surveillance networks and the setting up of mobile ones both go hand in hand with a third technological development: the designing of new field stations, including new types of detectors. One recent initiative aims to devise a single station capable of collecting and transmitting information about both seismic activity and ground deformation.

The essence of emergency intervention is rapid deployment. Because these mobile units will always be activated at a time of pre-eruption crisis, the stations must be light as well as smart, which presents the engineers with a challenge: the technology currently exists to achieve this, but it is their task to apply it.

A weak point of current surveillance networks is their power supply. The instruments cannot work without power, even though they use only small amounts. Almost all field stations are powered by solar panels, with battery storage to cater for cloudy periods, but if an eruption should commence with major phreatic explosions generating large amounts of ash fallout, it could coat the panels with ash, rendering the networks blind, or dumb, or both.

To deal with this eventuality, at least so far as volcano deformation surveillance is concerned, a European program is developing an all-weather radar imaging system that will work over reasonable distances. This will give a relief picture of a volcano's slopes, either by using a large number of metal targets placed around the mountain in advance, or by imaging the rocks directly. The precision aimed at is something approaching one centimeter in ten kilometers (an inch in nearly sixteen miles). At the very least, such a system would make it possible to monitor the swelling of a volcano, which is an extremely important factor in the eruptive mechanism of explosive volcanoes.

Of course, satellites are the obvious answer to observing the earth and all the natural phenomena on its surface. Various types of satellite image have been available for many years now, and the use of these has improved volcanological mapping, helped scientists to work out the eruption patterns of some volcanoes, and enabled temperature variations on volcanoes to be tracked from year to year. Best of all, satellite images make it possible to follow the spread of eruption plumes and clouds, as well as to determine their composition. We have already seen how vital this can be for safeguarding air traffic.

Satellites are also used for communications – but this idea is not a new one. More novel is the way the Argos satellite is used: it collects data as it passes over a volcano and transmits it to a processing center. The interpreted data is then sent back to the local area. This procedure could be of enormous value to a country which does not have the resources to maintain permanent observatories: it makes surveillance feasible by means of detectors on the mountain combined with Argos transmitting sets, and the results are returned after an interval of one to several days, depending on the setup. However, the cost of implementing such systems is still considerable. One very promising satellite system is Synthetic Aperture

It is vital to be able to receive data from apparatus permanently installed near the craters. Speed is the essence of risk reduction, and the most widely-used means of rapid transmission is radio. Power is supplied by the sun, with standby batteries. The device shown here is sited high up on Piton de la Fournaise.

Radar (SAR), which uses differential radar interferometry. Devices of this sort were at first mounted on aircraft, for the study of local danger points, but now the system has been installed on satellites. Very precise, high-resolution radar images are taken of the chosen target each time the satellite passes overhead, and the processing of successive images produces a topographical map which reveals any changes during the intervening period. If a volcano is swelling between one pass and the next, its progress can be followed with minute precision.

In spite of software advances, however, image processing is still slow, and it is not entirely automated even today. Moreover, what images can be obtained depends on the satellites' orbits and how frequently they pass over the volcano in question. At present, because of the polar orbits of observation satellites, only one or two pictures can be taken every month, so this technique can only contribute to the more long-term forecasts: we are still a long way from real-time prediction.

Another difficulty is presented by the fact that, even though satellite images can be acquired in all weathers, they are affected by the nature of the ground, and even more by vegetation. This can be a serious obstacle in tropical and temperate regions, where it is not easy to get a good image. All the same, techniques are developing so quickly in this field that there is no doubt the present century will see satellite surveillance being applied very effectively – and we can also be confident that some completely new methods will emerge. ∎

CONCLUSION

Volcanoes: a source of life, or the Source of Life?
The release of gases from within the earth, which is what originally created the atmosphere and the oceans, takes place via volcanoes: they are the exhaust pipes of the planet. The process is still going on, though feebly enough by comparison with the rate when the earth, now aged four and a half billion years, was only a few hundred million years old. Were volcanoes responsible for the emergence of life on earth? This question takes us into the realm of speculation, but why shouldn't volcanologists speculate? No volcanoes, no atmosphere, no water, no life!

Along the mid-ocean ridge, where the ocean floor is continually being renewed, there are black smokers and white smokers, hydrothermal vents in whose fluids bacteria live, surviving at over 200°C (400°F): these are thermophilic archeo-bacteria. Similar bacteria have been found in fumaroles and in the eruption gases of the hot-spot volcano MacDonald in the extreme southeast of Australasia. The bacteria in hydrothermal vents live by chemosynthesis: they synthesize the organic molecules they require, not by using energy from sunlight, as all other living creatures do directly or indirectly, but by exploiting energy from the chemical reduction of the metallic sulfides that issue from these smokers. On them a whole food chain depends, flourishing within a radius of a few meters around these sources: an oasis of highly distinctive marine life, whose workings are still imperfectly understood.

More prosaically, the ash thrown out by explosive volcanoes becomes, in areas where water is available, the most remarkable natural fertilizer. In humid tropical areas, it is not unusual to find farmers gathering two or even three harvests a year; no wonder, then, that people remain attached to their rich land and the homes of their ancestors, in defiance of the danger.

Volcanoes under surveillance
Yet volcanoes can be fearsome killers, if not kept under surveillance: they can cause real tragedies, and have proved it time and again. The people living on their slopes often have no other place to go, nor any other option than to put their trust in their protecting deities, and make offerings in hopes of appeasing the wrathful ones. For many, "science" is something amorphous, incomprehensible, and inaccessible.

Scientists therefore have a dual role: investigative, but also educational so far as the rest of the population is concerned. When it comes to surveillance and disaster prevention, there are two approaches available to them and to the civil authorities. The first is to keep watch on volcanoes so that eruptions can be predicted and people who are clearly at serious risk can be evacuated before it is too late. Surveillance and forecasting are inextricably linked to fundamental research on how volcanic eruptions come about. Technology has progressed considerably in recent years, and as a result there will be major advances in this field over the next few decades: soon every eruption will be forecast in reasonable time.

The second approach consists of carrying out construction works to mitigate some of the hazards of volcanic eruptions. Three case histories illustrate the kind of preventive action that is possible. The first concerns lahars, or mud flows: in Japan, many valleys down which lahars are liable to rush have had a system of dams installed. These are gigantic filters with a mesh that is less and less coarse the further down the valley they are sited. The riverbeds in the valleys below are channeled as well, so that when a lahar comes sweeping down from above, all that is left of it on arriving in populated areas is a muddy but well-behaved torrent that keeps to its bed. Once the lahar has passed, the dams are cleared of the debris of rocks and other material heaped up against them. There is a very similar program under way in Indonesia. The second case concerns the minor explosions that occur on some Japanese volcanoes which are popular tourist attractions as well as centers of religious pilgrimage. Concrete shelters have been built on Aso San and elsewhere, where visitors can take refuge at the first alarm.

Thirdly, lava flows can sometimes be turned aside. The first recorded attempt to do this was made by the people of Paterno, a small town on the slopes of Etna in Sicily, in 1669. Under Sister Papalardo's direction, wearing sheepskins soaked in water, the townspeople used picks and mattocks to divert one branch of the lava flow that was approaching their town. They were then set upon by the inhabitants of the next village, which was now threatened! This was the flow that destroyed a large part of the city of Catania.

The town of Zafferana, also on Etna, was saved in 1991–92 by works carried out under the direction of the volcanologist Franco Barberi. First of all, barriers of boulders were built at points above the town where they might slow the lava's progress. Then, the lava tunnels through which the molten lava flowed, retaining its heat, were blocked at their entrances so as to divert the lava into another area, and by the time that area was swamped with lava, the eruption had ended.

There have been other examples of countermeasures, too: at Heimaey in Iceland, during the eruption of 1973, the flow was slowed and eventually stopped by the use of a huge number of water pumps, constantly drenching and cooling the lava that threatened to close the island's main fishing harbor. At Kelut in Indonesia, tunnels were dug one above another in order to drain, at least partially, the lake of hot, acid water which had caused a lahar during the 1919 eruption and killed more than 5000 people. Lake Nyos in Cameroon, which in 1986 had suddenly released gas, killing nearly 1800 people, was later subjected to an experiment in controlled degassing.

Another line of defense is to simulate volcanic crises and hold evacuation drills, in order to test the reaction and response times of the civil defense services and the behavior of the public. Well-planned simulations of a volcanic emergency should be conducted in all high-risk zones, to prepare the public services and the public itself for evacuation. The few thousand people living at the foot of Sakurajima in Japan are familiar with these "full-scale" drills, and their example should be followed. Similar exercises have already taken place in Italy, near Vulcano and elsewhere, and others are planned.

Volcanoes as sources of energy

Where an aquifer lies close enough to a magma chamber for steam to be produced, the steam may be retained by a lid consisting of overlying layers of impermeable rock. Such situations have the makings of a powerful steam engine: all that is needed is to bore down through the lid, collect the emerging steam, send it through turbines, and there you have electricity! This is the principle of geothermal energy and, although in practice the process is a little more complicated, there are sites where it works extremely well: in New Zealand, Greece, and the United States, for instance. At Larderello in Italy, the oldest of all geothermal power plants produces enough power to run the entire Italian railway system, and Iceland is a geothermal paradise where the volcanoes provide electricity in abundance, heating homes, greenhouses, and bathing water.

Volcanoes as tourist and leisure attractions, and volcanoes as preservers of our heritage

There have been eruptions which were catastrophic in human and economic terms: those that destroyed Saint-Pierre on Martinique in 1902, Armero in Colombia in 1985, and Herculaneum and Pompeii at the foot of Vesuvius in 79. Civilizations have been extinguished, like the Minoan one in 1620 B.C., but at the same time, by covering whole towns in ash or pumice, some eruptions have paradoxically preserved them intact as part of our history. How much would remain today of the sumptuous villas of Herculaneum or Pompeii, if mud, ash, and pumice had not overwhelmed them? Would the temple of Sambisari still exist, if it had not been enveloped for millennia in a layer of protective ash from Merapi? What traces of the Minoan civilization would have been preserved until now without the eruption of Santorini – would we even have known of it at all? What would be left of the frescoes of Akrotiri, and all the other evidence of that forgotten civilization, now on view at Thera and helping us to reconstruct that chapter of our history? Although volcanoes were certainly responsible for casting these episodes of our past into oblivion, they have resurrected a great deal of our history from that same oblivion. As the 21st century dawns, volcanoes still challenge us head on, and research volcanologists continue to shoulder the responsibility of helping humankind to live in harmony with them. ∎

GLOSSARY

Alkaline magma series (alkaline basalt, hawaiite, mugearite, trachyte): Alkaline volcanic rocks (*see* Igneous rocks) formed by partial melting of mantle peridotite, ranging from silica-poor (alkaline basalt) to silica-rich (trachyte). Rocks of this series are associated with mid-plate volcanic activity (e.g. Hawaii, the French Massif Central): *see* pp. 92–93.

Andesite: *see* Calc-alkaline magma series.

Andesitic stratovolcano: *see* pp. 104–5.

Ash, volcanic: *see* Pyroclastites.

Asthenosphere (Greek *asthenos,* without strength): The layer of the earth's upper mantle that lies below the lithosphere. It is solid, but not rigid, and can be deformed, allowing the lithospheric plates to move.

Basalt: *see* pp. 90–93, Alkaline magma series, Calc-alkaline magma series, Tholeiitic magma series.

Calc-alkaline magma series (calc-alkaline basalt, andesite, dacite, rhyolite): Calc-alkaline volcanic rocks (*see* Igneous rocks) formed by partial melting of mantle peridotite, of which rhyolite is the richest in silica. Rocks of this series (also called the andesitic series) are typical of subduction zones (e.g. Japan, the Andes): *see* pp. 92–93.

Caldera: *see* pp. 110–11.

Cryptodome (Greek *kruptos,* hidden): A mass of magma "hidden" inside a volcanic structure, most frequently an andesitic stratovolcano.

Dacite: *see* Calc-alkaline magma series.

Diatreme (Greek *diatrêma,* perforation): A wide cylindrical or conical volcanic chimney formed by phreatomagmatic explosion (see pp. 100–3) and filled with breccia, angular volcanic rocks resulting from an accumulation of pyroclastites (*q.v.*). It is usually topped by a maar (*q.v.*).

Extrusion (Latin *extrudere,* to expel): The emission of magma at the earth's surface by effusive rather than explosive volcanic activity. Also, a dome or spine of viscous lava formed in this way. A protrusion (*q.v.*) is a type of extrusion.

Gabbro: A coarse-grained plutonic (intrusive) igneous rock (*see* Igneous rocks) with a chemical composition similar to that of basalt, but formed by crystallization at depth.

Geothermal (Greek *gê,* the earth, and *thermos,* hot): Used of the internal heat of the earth, the scientific discipline which studies this, and the energy produced from its exploitation.

Hot spot: *see* p. 84.

Hydrovolcanic activity (Greek *hudor,* water): A range of volcanic activity types caused by the interaction of magma and water.

Igneous rocks (Latin *ignis,* fire): Rocks originating from the cooling of a magma. There are two broad categories of igneous rocks:
– plutonic (intrusive) rocks, which are coarse-grained (with large crystals) and have cooled slowly deep in the earth (e.g. gabbro, granite);
– volcanic (extrusive and pyroclastic) rocks, which are finer-grained (with smaller crystals) and have cooled quickly at the surface (e.g. basalt, rhyolite).
The same magma may give rise to either a plutonic or a volcanic rock, depending on whether it reaches the surface. Gabbro and basalt come from the same magma and thus have a similar chemical composition; so do granite and rhyolite.

Ignimbrites (Latin *ignis,* fire, and *imber, imbris,* rain): In a broad sense, all large pyroclastic flow products, associated with the formation of large calderas. Originally used for heat-fused products only, and this narrower meaning is still current, particularly among French authors.

Lapilli (Latin, plural of *lapillus,* small stone): *see* Pyroclastites.

Lithosphere (Greek *lithos,* stone): The outer layer of the earth, comprising the crust (oceanic or continental) and part of the upper mantle, known as the lithospheric mantle. It is rigid, and able to withstand fairly high pressures (around 100 kbar or 1.5 million psi). The lithosphere is dissected into a number of plates which can move in relation to each other.

Lithostatic pressure (Greek *lithos,* stone): The pressure exerted by the weight of overlying rocks, which increases with depth.

Maar: A crater produced by phreatomagmatic explosion (see pp. 100–3), usually edged by a ring or crescent of tuff (*q.v.*) and often containing a shallow lake. (*See* Diatreme.)

Magma: *see* pp. 88–89, Alkaline magma series, Calc-alkaline magma series, Tholeiitic magma series.

Mantle plume: A body of hot material rising from deep in the earth's mantle (*see* pp. 88–89). Broadly synonymous with hot spot, though the area of lithospheric plate affected by a mantle plume is much larger.

Mantle: *see* pp. 70–71.

Mid-ocean ridge: *see* pp. 90–91.

Nuée ardente (French, glowing cloud): A term coined by Alfred Lacroix (*see* p. 68) to describe the pyroclastic flows (*see* Pyroclastites), accompanied by a hot ash cloud, which he observed on Mount Pelée.

Obsidian (from Obsius, who according to Pliny the Younger was the first to discover this rock): A black, glassy volcanic rock (*see* Igneous rocks) formed by the rapid cooling of acidic, differentiated magmas (i.e. those rich in silica and therefore viscous).

Ophiolites: *see* p. 91.

Pelean eruption type: *see* p. 101.

Peridotite: An igneous rock composed mainly of olivines, greenish minerals with a high iron and magnesium content.

Petrography (Greek *petra,* rock, and *graphein,* to write): Broadly, the science of rocks (also called petrology). This includes their description (petrography in the strict sense), their classification, and the study of their formation.

Phreatic eruption (Greek *phreas, phreatos,* a well): An explosive volcanic eruption due to magma encountering groundwater or surface water and converting it to steam, which expands rapidly. If significant amounts of magma are ejected along with the steam, the eruption is known as phreatomagmatic.

Pit-crater: A roughly circular crater formed on a basalt shield volcano by the ground collapse that follows emission of a large quantity of fluid lava (e.g. the Dolomieu and Bory Craters on Piton de la Fournaise).

Plinian eruption type: *see* p. 101.

Protrusion (Latin *protrudere,* to push out in front): A mass of highly viscous lava which, as it leaves the vent, retains the same diameter, forming a spike extruded like a piston.

Pyroclastites, adj.: pyroclastic, (Greek *pur,* fire, and *clazein,* to break); synonym, tephra: Igneous rocks (*q.v.*) fragmented by explosive volcanic forces. They are classified according to particle size as:
– volcanic dust, particle size below one millimeter (0.04");
– volcanic ash or cinders, particle size in the millimeter range;
– lapilli, particle size in the centimeter (0.4") range;
– volcanic blocks or bombs, size ranging from centimeters to meters (one inch to several feet).

Pyroxene (Greek *pur,* fire, and *xenos,* foreign): A mineral of the ferromagnesian silicate family, which crystallizes at high temperature. As a primary magma cools, this is one of the first minerals to crystallize.

Rhyolite: *see* Calc-alkaline magma series.

Rift or **Rift valley**: A trough (or graben) that forms at the margins of diverging tectonic plates. Rifts in oceanic crust are found along slow-spreading oceanic ridges; the only known active continental rift is the East African Great Rift.

Rift zone: An area of terrain riddled with a dense network of dikes and radial sills, from which most eruptions on basalt shield volcanoes emerge. Landslides tend to occur between two rift zones on the slopes of a volcano (e.g. on Piton de la Fournaise and Kilauea).

Scoria (Greek *skoria,* droppings, slag): A term borrowed from industry, used for fragments of foamed, low-density lava.

Serpentines (from "serpent"): Greenish rocks associated with the ophiolite sequence (*see* p. 91).

Shield volcano: *see* pp. 106–7.

Stratigraphy (Latin *stratum,* layer, and Greek *graphein,* to write): The scientific study of sedimentary deposits, which are often laid down as successive layers or strata.

Subsidence (Latin *subsidere,* to sink): A term used in general to describe the gradual sinking of a sedimentary basin over a relatively long period. It is also used for the identical phenomenon caused by the accumulation of large masses of volcanic material in basalt shield volcanoes.

Sulfur dioxide: A gas (SO_2), sometimes of volcanic origin, which in combination with water can produce sulfuric acid.

Surtseyan eruption type: *see* p. 100.

Tephra (Greek *tephra,* ashes): *see* Pyroclastites.

Tholeiitic magma series (tholeiitic basalt): Tholeiitic volcanic rocks (*see* Igneous rocks) formed by partial melting of mantle peridotite. Rocks of this series are found at the mid-ocean ridges: *see* pp. 90–91.

Trachyte: *see* Alkaline magma series.

Tuff: Finely-fragmented ejecta from volcanic eruptions, usually fused by heat.

INDEX

The page numbers in *italics* refer to illustrations and their captions;
those in **bold** refer to the pages where a topic is covered in depth.

Aa flows/lava, *see* Lava, aa
Acid, sulfuric, 108, 109, 123, 132
Acid lakes, 109, *109*, 155
Acid rain, 121, *123*, 133
Adams (Mt.), *18*
Aetas, 37, 40, *42*, 44
Agricola, 63
Agung (Mt.), *11*, 61, 78, 119
Air safety, 55, 119, 124, *124*, **126–7**
Albertus Magnus, 63
Albite, 94
Aleutians, 79
Alps, 73, 91, *91*
Alvin (submersible), 81
Amphiboles, 94
Anaximander, 62
Andes, 22, 73, 74, 78, 79, *79*
Andesite, 78, 79, 92, 149
Anorthite, 94, 95
Aoba, 148
Archimède (bathyscaphe), 81
Archimedes, 94
Arcs, island, *see* Island arcs
Arenal, *10*, 18, 120, 122, *122, 127*
Argos (satellite), 148, 153
Aristotle, 62, 63
Armero, 22, 23, *128*, 129, 135, *135*, 155
Asama (Mt.), *63*, 68, 136
Ash, *39*, 42, *42*, 43, *43*, 44, *45*, 54, 109, 121, **123–5**, 126–7
Aso San, 68, 154
Asthenosphere, 71, 78, 79, *88*, 89, 94
Atlantis, 59, 122
Atolls, 106
Augustine, *10*, 78, *125*, 127
Austral (islands), 93
Auvergne, 64, 65, 66
Avalanches, 50, 51, *see also* Debris avalanches
Awu, 120

Baker (Mt.), *18*
Banda (islands), 79
Barberi, Franco, 28, 135, 155
Basalt, 70, 71, 80, 82, 86, 88, 93, *99*, 124, 149
  alkaline, 90, **92–3**, 106
  mid-ocean ridge (MORB), 80, **90**, 92
  mid-plate, **92–3**
  oceanic, 73, **90–1**
  ocean-island (OIB), **92–3**
  subduction-zone, **92–3**
  tholeiitic, **90–1**, 93, 106, *106–7*, 114
Batur, *11*, 112
Bauer, Georg, 63
Black smokers, *90*, 91, 154
Blum, P. A., 146
Bombs, 53, 100, 102–3, *123*
  "breadcrust", 100, 103, *103*
  "cauliflower", 103, *103*
  "cowpat", 102
  "ribbon", 102, *102*
  "rotational", 102, *102*

Bora-Bora, *107*
Bory Crater, 30, 31, 65
Bory de Saint-Vincent, Jean-Baptiste, 30, 65
Bromo (Mt.), 61, *61*
Bruno, Giordano, 63
Buffon, Count, 64

Calcium carbonates, 96
Calderas, 12, *17*, 28, *36*, 52, 54, 55, 59, *59*, *105*, **110–13**, 130, 141, 142, 144
  avalanche, 16, *105*, 112, *129*
  basaltic, 112
  ignimbritic, 54, *111*, 112–13
  on andesitic stratovolcanoes, *105*, 110–12
  on shield volcanoes, 112
Cameroon (Mt.), *11*, 86
Canary Isles, 65, 66, 111
Carbon-14 dating, 151
Carbon dioxide, 28, 96, *98*, 109, 133, *133*, 149, 150, 151
Carbonatites, 96, *96*
Carlsberg Ridge, 139
Carteret, Philip, 54
Cascade range, 18, *18*, 74, 79
Cascades observatory, 136
Cerro Azul, 78
Chichón, El, *10*, 78, 119, 120, 123, *123*, 125, *125*, *127*, 128, 133, 141
Chlorine, 133
Civil Aviation Organization, International (ICAO), 126
Cloud columns, Plinian, *17, 36, 38*, 99, 101, 103, 110, *125*
CNRS ((French) National Center for Scientific Research), 136, 137, 138, 139
Coan, Titus, 12
Colima, 132
Colo (Mt.), *11*, **46–7**, *127*
Comoros (islands), 137, 139, *141*
Cones:
  adventive, 102
  andesitic, *111*
  cinder, 101, 102, *102*
  scoria, 14, 67, 100, 101, 102
  spatter, 102, *102*
  Strombolian, 27, 102
  tuff, 100, 101, 103
Continental drift, **72–3**, *85*, 86
Continental rifts, 74, *74*
Convection, 71, *72*, 76, *89*, 90, 93
Cook (islands), 93
Coral reefs, 54, *107*
Cordilleras, 22, 73, 74, 77, **79**, 88, 92
Core, earth's, 70, *71*, 88, *88*, 89
Correlation spectrometer, 132, 151
Cotopaxi, *79*, 129
Crandell, Dwight, 16, 18, 151
Crater Lake, *10*, 18, *18*, 60, *60*, *110*, 112
Crater lakes, 108–9, *109*, 112, 128, 133, 148, 149

Crust, earth's, 70–1, 72, 73, 89, 94
  continental, 28, 70, 71, 79, 80, 86, 89, *92*, 93
  oceanic, 70, 71, 78, 79, 80, 86, *88*, 89, 90, 91, 92, *92*, 93
Cryptodome, 17, 19, *129*
Crystallization, fractional, 91, 94–5, 96
Cyamex (*Cyana* Mexico) project, 81
Cyana (submersible), *80*, 81, 83

Dacite, 92, 143
Dana, James, 12
Daubeny, Charles, 67
Day, Arthur, 67
Debris avalanches, 16, *21*, 48, 112, 121, *123*, *129*
Deccan, 86
Degassing, controlled, 155
Descartes, René, 63
Desmaret, Nicolas, 65
Devil's Tower, 60
Diapirs, *88*, 90, *92*, 94
Diatremes, 101, 103
Dieng, *11*, *104*, 133
Dispersion, 100, 101, *100–1*
Distancemeters, 147
Djibouti, 137, 139
Dolomieu, Déodat de Gratet de, 65–6, *65*
Dolomieu Crater, *30–1*, 31, 32, 34, 65, 139, 145
Domes, 16, 20, 41, 50, 51, 99, 101, 103, *104*, *111*, 112, *123*, 143
  flow, 103, 143
  Pelean, 103
  resurgent, 112
Domite, 66

Earth, structure of, **70–1**
Earthquakes, 22, 52, 66, 79, 119, 122, *129*, 130, 139, 144
El Chichón, *see* Chichón, El
El Misti, *10*, 60
Eldfell, 26, 27, 124
Electrical field surveillance, 137
Elevation of craters, 66–7
Ellis, William, 12
Empedocles, 59, 62
Erta Ale, *11*, 72, 96, 106, *151*
Eruption mechanisms, **98–9**
Eruption products, **102–3**
Eruption types, *see also* Hawaiian, Pelean, Plinian, Strombolian, Surtseyan, Vulcanian eruptions
  andesitic, 123–4
  effusive, 14, 98, 99, 100, *104*, 109, 120, 140
  explosive, 12, 54, 95, 98–9, *104–5, 107*, 119, 120, 123, 129, 141
  gas-driven, 100–1
  phreatic, 22, 25, 37, 46, **100–1**, *129*, 143, 151, 153
  phreatomagmatic, 34, 46, **101**, 130

undersea, 81, 93, 102, 103, *106*, 122, 130
  water-driven, 100–1
Etna (Mt.), *11*, **28–9**, 59, 61, 62, 64, 65, 66, 67, 68, *98, 99, 131*, 155
Evacuation, 15, 18, 26, 32, 37, 40, *42*, 42–4, 46–7, 50, 53, *53*, 54, 119, 124, 128, *131*, 132, 143, 144, 148, 155
Explosion craters, 103
Extension zones, *74*, 77, 80, 83, 86, 89, 91
Extensometers, 146, *146*
Extraterrestrial volcanoes, *114*, 114–15, *115*
Extrusions, 103

Famine, 120, 121, 124
Famous (French–American Mid-Ocean Undersea Survey), 80, 81
Faults, 73, *74*, 83, 113
Fissures, 53, 94, 143, *144*, 145, 146, *146*, 149
Fissurometers, 53, 146
Fluorine, 133
Forecasting eruptions, **134–53**, 154
Fouqué, Ferdinand, 67, *67*
Fouqué enclosure, 31, 32, 132
Fractional crystallization, 91, 94–5, 96
Fragmentation, 100, *100–1*
Franklin, Benjamin, 123
Fujiyama, *11*, 61, *127*
Fumaroles, 22, 46, **108**, 109, *123*, 135, 138, 140, *140*, 143, 149, *149*, 150–1

Gabbro, *90*, 90–1, 93
Galeras, 119, 132
Galunggung, *11*, 120, 124, *124*, 126, *127, 129*
Garibaldi (Mt.), 18, *18*
Gases, magmatic/volcanic, 14, 54, *84*, 88, 95, 96, *98*, **99**, 100–1, 102, 108, *108*, 109, 121, 123, 124, 125, 126, **132–3**, 149–51, *150, 151*, 154, 155
Geochemical surveillance, 30, 138, **149**, 150–1
Geognosy, 64
Geological Service, United States (USGS), 135, 152
Geophysical surveillance, 138, 139, 149, 150
Geothermal energy/fields, 108, 155
Gesner, Conrad, 64
Geysers, 108, *108*
Glacier Peak, *18*
Glicken, Harry, 18, 128, 140, 143
Global Geophysics, Paris Institute for, *see* IPGP
GPS (Global Positioning System), 146, 147
Graben, 83
Granite, 70, 71, 86, 89, 95, *95*

Granodiorite, 70
Gravimetric surveillance, 137,
    147–8, 150
Great Rift, East African, 74, *76,*
    77, 88, 96, 106
Ground deformation, 53, 95, 138,
    140, 141, **143–5,** 146, 147,
    148, 150, 152, 153
Guadeloupe, *10,* 48, 119, 129,
    136, 137, 138, 151
Guettard, Jean-Étienne, 64

Halides, alkaline, 150
Hall, James, 65
Hamilton, Sir William, 66
Hawaii, 12–15, 65, 67, 68, 74, *76,*
    77, *85,* 86, 93, 99, 112, 130,
    140, 142
Hawaiian eruptions, 13, 26, 28,
    100, 102
Hawaiites, *107*
Hazards, volcanic, 38, 66, **118–33**
Heimaey, *11,* **26–7,** 124, 155
Helgafell, 26
Herculaneum, 119, 155
Hess, Harry Hammond, 72–3
Hibok-Hibok, 119
Himalayas, 73
Hood (Mt.), 18, *18*
Hooke, Robert, 63
Hot ash flows, *see* Pyroclastic
    flows
Hot spots, 15, 26, 74, *74, 76–7,* 77,
    84–6, 88, *88,* 89, 92, 93, 106,
    107
Huaynaputina, *10,* 60
Hubert, Joseph Henry, 30
Hummocks, 112
Hutton, James, *64,* 64–5
Hyaloclastites, *107*
Hydroacoustic surveillance, 148
Hydrogen chloride, 150
Hydrogen sulfide, 150
Hydrophones, 109, 148
Hydrovolcanic activity, 27,
    100–1, 102, 103, *107,* 109, 112

Iceland, 26–7, 74, *76,* 77, 86, 108,
    124, 129, 155
Idjen, *11*
Igneous rock, 89
INSU ((French) National
    Institute for Sciences of the
    Universe), 136, 137, 138, 139
Io, 114, *114,* 115, *115*
IPGP (Paris Institute for Global
    Geophysics), 34, 136, 137,
    139, *139,* 151
IPOD (International Program of
    Ocean Drilling), 73
Irazú, 150
Island arcs, 46, 52, 54, 73, 74, 77,
    78–9, 88, 92, 143

Jaggar, Thomas, 12, 68, 136
Jameson, Robert, 65
Java, 48–9, 61, *104,* 112, 130, *130,*
    133
Jefferson (Mt.), *18*
Johnston, David, 18, 19
Jupiter, 115

Kagoshima, 52, *52,* 53

Karthala, *11,* 139
Katla, 129
Katmai, 44, 78, *123*
Kawah Idjen, *108,* 109, *109*
Kelut, *11, 98,* 109, 119, 120, 128,
    148, 155
Kilauea, *10,* **12–15,** 30, 67, 68, 86,
    94, 100, *106, 127,* 130, 136,
    141, 142, 144
Kilimanjaro, *11,* 60, *60*
Kircher, Athanasius, 63
Kirgurich, 149
Kirwan, Richard, 65
Krafft, Katia and Maurice, 38,
    122, 128, 140, 143
Krafla, *11,* 144
Krakatau, *11,* 67, 78, 111, **112,**
    120, 123, *123, 127,* 130, *130*
Kuriles, 79
Kyushu (island), 52

Lacroix, Alfred, 25, 30, 68, *68,*
    100, 135, 136, 137, 139
Lacroix classification, 68, 100
Lahars, *22,* 37, *40–1,* 44, *45,* 50,
    109, 120, 121, 128–9, 135,
    154, *see also* Mud flows
Lakes, *see* Acid, Crater, Lava,
    Undersea lava lakes
Laki/Lakagigar, 120, 123, *123,* 124
Lamington, 119, 120
Landslides, 32, 48, 112, *113, 123,*
    128, **129–30,** 143, 144, *see also*
    Debris avalanches
Lapilli, *27,* 102, 121, 124
Larderello, 108, 155
Lassen Peak, *10,* 18, *18*
Lava:
    aa, 28, *32,* 101, **102,** *106, 107*
    basic, 88
    blocks, 102, 103, *104*
    bombs, *see* Bombs
    differentiated, 88
    flows, 28–9, *29, 34, 35,* 81–2, 83,
        84, 96, 99, 100, 112, 121, *123,*
        130, *130, 131,* 139, 154–5
    fountains, *14, 26,* 32, *33, 96,* 99,
        100, 102, 124
    lakes, *12–13, 14, 72, 96,* 100,
        132, *132*
    pahoehoe, 12, *32,* 83, 100, **102,**
        106, 107
    pillow, *81,* 81–2, 86, 90, *90,* 103,
        103, 106
    "pudding", *15,* 102
    ropy, 12, 66, 83, 102, *102*
    strands, *15*
    tunnels, 12, 29, *29,* 130, 155
    viscosity of, **100–3,** 106, 120,
        130, 132
Lava-block flows, 103, *104*
Les Puys range, 64, 66, 101
Lesser Antilles, 79
Lister, Martin, 63
Lithosphere, 71, *77,* 78, 79, 84, *85,*
    88, 89, 92, 93, 94, *107*
Lithospheric plates, 71, 77, 84,
    85, 92
Lithostatic pressure, 94, 98, 140
Loihi, 112
Loki, *115*
Long Valley, 141, 144
Lonquimay, 133

Lucretius, 62
Luzon (island), 36, 37, 42
Lyell, Charles, 67

Maars, 101, 103
Maat Mons, *114*
MacDonald (Mt.), *10,* 86, 122, 154
Magellan mission, 114
Magma, 70, 76, 78, 79, 80, 86,
    87–96, 98
    acidic, 54, 88, *95,* 123
    alkaline, 88, *88,* 93, 96
    andesitic, 79, 92, 93
    basaltic, 94, 95, 99, 124
    basic, 89, 123
    calc-alkaline, 88, *88,* 92–3
    carbonate-rich, 96
    differentiation of, 88–9, 90, 92,
        93, **94–5,** 96, 114
    mid-plate, 89
    mixing of, 95, 96
    origin of, 78, 79, **87–9**
    primary, 89, 90, 92, 93, 94, 95
    rhyolitic, 99
    storage of, 89, **94–5**
    tholeiitic, 88, *88,* 90
    transport of, 89, **94–5**
    viscosity of, 89, **98–9**
Magma chambers, 89, 90, *90,* 91,
    91, 92, 93, 94, 95, *95,* 98, *107,*
    111, 112, 113, *129,* 144
Magmatic gases, *see* Gases,
    magmatic/volcanic
Magmatic series, 88, 90–3
Magnetic field, 70, 72, 73, 148
Magnetic surveillance, 30, 137,
    140, **148,** 150
Magnetite, 72
Magnetometers, 30, 148, *148*
Maillet, Benoît, 63
Makian, 120
Mantle, earth's, 70–1, 72, 73, 76,
    77, 84, *88,* 89, 91, 93, 94
    lithospheric, *88,* 92
    lower, 70–1, *77,* 84, *88,* 89, *92*
    plumes, 84, 86, 92–3
    upper, 70–1, *77,* 80, *88,* 89, 90,
        92, 92, 93
Marianas (islands & Trench), 79
Mars, 115, *115*
Mascarene Island plateau, 86
Massif Central, 133
Mauna Kea, 112
Mauna Loa, *10,* 12, 86, 100, 106,
    142
Mauritius, 86
Mawensi, *11,* 60
Mayeyama, 130
Mayon, *11, 136*
Mazama (Mt.), 18, *18,* 60, *110,*
    111–12, *123*
McLoughlin (Mt.), *18*
Measurement:
    continuous, 139, 145–50, 152
    reiterated, 144, 149, 150–1
Medicine Lake volcano, *18*
Melville, 86
Merapi, *11,* **48–51,** 61, *98,* 119,
    127, 155
Mica, 94
Mid-Atlantic ridge, 26, 73, 74, *76,*
    77, 80, 83, 86
Mid-ocean ridge, 26, 72, 73, 74,

    74, 76–7, *76–7,* **80–3,** 86, 88,
    88, 90
Minoan civilization, 122, 155
Misti, El, *10,* 60
Modern Caldera, 13
Mogi, K., 144
Moluccas, 79
Monte Nuovo, 63, 144
Montlosier, Count, 65
Moon, 114, 115
MORB (mid-ocean ridge basalts),
    80, **90,** 92
Moro, Lazzaro, 63
Mud flows, 20, *21, 22–3,* 40,
    48–50, 121, *123, 129,* 135, *see*
    also Lahars
Mugearites, *107*
Mullineaux, Donal, 16, 151

Naples, 61, *62,* 66, *66, 140,* 141
Nea Kameni, *59,* 63, 67
Neckam, Alexander, 63
Neptunists, 63–5, 66
Nevado del Ruiz, *10,* **22–3,** 119,
    120, 121, *128,* 129, 135, *135*
Newberry volcano, *18*
Novarupta, *see* Katmai
Nuées ardentes, 24, *24–5,* 25, 49,
    68, 101, *123,* 125
Nyamlagira, *11,* 96, *96,* 106, 132
Nyiragongo, *11,* 60, 96, 130, *130,*
    132
Nyos, Lake, *11,* 109, 119, 133,
    133, 155

Observatories:
    underground, 53, *152*
    volcanological, 12, 30, 37, 51,
        68, 127, **135–40,** 152
Obsidian, 103
Ocean floor, 79, 80, 90, 91, 106
Oceanic ridges, 73, *76,* 89, 93
Oceanic rifts, 73, 80, 83, 84, 88
OIB (ocean-island basalts), **92–3**
Ol Doinyo Lengai, *11,* 96, *96*
Olivine, 90, 91, 94, 95
Olympus Mons, 115, *115*
Omori, F., 144
Ophiolite sequence, 91, *91*
Ophiolites, 82, 91
Ortellius, A., 72
Ovid, 62

Pacific Ring of Fire, 16, 18, 122,
    127
Pahoehoe, *see* Lava, pahoehoe
Palmieri, Luigi, 141
Papadajan, 120
Paricutín, *10, 127, 131*
Payen, Louis, 30
Pele, 15, *85*
    Pele's hair, 15, 102, 124
    Pele's tears, 102
Pelean eruptions, 25, 49, 100,
    101, 103
Pelée (Mt.), *10,* **24–5,** 51, 67–8,
    100, 103, 119, 120, 121, *123,*
    125, 128, 135–6, 137, *139,* 141
Peridotite, 90, *90,* 91, 92, 93, 94
Peridots, 95
PHIVOLCS (Philippines Institute
    of Volcanology and
    Seismology), 37, *136*

Phlegrean Fields, *11*, 63, *140*, 141, 144
Phreatic eruptions, *see* Eruption types
Phreatomagmatic eruptions, *see* Eruption types
Pinatubo, *11*, **36–45,** 78, 98, 99, 101, 110, 113, 119, 120, 122, 123, *123*, 124, *125*, 126, *127*, 128, *129*, 132–3
Pit-craters, 12, *31*, 34, 112
Piton de la Fournaise, *11*, **30–5,** 65, 86, 94, *113*, 132, 136, 137, 139, 140, 142, 145, *145*, *146*, 147, *148*, 150, *153*
Piton de Sainte-Rose, 32
Piton de Takamaka, 32
Piton des Neiges, 31, *113*
Plagioclase feldspars, 91, 94, 95
Plate tectonics, **69–86**
Plates, lithospheric, 71, 77, 84, *85*, 92
Plates, tectonic, *see* Tectonic plates
Plato, 59, 62
Playfair, John, 65
Plinian eruptions, *17*, 25, 36, 48, 54, 100, **101,** 103, *105*, 119
Pliny the Elder, 62–3
Pliny the Younger, 63, 101, 119
Plutonic rock, 89
Plutonists, 63–5, 66
Plutons, 89
Poas, *10*, *109*
Pompeii, 63, 119, 155
Popocatépetl, 119, 132
Potassium, 92
Powers Caldera, 13
Pozzuoli, 144
Prévost, Constant, 67
Products of eruptions, **102–3**
Protrusions, 16, 101
Pumice, 48, 55, *55*, *59*, 103, 110, *111*, 112
Puy Chopine, 66
Puy de Dôme, 64, 66
Puy de la Nugère, 64
Puys range, 64, 66, 101
Pyriphlegethon, 62, 87
Pyroclastic flows, 22, 37, 41, 43, 44, 47, 49, 50, *50*, 51, 101, *105*, 110, 120, 121, *123*, **125–8,** 130, 143
Pyroxene, 91, 94, 95

Rabaul, *11*, **54–5,** 68, 78, 101, *125*, *126*, *127*, 141, 144
Radar, 43, 153
Radon, 28, **149–50**
Rainier (Mt.), 18, *18*
Redoubt, 126
Re-emergent sources, 29, *29*
Réunion (island), 30, 31, *35*, 65, 74, 86, *113*, 137, 139, 140, 142
Rhyolites, 86, 88, 92
Ridges, *see also* Mid-Atlantic, Mid-ocean, Oceanic ridges
    fast-spreading, 80, 82, 91
    intermediate, 80, 83, 91
    slow-spreading, 80, 82, 91
Rift, Great, *see* Great Rift
rift zones, 12, 14, 32, 112
rifts, continental, 74, *74*
rifts, oceanic, 73, 80, 83, 84, 88

Ring of Fire, Pacific, 16, 18, 122, *127*
Rita zone, 83
Rittman, Alfred, 68
Rockies, 74
Ruapehu, 148

Saint Helens (Mt.), *10*, **16–21,** 44, 48, 78, 101, *105*, 109, 112, 119, 123, *123*, 126, *127*, 128, 129, *129*, 136, 143, 151
Saint-Pierre, 24–5, *25*, 67, 101, 128, 136, 155
Sainte-Claire Deville, Charles, 67, *67*
Sakurajima, *11*, **52–3,** *127*, *152*, 155
Sambisari, temple of, 50, 155
Sangihe (islands), 79
Santa María, 78, 119, 120, *123*, 135
Santorini, *11*, 59, *59*, 63, 67, 112, 119–20, *123*, 130, 155
Sarcoui, 66
Satellites, 43, 144, 147, 152, 153
Sciences of the Universe, National Institute for, *see* INSU
Scientific Research, National Center for, *see* CNRS
Scoria, 66, 100, 102
Scrope, George Poulett, 67
Sea-floor spreading, 72–3
Seamounts, *81*
Sediments, 79, 89, *90*, 91, 93
Seismic activity, 22, 43, 46, 53, 54, 109, 121, 141, 143, 144, 145, 152
Seismic surveillance, 30, 137, 138, 139, **141–2,** 143
Seismic swarms, 142
Seismographs, 43, 46, 53, 137, 141, *141*, *142*
Seismometers, 30, 141, 142
Seneca, 62
Serapis, temple of, 144
Serpentines, 91
Shasta (Mt.), *10*, *18*, 60
Shepherd, Ernest, 67
Sial, 72
Silica, 88, 89, 92, 93, 96, 99, 102
Silicates, 70, 71, 72, 88, 89, 94, 95, 98–9, 149
Sima, 72
Smithsonian Institution, 10, 122
Smokers, black, *90*, *91*, 154
Solar power, 146, 150, 152–3
Solar system, 114–15
Solfatara Crater, *140*
Solfataras, 108
Soufrière de la Guadeloupe, *10*, 48, 119, 129, 136, 137, 138, 151
Soufrière de Saint-Vincent, 119, 120, 135, 144
Spikes/Spines, 25, *25*, 99, 103, *103*
Spirit Lake, 20
Springs, hot, 108
Strabo, 62
Strainmeters, *see* Extensometers
Stratosphere, 43, 78, 123, *125*, 126
Stratovolcanoes, andesitic, 22–3, 52, 79, *92*, 95, 103, **104–5,** 110, 123, *129*, 143
Stromboli, *11*, 65, *78*, 101
Strombolian eruptions, 26, 28, 46, 100, **101,** 102

Subduction, 77, **78–9,** 93, 143
Subduction zones, 22, 52, 54, 73, 74, *74*, 77, **78–9,** 80, 88, *88*, 89, 92–3, 104
Subsidence, 106, *106–7*
Sulfur, 46, 70, 108, *108*, 109, 115
Sulfur dioxide, 19, *98*, 108, 115, 132–3, 151
Sulfuric acid, 108, 109, 123, 132
Sumbing, *104*
Sunda (islands), 79, *104*, 111
Sundoro, *104*
Surtsey, *11*, 100
Surtseyan eruptions, 27, **100**
Surveillance networks, 136–9, **140–53**
    electrical field, 137
    emergency, 152
    geochemical, 30, 138, **149,** 150–1
    geophysical, 138, 139, 149, 150
    gravimetric, 137, **147–8,** 150
    ground deformation, 140, **142–5**
    hydroacoustic, 148
    magnetic field, 30, 137, 140, **148,** 150
    radar, 153
    radon, 149–50
    reiteration, 144, **150–1**
    seismic, 30, 137, 138, 139, **141–2,** 143
    telemetric, 136, 137
    thermometric, 149
    tiltmeter, 30, 138, 144, **145–6**
Surveillance of volcanoes, **134–53**
Survey crosses, 150
Swellings, ground, 129, 138, 140, 143–5, 146, 147, 153

Taal, *11*, 148
Tambora, 119, 120
Tarso Voôn Caldera, 112–13
Tavurvur, 54, 55, *55*
Teahitia, *10*, *81*, 86, *127*
Tectonic activity, 83, 89, 91, 94
Tectonic plates, 54, 74, *74–5*, 76–9, 80, 84–6, 91, 93
    African, 28, *74–5*
    Pacific, 14, *74–5*, 86, 143
Telliamed, 63
Ten Thousand Smokes, Valley of, 44, 111
Tenger, *11*
Tephra, 26, 27, 100, 112, 122
Tethys, 73, *73*
Thales, 62
Thera, 59, 155
Thermometric surveillance, 149
Three Sisters, *18*
Tiltmeters, 30, 138, 144, **145–6**
Toba (Mt. & Caldera), *11*, 113
Trachytes, *107*
Tremors, 16, 22, 66, 86, 109, 128, 135, **142,** 143
Tropopause, 123
Troposphere, *125*, 126
Tsunamis, 55, 59, 112, 120, 121, **130,** 143
Tuff, 100, 101, 103
Typhoons, *40*, 42, 44

Una-Una, 46–7, *47*
Undersea lava lakes, 81, *82*, 82–3, *83*

United Nations, 140, 152
    UNDRO, 135
    Unesco, 122
Unzen (Mt.), 119, 120, 121, 125, 128, 136, 143
Uranium, 149
Usu, 143

Van Padang, Neumann, 46
Varenius, 122
Venera probes, 114
Venus, 114–15
Verbeek, Rogier, 67
Vesuvius, *11*, 61, *61*, 62, *62*, 63, 64, 65, 66, *66*, 101, **119,** *123*, 128, 135, *140*, 141, 142, 155
Vibrations, 148
Viking probes, 115
Virgil, 61, 62
Volcanic Explosivity Index, 120, 122
Volcanic gases, *see* Gases, magmatic/volcanic
Volcanic rock, 89
Volcano Observatories, World Organization of (WOVO), 127, 136
Volcanoes:
    acidic, 123–4, 143
    active, definition of, 122
    (basalt) shield, 12, 28, 30, 84, 86, *92*, 94, 95, **106–7,** 114, 115
    basic, 124
    composite, 103, 104
    extraterrestrial, *114*, 114–15, *115*
    hot-spot/mid-plate, **84–6,** 88, 92, 93
    strato-, *see* Stratovolcanoes
Volcanological Survey of Indonesia (VSI), 46, 50, 51, *51*
Volcanology and Chemistry of the Earth's Interior, International Association of, 136, 152
Volcanology Association, International, 122
Volcano-tectonic cycle, 83
Volvic stone, 64
Von Buch, Leopold, 66–7
Von Humbolt, Alexander, 66
Voyager probes, 115, *115*
Vulcan, 54, 55
Vulcanian eruptions, 46, 54, **100,** 103
Vulcano, *11*, 61, 100, *133*, *149*, 155

Waimanger (geyser), 108
Watt, George, 65
Weather Organization, World (WWO), 127
Wegener, Alfred, 72
Werner, Abraham Gottlob, 64, 66
WOVO (World Organization of Volcano Observatories), 127, 136
WWO (World Weather Organization), 127

Yellowstone, *10*, 86, *108*, 122
Yogyakarta, 48, 50, 61, 119

Zafferana Etnea, 28–9, 155

PICTURE CREDITS

All photographs **Krafft/HOA-QUI** except:

METRIC UNITS

	Metric unit	US equivalent (approximate)
Length	1 millimeter (mm)	0.039 inch
	1 centimeter (cm)	0.39 inch
	1 meter (m)	3.28 feet *or* 1.09 yards
	1 kilometer (km)	0.62 mile
Area	1 square kilometer (km^2)	0.39 square mile
	1 hectare (ha)	2.47 acres
Volume and capacity	1 cubic meter (m^3)	1.3 cubic yards
	1 cubic kilometer (km^3)	0.24 cubic mile
	1 liter (l)	0.26 gallon
Mass and pressure	1 gram (g)	0.035 ounce
	1 kilogram (kg)	2.2 pounds
	1 tonne (t)	1.1 short tons
	1 kilobar (kbar)	14,500 pounds per square inch (psi)
Temperature	degrees Celsius (°C)	$\times 1.8 + 32 =$ degrees Fahrenheit (°F)